Natural
Dog Training

Natural Dog Training

The Canine Arts Kennel Program—Teach Your Dog Using His Natural Instincts

KEVIN BEHAN

WILLIAM MORROW AND COMPANY, INC.
New York

It is the policy of William Morrow and Company, Inc., and its imprints and affiliates, recognizing the importance of preserving what has been written, to print the books we publish on acid-free paper, and we exert our best efforts to that end.

Library of Congress Cataloging-in-Publication Data

Behan, Kevin.
    Natural dog training: the canine arts kennel program—teach your
dog using his natural instincts / Kevin Behan.
      p.   cm.
   ISBN 0-688-08783-3
    1. Dogs—Training. I. Title.
SF431.B416 1992
636.7′088′7—dc20   91-47905
                                                      CIP

Printed in the United States of America

First Edition

1 2 3 4 5 6 7 8 9 10

BOOK DESIGN BY BERNARD SCHLEIFER

To AGI—nourished by her faith in me,
I've learned love and harmony.

Acknowledgments

WHATEVER REWARDS A dog owner reaps from this book are due as much to what is *not* in the book, as to what *is* in it.

The reader might be gratified to learn that a self-editing mechanism has been at work sparing them from reams of my musings about dogs. When I first started this project, I thought that writing a book meant being able to jot down everything I possibly could think of concerning dogs and their behavior. I was in for a rude awakening. Simple language and direct expression of ideas are the true hallmarks of effective communication. That there may be some elements of these in this book is due to some specially dedicated people.

The first in line for my heartfelt thanks is my wife Agi, who suffered through my most tortured writing attempts and was able to nudge out of me what I was really trying to say, simply. I'd also like to express my appreciation to my friend and agent Joan Raines. A special pat for her dog Spruce is in order, for not only did he often drag Joan about, but in so doing he also dragged her into my life, and without her this book would not have become a reality. Little did Joan realize exactly what Spruce would cost her, in red pencil alone. A special thanks to my editor, Randy Ladenheim-Gil, who saw potential in this project and was always encouraging and patient.

Both sides of my family have been supportive in many ways, which has been inestimably sustaining. I'm indebted to my children, Sondra, Sean, and Cara, for their innocent wonder about the world, their sensitivity and kindness toward animals, and their simple but profound questions. They have been a source of deep inspiration.

I have been especially touched by my clients' compassion for their pets, and I would like to acknowledge Ellen Nickelsberg in particular for her provocative questions and, especially, for her drive to learn.

Finally, I am indebted to my father, John Behan. He was a pioneer in dog training, and at his knee I learned to be an independent thinker.

Contents

Natural
Dog Training

Introduction

DOG TRAINING CAN BE extremely simple and fun for both dog and owner. It needn't be a test of wills. Everything a dog needs to do so that your home will be clean, so that he will behave calmly around strangers and children, so that he will come when called no matter what may be going on around him, is easy to achieve and reasonable to expect. It's easy and reasonable, that is, if only we as dog owners understand the way in which dogs learn to cooperate.

The dog was domesticated from the wolf, a pack animal that lives in an intensely social manner. To this day, all dogs, whether they be purebreds or all-American mutts, still react and learn with the same instincts forged by the wolf through millions of years of its evolution in the wild.

There are two types of instincts. One is concerned with survival and is typified by defensive, submissive, and dominant behaviors. These kinds of instincts are only concerned with how *not* to do things. Survival impulses, while necessary in the wild scheme of things, have long been the focus of traditional dog training and behavioral studies as they've been misidentified as being a positive influence on behavior.

The other type of instinct is concerned with being in harmony both with the environment and with fellow group members. I call these the "harmonic pathways of learning," and they're evidenced by such group behaviors as found in hunting, playing, breeding, and caring for the young. This second class of instincts is of the utmost importance in dog training because it is how the dog learns to function smoothly in a group and for the group's highest good. It's the way a dog learns *how to do things*, the very avenue through which a dog can be domesticated. This "harmonic" endowment, heightened even further by selective breeding, makes it possible for a dog to fit into man's world, something a wolf could never do.

Have you ever noticed how quickly and infallibly a dog learns he's going out for a walk, or for a ride in the family car? Have you ever wondered why it is so much easier to train a dog to wait patiently for his food, or for a ball to be thrown, or to perform a trick for a treat than at other times in dealing with the dog? The examples abound whenever the dog senses that he and his owner are on a common wavelength and share a collective purpose.

Most important, stored within these pathways is every behavior that we need from the dog in his training. There is an automatic reflex that causes a dog to sit, to stay, to lie down, and to want to be with his owner. To train a dog all we have to do is gain access to this genetically coded information with a little bit of understanding and some simple techniques.

When a dog masters a lesson along a harmonic pathway it is the most durable way for him to learn; the "answer" to the training problem comes from inside the dog, from genetic information naturally available to him. Properly inspired by the right technique, the dog works hard to stay in harmony with his owner. Since the harmonic pathways liberate the dog's spirit, in addition to becoming obedient, he becomes happily compliant.

The significance of this kind of learning transcends the clinical sense of the term *instinct* because it is also how a dog develops the character traits of self-confidence, persistence, and calmness, the best of traits and those that make a dog a joy to live with.

The pleasure of companionship springs from the harmonic pathway, and yet this undeniable connection has been ignored; the dog remains as misunderstood as his ancestor the wolf. Since a distinction has not heretofore been made between the survival and the harmonic instincts, we find that traditional dog training fails to take the harmonic pathway into account. These other methods generally focus on either rewards and corrections, discipline, or outright punishment, but unfortunately, with any of these approaches, the survival instincts as opposed to the harmonic instincts are going to be reinforced. Ultimately, the dog learns either a generalized nervousness or a resistance to cooperative behavior. While the dog may appear to be acting hyper, sluggish, defiant, or submissive, in reality, he is merely confused.

All so-called "disobedience" and problem behaviors are basic responses of survival to such a state of confusion. This is tragic because the dog is being made more and more wildlike, actually limiting his ability to adapt to our rules and regulations. He's destined to become either our prisoner or a constant source of anxiety.

So aside from the practical aspects of training a dog efficiently, the greatest opportunity presented here is for the chance to discover the true nature of a dog and to free him from resistance and confusion. I invite the reader to explore nature by reading on, and to become what his pet truly needs, a master, at whose side his dog can walk calmly and obediently.

1

What Is the Problem?

OUR LOYAL FRIEND THE DOG is totally misunderstood. As evidence, let's consider the state of affairs in this country as it concerns the dog.

On the one hand, the American dog has it better than perhaps any other dog in the world. A multibillion-dollar industry looks after his medical needs, his nutritional requirements, and his education; all this attention reflects an intense commitment of love, energy, and money that the American dog owner willingly invests in his pet. When we hear people say, "In my next life I'd like to come back as my dog," there is a wisp of truth to the statement, as the life of the American dog is quite cushy. Yet, in stark contrast to such love, millions of physically healthy dogs are destroyed each year. Are the dogs at fault?

Clearly not, and I think trainers and behaviorists would agree with me on this point. I've met tens of thousands of dogs in my life and can only recall a few that could be called unsound, and those rare misfits were the result of faulty breeding practices: once again, the hand of man, not the influence of nature. So it would seem that the smoking gun can be found in the hand of the dog owner. But a simple indictment of dog owners isn't warranted either; after all, upon their good intentions the dog industry is supported. Certainly, most dog owners can't be accused of wanting anything less than the best for their pets. Dog-food manufacturers recognize this demand as they compete to be recognized as purveyors of the finest premium dog foods. Pet stores and catalogs keep pace as well, dazzling the canine consumer's insatiable desire for more equipment, accessories, and, of course, toys to make Scruffy's day joyful. Additionally, dog owners invest their time as well as their money in an effort to get their dogs to behave properly; they buy books and consult experts. Nevertheless, few dogs are well trained or calmly adjusted to their owner's life-style, and so the ranks of the unwanted swell yearly. Our animal shelters and dog pounds aren't overflowing with dogs ruined by outright abuse; normal dogs are being killed, and they have been discarded by average families, because neither party could learn to get along over the simplest of domestic issues.

Given this wide gap between the best of intentions and the results we obtain, is there a uniform rule for success that the typical dog owner is ignoring?

If so, it's not apparent from surveying the informational marketplace on dogs and their behavior. When the American dog owner turns to the experts for help, he has to sift through a dizzying blizzard of methods and theories about how to raise or train a dog. In the warehouse of training books, theories, and advice, there seems to be considerable disagreement in the basic formula. One book says "love," the other says "dominate." One system of training will prescribe food as a positive inducement for learning and another will decry the use of food as tantamount to bribery, a wholly corrupting influence. Even within any one given method, an owner will find techniques that don't support the governing theory. For example, an expert may claim that a dog can be motivated to behave properly through a desire to please its owner, and yet this same trainer will then advocate the use of a crate in housetraining (to confine the dog so that it isn't free to wander about the home and have accidents). Why has the crate now become a more reliable motivator for cleanliness than the supposed desire to please? Another book will state that a prong collar is cruel and inhumane; however, if a dog is bad enough, the owner is advised to throw a can filled with marbles at him to make a hellish racket. I wonder what the dog's definition of cruelty might be in this matter. Another book suggests that making a dog submissive, as a superior member of a wolf pack would to an inferior, is the most positive way to engender respect from one's dog. But in the later chapters we read that pack leaders are destined to be violently deposed and that fights over bones and status are commonplace. Why would we want to live in a wolf pack as a packleader? Besides, what wolf is expected to come on command when in full stride after a rabbit, to hang around the den, to admit strangers into his territory, to tolerate a vet's exam?

Our national pattern of misunderstanding runs so deep that in addition to the yearly carnage of euthanasia, dog owners are advised to spay bitches at six months of age, to lop off a male dog's testicles, to give female hormones to aggressive dogs, to sedate rowdy dogs that have behavioral problems, to remove the vocal cords in noisy dogs, and even to remove the canine teeth in some cases of aggression! How ironic that in a country given to endless romanticism and sentimentality about dogs, we fail to consider the animal's whole being. It is as if we think of the dog as an appliance, and that we can pick and choose from a list of optional accessories so as to machine tool the dog precisely to our life-style. Besides, is this to be the height of understanding and knowledge that we should dare to strive for?

If this kind of confusion existed in the air industry, no one would fly. How would we feel as our jet is taxiing toward takeoff if we knew that the designers at Boeing, Lockheed, and McDonnell Douglas disagreed on the basic physics of flight? On a bumpy flight it's reassuring to know there is a consensus among scientists on how planes fly and what they can fly through. By comparison, what standard does the dog owner have to go on?

With so many conflicting messages, it isn't surprising that dog owners are confused, and out of misunderstanding we get misinterpretation. Finally, we end up with myth: Dogs want to please; dogs need discipline; dogs roam to breed; dogs can turn on their masters; dogs can be stupid, smart, or vicious. Being misinformed allows the worst tendencies in handling to take root. It is so easy to lose faith in a dog if our view of him is based on an illusion.

Unfortunately, science, at least in the popularized form that reaches us lay people, serves to perpetuate myth and deepen the gap between dog and owner. Because science can describe the genetic and hormonal influence on behavior and the learning process, it is assumed that behavior and learning are understood. I beg to differ; behavior is a mysterious process, and terms such as intelligence and instinct have been hackneyed into oblivion in their everyday use. Other terminology such as *drive, emotion, feelings, dominance, submission, personality, temperament, character, disposition*, and the like, are bandied about without any overall coherency. In such an atmosphere of inconsistency, what can a dog be expected to learn from his human supervisors?

In an attempt to clarify such muddied discussion, I'm going to be introducing many concepts that the reader might find difficult to accept. My ideas directly contradict more familiar ones that are currently in fashion, but don't let an initial sense of resistance distort my message. If you've bought this book, you're already determined to succeed with your dog or puppy. All you need now is dog sense.

There are two irresistible forces in our favor. First of all, Americans love dogs, and that emotion is a powerful ally. Second, there is a wealth of training talent available to the dog-owning public that can get dog and owner back on the right track. Unfortunately, these professionals and owners aren't speaking the right language to each other. The techniques that may indeed be effective are driven by a native talent in the trainer, but they are couched in old, outdated frames of reference. So we have the paradox of the right techniques being housed in the wrong philosophy. Out of a love for the philosophy, many counterproductive techniques can coexist with effective ones, and their downward weight goes undetected. Therefore, the trainer isn't able to articulate correctly the real reasons for his success. The danger here is that an owner without an inner sense guiding him or the means of cultivating it ends up with the wrong attitude. He may attempt to imitate the trainer, but he has only the explanations to go on and can never learn to understand the subtleties of a dog's learning process. He and his dog will never be on the same wavelength.

My greatest hope is to redefine the discussion so that the public can start to appreciate the dog's point of view; then methods that don't work can be painlessly discarded.

In the course of writing this book, I have come to two inescapable conclusions: Everything Americans feel about their dogs is right; but everything we think we know about dogs is wrong. To reconcile what we feel about dogs with what we know about them, I would like to offer a much simpler model to account for the diverse and complex ways dogs behave and learn.

First, we must recognize that everything a dog does, whether it is a simple or complex behavior, *is emotional*. There are many who might like to debate whether or not dogs have emotions and feelings; however, I'm going to assume that my reader has little problem with this concept. It is obvious that a dog is an emotional animal. In order for him to act, the mere feat of putting one paw in front of another or the pricking of an ear toward a distant sound requires the energizing effect of emotion. We witness these effects daily. Upon our return home, our pets bound with the joy of overwhelming ecstasy. The opposite but equally emotional reaction of stress can be evoked by the prospect of a bath, a nail trimming, or a veterinarian's needle. If dogs didn't reflect our emotions as well as expressing their own, they wouldn't have emerged to become man's best friend in the first place.

We need to see that emotion is linked to instinct. A term such as instinct can sound a little intimidating at first. I've noticed that trainers and behaviorists tend to club questioners over the head with it. "Why does my dog do this or that?" one might ask: "Because it is an instinct," or "The behavior evolved due to survival of the fittest." The discussion ends to everyone's apparent satisfaction. But there's no reason to be threatened or appeased by the clinical and scientific sound of the word. To call a behavior instinctive—the result of hormones or influenced by genetics—is not the bottom line in our understanding of behavior. There is a reason why dogs snap, growl, chew, jump up, etc., and these underlying motivations are what the owner is groping for as he seeks answers. Merely explaining a dog's behavior by relating it to instinct and evolution does nothing to explain the dog's actions in any meaningful way. What is the dog's instinctive point of view—what is in his mind?

The basic function of an instinct is to provide a pathway through which emotion can flow, like a pipe carrying a stream of water. A dog has a distinct point of view based on whether or not his emotions are flowing through this "pipe." The next question for the dog: How much water is moving along?—the more being the merrier. We can recognize when a lot of water is flowing, because the dog will be acting excited and experiencing pleasure. Conversely, when juice isn't circulating, the dog will be under pressure and will exhibit stressful or explosive types of reactions.

The interplay between emotion and instinct can get very complex, but it always follows a natural plan, delivering us a dog that is born incomplete. His instincts make him a social being needing others of his own kind. On the lowest level, an instinct connects him to that which he needs to survive, and once connected, the dog becomes in balance. However, there is a much more profound aspect to behavior beyond mere survival. When emotion flows through instinct at full strength *the dog becomes whole*.

The dog descended from the wolf, and since the wolf earns his living by killing, we will find that not surprisingly, the prey instinct—the desire to chase and bite that which is moving—is the mainspring in the dog's internal mechanism. The prey instinct is the faculty that can accommodate the full gush of an emotional outpouring. It's like the main pipe that brings water from the well to the house, or the high-voltage line that transports electricity from the utility pole to the circuit panel in the basement. Even if your dog seemingly displays the predatory impulses of a couch potato, the mighty heart of an Arctic carnivore roars somewhere in the deepest recess of his temperament. If you listen closely, you can hear its faint murmur. Until you read the next few chapters, this connection may be hard to find. But if you step outside the traditional ways of looking at the dog, you'll notice that what leaves your dog feeling totally fulfilled are those times when his prey instinct is completely exercised, rendering him emotionally exhausted. For your dog, this may mean a game of fetch, or putting a flock of geese to flight, or play-predator games with his dog buddies. Perhaps you've seen a hunting dog sacked out after a full day in the field. The glazed eyes, the tongue lazily and carelessly dangling from a slack jaw, indicate a mood of complete contentment. *Fulfillment is the condition of wholeness.*

This is vital information to anyone interested in training or living with a dog, because the prey instinct does more than fetch a meal; it puts the dog into harmony with anything or anyone that can lead him to the natural bliss of wholeness. The prey instinct does more than reinforce behavior—it determines the dog's perspective and range of responses. Its effects cannot be overstated; it is the agency through which the dog learns self-confidence and calmness or their negative counterparts, unsureness and anxiety. *Everything a dog feels, acts, and learns, everything he is about, is due to the overwhelming influence the prey instinct has on the canine species.*

We will be exploring this connection in great detail as we go on, but for now let me say that when this linkage is ignored, the dog cannot be trained in a manner consistent with his natural process of learning. He is destined to become stressed, and this nervousness in turn will activate defensive and survival instincts, reverting him to a state of near wildness.

The key to success in raising or training a dog is to know the rules by which the prey instinct influences a dog's emotions and behavior. It is virtually a mechanical process. This realization shouldn't diminish for a second the degree of affection we hold for our canine companions. The spirit of a dog, that essence toward which we are emotionally attracted and wish to befriend, is trapped within this instinctive mechanism. By working with his wildness, we can truly set our dog free.

2

Call of the Wild

ONE FALL EVENING, I took my family to a local school where an Audubon group was hosting "The Night of the Wolf." As the featured pair of wolves emerged on stage, a buzz hummed through the crowd. People were startled, particularly those who owned shepherd or husky dogs; these wolves looked and acted much like their dogs at home. Their mannerisms were so familiar it was difficult to think of them as wild. The female wolf was allowed to explore the auditorium, but as she sniffed those of us in the front row, her handler requested that we resist the urge to hug or pet her. As a dog lover this was hard to do.

The surprise the wolves evoked in the audience was understandable, because we tend to think of the dog as an animal totally distinct from the wolf. We call the wolf wild, and we call the dog domesticated. Living so closely with the dog, it is easy to think that he is more of man's world than of nature's realm. In reality, domestication has meant nothing more than a remixing of primal patterns of wild behavior; no new genes have been added to the chromosomal pool. We've merely blended ancient balances of nature into new ratios to serve our modern needs. Given his instinctual roots to the primordial past, the modern dog remains much closer to nature and to those wolves on stage than he is, or can ever be, to man.

A dog is born wild, with the same innate instincts that his forebear the wolf possesses. The wolf and the dog use their bodies in the same ways and for the same reasons. Dogs mark their territory when they eliminate, defend a bone, give chase, dig up a flower bed, tug at a pant cuff, or lick their owner's face—all actions that wolves do. These instincts produce a style of group living that enables wolves to hunt effectively and survive almost anywhere there is enough wild habitat. For a better understanding of what is special about dogs, let's look at the wolf.

What is particularly special about wolves is the teamwork displayed in their manner of stalking, herding, and killing an animal of prey that is much larger than themselves. A buffalo, moose, muskox, or caribou is not an easy mark. These prey animals may seal themselves off behind a defensive formation or confront their attackers directly. A group of wolves faced by a prey brandishing a rack studded with sharp tines and possessing brute muscle power that can turn a hoof's dull rim into a razor-sharp cutting edge must act as one to achieve its goal. In the hunt, each individual has a specialized job, such as outflanking the herd, cutting a weakened specimen from the safety of its numbers, or simply harassing and slowing an animal until reinforced. In the chase, each wolf will target a different body part: Some will bite and grab the nose while others will strike at the neck, shoulders, or haunches. All this happens at blazing speed and yet each individual's action is perfectly coordinated to the efforts of the other group members. Specialization and cooperation in overcoming a formidable obstacle are the hallmarks of a successful attack.

The spoils of the hunt are well worth the risks, as there is a big social dividend to be gained when one kill can yield so much fat and protein. The offspring are afforded a prolonged period of upbringing, giving them the time to learn the intricacies of hunting and group behavior. They aren't born fully developed and instinctively "hard wired" in their adaptations to the outside world. They can be born impressionable, and then through group life, be gradually exposed to the stresses of the world in a process of learning that leaves them deeply affected by environmental influences. Puppies are endowed with a basic "software," the prey instinct, the full scope of which is intact, but advanced aspects of it lie dormant until catalyzed by the outside world. It is a subtle process of molding and sculpting a malleable mind, requiring the better part of two years. The big evolutionary advantage to this kind of programmable flexibility is a vastly improved degree of adaptability.

The luxury of flexibility in the young is possible because there are adults in the group besides the parents to protect them, and to kill for them. Researchers have long marveled at the elaborate and affectionate system of nurturing and development that characterizes the overall effort of the wolf pack tending to its brood. A hunter returning to the den, parent or otherwise, regurgitates its portion of a fresh kill to the cubs while another adult, which is not necessarily a parent either, has stayed behind at the den to guard them.

This extended period of care-giving wouldn't be necessary if the puppies were born prepackaged and more complete. And it wouldn't be possible if wolves hadn't evolved to hunt large game as a group.

To a civilized person, hunting might conjure up all kinds of negative imagery—the relentless chase, the gnashing of teeth, the mauling and suffering of a prey animal—but that would be an unfortunate aspect of the hunt on which to dwell. In both hunting and den life, clearly the interests of the group stand above the individual, and cooperation if not altruism seems to be the overriding theme. And we shouldn't be surprised that what makes the wolf special is also what makes the dog special to us as well. Everything we love about a dog—what we know as his intelligence, adaptability, sociability, and cooperative good nature—has been passed down from the wolf in the form of the canine love for the hunt.

What does hunting look like? It needn't mean an expedition to the Yukon complete with Wellies, rain gear, and a large-bore rifle. From your dog's point of view, a hunt can be as simple as a walk around the block, a game of fetch, or an electrifying leap to snatch a Frisbee in midair. It can also be a jog down a street or woodland trail, or a car ride, because fundamentally, hunting means a change of scenery, new sights and smells, and the potential for emotional energy to be cut loose. Hunting means being connected to a group and to nature. No matter how well fed our pooches may be, they'll yearn to follow the call of the wild broadcast through every strand of DNA constituting their genetic makeup. Because this urge runs so deeply in all breeds of dogs, we cannot remove hunting from either a dog's mind or his behavior. Nor should we try, for to do so would require training him not to look, listen, or smell, and that's a pale state of existence for any being intoxicated with nature.

The call of the wild lies just a scratch below the surface in any dog. Just because dogs are instinctively responsive to man, making them what we call tame, doesn't make these instincts any less wild! Whenever a dog gets loose, he looks for other dogs, they form a group, and off they go searching for things to investigate and ultimately to chase. It is an activity that reinforces itself even if nothing is caught or put to flight; it is a natural and wild state of being. In parks, along city streets, in backyards, and in country fields, we can find dogs doing what they love and know best—hunting.

As I view the dog as a product of nature, please allow me in the upcoming chapters a degree of poetical and philosophical latitude. When I speak of the dog, I am talking about the wolf in the same breath. And when I talk about the wolf, dogs are in the wings as well. For this reason, there won't be a clear demarcation between wolves and their evolution and dogs and their behavior. Every sentence of this book is part of one central synthesis with but the subtlest of separation between subject matters. In my view, a discussion of dog training cannot be reduced to a manual on technique. We need to engage ourselves with nature on intellectual, emotional, philosophical, and spiritual levels.

The premise that the dog is linked to the wolf is nothing new. What is newly being presented here is the idea that sociability is a by-product of, and is dependent on, the prey instinct. Since killing large animals makes advanced social living possible, it makes sense to look for a connection between the higher levels of social development and the prey instinct. Foxes and coyotes, for example, which almost exclusively hunt prey smaller than themselves, do not exhibit this kind of elaborate social structure.

Dogs are socially flexible because the prey instinct in wolves evolved to be flexible. Flexibility in the prey instinct is necessary not only because wolves hunt a wide variety of game—everything from mice to moose—but most important, because they hunt a prey that is fast and dangerous. Circumstances in the hunt are going to be changing constantly. And when I talk about flexibility, I don't just mean the individual's ability to react to change; I mean that all the members adjust to change *as a group*. This kind of collective coordination is the bedrock of sociability. Normally, this kind of co-ordination might be thought to fall more under the realm of communication, learning, and intelligence rather than of instinct. My premise, though, is that the prey instinct coordinates behavior and controls the learning process. It exerts an influence that exaggerates slight differences in each individual's temperament into gross differences of behavior, thereby producing the phenomenon of specialization. It's quite like passing an electrical current through a chemical solution such as in a battery. As each molecule is charged, it migrates to either the positive or negative polarity. The group has more polarities than that, one for each member, and you can visualize its structure as a wheel with spokes radiating outward from a hub. For each individual to be balanced, it needs to be in position along a spoke. Once aligned, the group can come into sync and the wheel is ready to roll. From each particular spoke, the world will look quite different to any one individual than it will look to his peers. He acts accordingly. And so, each member of the group, once charged by the prey instinct, gravitates to a different task in the hunt. Then, as circumstances in the hunt ripen for the kill, the group is guided back together again for the finish. The wheel spins faster as the spokes grow shorter.

The kill indicates that no matter how different each job may seem, they are all variations on a central theme. Each is a balance of strong emotional attraction weighed against resistance, resistance being the work required to catch up, secure a bite, and then subdue the targeted animal. Resistance takes a toll physically but, much more important, emotional reserves are depleted commensurate with the physical energy expended. In fact, a canine doesn't feel physical fatigue without first experiencing emotional resistance.

Tabulating the degree of attraction to the prey relative to the amount of resistance experienced in the chase and fight is a balancing act that has a profound effect on the nervous system of the hunter, and he is then reaffected emotionally. He grows either apprehensive or positively expectant, depending on how the scales are tipped. If the prey becomes highly agitated, confused, or displays weakness, the collective energy of the group peaks, and its specialized skills and coordinated action add up to a kill. If the prey remains resilient or composed, the group will grow inhibited and the prospective victim will live for another day.

As an individual learns one role in the hunt, indirectly he's halfway to learning another. Each job is not so much a skill as a different emotional state of inhibitedness relative to rushing in on the prey. The more uninhibited a member is, the less sensitive to resistance he'll be, and the more direct and straightforward in his drive to bite. He'll be the leader. The more inhibited an individual might be, the more circumspect and restrained he'll act, and he will be a follower. In this way, not only does the prey instinct "train" each member to his place in the hunt, but also to what his range of reactions can be. In such a flexible system of learning, where each job is emotionally linked to another, there can be social migration through the ranks, both upward and downward, as the emotional environment of the group changes over time and the group constantly adapts to retain the overall balance and synchronization. Therefore, while learning is dynamic and responsive to outside elements, it is also predetermined.

Given such social mobility, temperament is highly flexible in the canine species. Temperament is a faculty we'll be discussing at length, but my definition of it is quite simple: Temperament is how the canine categorizes stimuli, and the standard by which all life is measured is the prey instinct. A stimulus is analyzed by the temperament either in terms of its emotional attraction or to the degree of resistance it is offering.

Temperament, throughout an adult canine's life, remains responsive and flexible to the emotional climate of the group. As the group changes, temperaments shift, which is why we find not only wide diversity in wolf and dog behavior (commonly referred to incorrectly as personality), but remarkable uniformity as well. *Making prey is the entire scope of the learning process in canines and is responsible for the species' advanced form of social living.*

To understand more fully the relationship of the prey instinct to social life, consider the emotions of a puppy. He is so deliriously happy with life and every being he finds in it, simply because he can find something bite-worthy in all of it. Any new person or dog is by definition a group member because he arouses the pup's prey instinct. A hand, a tail, a leaf, anything that moves, is to be pounced on and examined for its crunching potential. And if it doesn't move, it might as well be tugged at, gnawed on, and tasted just the same. A puppy looks cute to us precisely because his instincts are so deadly serious; but humorously, he lacks the power of concentration and the motor skills to carry it off. He attempts to pounce and strike with the finesse and aplomb of a fearsome predator, only to crash-land in a heap on his chin. The contrast between his zeal and his limitations is what makes us laugh, not any inherent quotient of cuteness independent of the above dynamic of contrast.

A puppy's state of total uninhibitedness is the first phase of a flexible prey instinct, and it is the bedrock of sociability. When a puppy is attracted to a living being through his prey instinct, he becomes emotionally committed, for he feels as strongly connected to that being as if he were of his group. If a puppy is not attracted with his prey instinct—observable by some manner of using his teeth and jaws—he's not very attracted, and he won't be either outgoing or particularly healthy. It has been shown that wolf cubs, if captured early enough (while they're still uninhibited), can be raised with man with some degree of success. (However, for a host of reasons, this is a bad idea.) As a pup or cub matures, he loses this flexibility and becomes more and more selective over who belongs in his group and who is an outsider. His positive orientation to the world becomes more narrowly defined and specific to familiar group routines. But the more of the puppy's uninhibitedness that survives into adulthood, the more outgoing and assertive he'll prove to be.

Normally, as I've said, the high traits (intelligence, cooperation, ability to communicate, etc.) have been assigned to the social sphere as if they were distinct means of experience unto themselves. The usual interpretation is that the social capabilities of the wolf evolved first or alongside advancement in hunting technique. Then, as the ability to form lasting emotional bonds evolved, the formation of packs became possible and hence the ability to hunt in a cooperative and specialized style. The conclusion drawn is that these higher qualities can stand on their own. This interpretation is part of what I call the Pack Theory of canine behavior.

Seeing the pack as the fountainhead of cooperative and intelligent action in the hunt leads one to believe that these characteristics are genetically transmittable, as if there can be a gene, or series of genes, for smartness, and then a gene or two for friendliness, adaptability, and so on—and furthermore, that these characteristics were specifically selected for in the domestication process. Early man presumably captured a litter of wolf cubs and favored the cutest, friendliest, and maybe the smartest. These were most likely to be tossed a bone and so, were more likely to survive and hang around. Selecting for cuteness is allegedly why so many breeds of dogs carry infantlike features and behavioral patterns into adulthood. (This sequence of events may well have happened, but my point is that what was actually being selected for has been completely misinterpreted.) In the Pack Theory, apparently the emerging dog was evolving to be able to resist the call of the wild because the above traits were coming to dominate his character. Then, it is postulated, as breeding practices advanced into the modern era, the primitive hunting instincts of the wolf were gradually dampened. Meanwhile, social characteristics were specifically selected for to make the dog more and more well rounded as a companion. Heightening this view is the observation that dogs that run free tend to scavenge from garbage cans and hang around dumps for food. They don't live and kill as pack animals, preferring eventually to return to a human household. Clearly, dogs seem to be fundamentally different from wolves.

In this vein, we often hear breeders say that their stock has good temperament, meaning that their dogs are friendly, or that they like children; perhaps it is presumed that this is due to a concentration of the alleged friendly gene in their makeup, the keystone to being domesticable. This is a monumental misinterpretation. Search as we might, there is not a friendly gene to be found in the canine species. Neither, I must also add, is there a mean bone to be found in its body.

Allow me to propose an alternate theory: the Group Theory. Its central tenet is that a hunting life begets a social life, and that the prey instinct is the connecting and underlying theme in all canine behavior.

The unifying current in canine behavior is neither intelligence as it is commonly defined nor some vague concept such as altruism or cooperation, but is instead the prey instinct. Agreeableness, sociability, and collective harmonious action are by-products of, and are dependent on, this deep-rooted urge. Since in my view this instinct is the supporting framework, were one to tinker with it genetically there would be an inevitable ripple effect throughout the temperament and body characteristics in ways that might seem unrelated. What we view as social traits are in reality modifications of the prey instinct. If we reevaluate the domestication process in this light, a different pattern becomes clear.

Several years ago, in a story in *U.S. News and World Report*, an interesting theory was covered suggesting that the wolf adopted man and became the dog rather than the other way around. As hunters of large game, man and wolf were on parallel evolutionary tracks, both probably following the same migrating herds and living almost the same kind of nomadic life. Man was, of course, prolific in his ability to figure out the killing craft, and in his efficiency would drive whole herds of prey over cliffs. Amid such abundance, some wolves might have taken to scavenging around kill sites and following human hunters from camp to camp. Perhaps man started to feel secure having the wolves bivouacked nearby as an early warning system against saber-toothed tigers and other woolly beasts of the night. Also, in leaner months, man might have learned to admire the wolf's ability to track wounded animals or its uncanny ability to locate prey. Slowly, a symbiotic relationship could have easily developed. And even if man didn't make the first move by capturing a young litter of cubs, it isn't inconceivable that a bold cub or yearling might just wander in on his own. If his "cuteness" was endearing and garnered him a cozy spot at fireside, man wasn't in truth favoring friendliness; rather, he was selecting for the flexible prey instinct! He was fanning the flame of something already baking in nature's oven.

As the dog evolved to adapt his prey instinct to man's ways—which was inevitable, for he was already socially flexible given his preadaptation to group life—the prey instinct was fine-tuned even further to a precise tolerance through eons of history and right up into the modern era. Each breed ended up being a magnification of a small slice of the larger pie. But while fundamentally different in this sense, the main code still exerts an overall influence, making them the same as wild wolves in another and even more profound sense.

Consider for a moment the names of the breeds of dogs we live with today. It is quite clear that the needs of the hunt directed man's initial interest in the dog rather than any domestic concerns or interest in friendliness. The whole class of terrier dogs (*terra* is earth in Latin) is so named because of the dogs' intense drive to go to earth to kill prey. They'll recklessly follow a varmint into its very lair underground. A poodle, today the most demure of parlor dogs, means "puddling wet" in German, referring to its aptness as a hunter of marshy swamplands. Even its fancy clipping style has a purely utilitarian purpose. With the body hair cropped close to prevent entanglement in the briars, puffs of hair were left on the joints for their insulation and protection. And a pom-pom was created for the tail so the hunter could see his dog while it was immersed in the swamp grass. We have elkhounds, otterhounds, deerhounds, coonhounds, and even *wolf*hounds, talking about the flexibility of the prey instinct. The *cocker* in the name of America's favorite family dog, the cocker spaniel, reminds us that it once was the preferred breed for hunting the elusive woodcock bird. Dachshund means badger dog in German. We have setters, springers, pointers, and retrievers, so named as to how they were bred to behave in their respective skills in the hunting of birds. Pinscher, Schnauzer, and spitz indicate that some aspect of the dog's biting capabilities or jaw structure were of interest to their early breeders. Even the species is named in recognition of the fact that the principal teeth of "making prey" are the canines, reminding us once again that it was the prey instinct that was being selected for in domestication. When a breed of dog is miniaturized to where it has absolutely no value to the hunt and is called a toy, the fangs remain a prominent feature of its dentition. The dog can be made smaller, but the prey instinct just isn't reducible. John McGloughlin's book *Canine Clan* offers insightful illustrations that show how many breeds of dogs end up looking, in body shape and features, very much like the prey they were designed to chase or kill. It seems that from a historical and a behavioral perspective it is conservative to see the prey instinct as being fundamental to social life.

To review, social traits weren't being selected for in the domestication process; some aspect or other of the prey instinct was. It is possible to breed a highly specialized style of hunting dog, because the prey instinct in the canine species had evolved to be flexible so that the group could uniformly adapt to rapidly changing conditions in the hunting of large game. Because the group crystallizes around the prey instinct, if you fiddle with the prey instinct, you affect the social nature as well. Any subsequent changes in a breed's character traits that were to prove to be desirable in a civilized world were totally inadvert. Initially, man didn't care about a dog's household manners or tolerance to outsiders, only his value to the hunt.

Not surprisingly, we find that each modern breed of dog has a specific social nature relative to its specialized style of hunting. Those most sociable tend to have been bred to search for small prey and leave the killing to the human hunter. These are the searching kinds of dogs; their emotional thresholds are so low as to propel them tirelessly through the fields, and as a result of such a low flashpoint, they're attracted to everything and everybody. Any small stimuli is a potential prey object and every being encountered is a potential hunting comrade. This combination produces a dog that is rarely aggressive, especially toward people. It isn't coincidental that gun dogs, goldens, setters, labs, pointers, and spaniels are so outgoing and beloved as family pets.

Terriers, meanwhile, sit on both sides of the fence. They hunt small game, but they're designed to kill it. While they are universally friendly, they can also be feisty, if not fierce as well.

Dogs that have been bred to have an uninhibited biting reflex toward large prey animals have a much higher emotional threshold, and they've become the prototype guard dogs: mastiffs, rottweilers, and the like. They are more concerned with biting than with searching for prey. It takes more stimuli to get them up to hunting speed, and it takes them longer to get to know someone, since an inner quotient to be satisfied is correspondingly greater as well. Then, should their prey instinct be impinged upon (the group has to shift, as when a stranger approaches), they become aggressive: The being is not of their group.

Herding breeds carry the prey instinct in its fullest and most flexible form, and so we find them running the gamut from search-

and-rescue dog, to police dog, to Seeing Eye dog. Their emotional thresholds can be like putty in a sculptor's hands, and they are pure delights to work with. Due to this versatility, they are called the working class of dog.

Of course, a discussion of breed traits must get much more specific than this in order to accommodate the many deviations from these general rules due to overlaps and the many more profound effects of the prey instinct that we will investigate as we go on.

I do not wish to represent myself as an expert on the ancestry of dogs. I am not a geneticist, anthropologist, biologist, wolf expert, scholar, or scientist of any sort. But from what I know about the dogs I live and work with, the scientific and Pack Theory of evolution, domestication, and behavior just hasn't made sense to me. I can't square this body of knowledge up with what I've observed in behavior and the practical experience I've had in training. My own theory is simply an alternative developed from questioning basic assumptions until they led me back to the most fundamental premises I could find. As for my opinions on wolves, for years I've noted how the Pack Theory of dominance and submission in the wolf pack has been projected onto the dog to explain his behavior. Since in my experience this is patently incorrect, I've taken what I know about dogs and have worked in reverse, projecting these ideas onto the wolf to discover an alternative theory for its behavior. For the moment, my theory seems to accommodate the most data, and squares up nicely with my training method. However, I always think of the two as being separate from each other; the journey of discovery is only just beginning.

It is important for me to convey to the reader that there is in fact a mystery here. Don't think of your dog as a completely known being; he is a barely charted frontier of nature. One needn't travel to an exotic place to peer at gorillas to get closer to nature; it exists in magnified proportions in our own pets. There they lie, forgotten by our feet, great wonders of nature—an important link between man and the wild kingdom. Don't take dogs for granted; study them closely, and when they're scratching at the back door, let them in, and let nature in with them.

Finally, we need to realize that our dogs sense life, and are *sensitive* to life, through their prey instinct, as incredibly paradoxical as this must seem. It is the dog's life force. When a breeding program selects for "friendliness," for a factor that doesn't exist, it will quickly stray from the original working purpose of the breed and a timeless balance will be upset. No matter how a dog is bred, if he's required to make prey in any one of its many specialized forms, he will always end up being balanced and adaptable when handled and trained properly. It isn't specifically inbreeding that has ruined so many formerly hearty and stable breeds of dogs in this country. An obsession with form in deference to the whims of fashion has displaced the traditional attention to function. Dogs used to be bred to work for a living and since this required the prey instinct, by definition the progeny were bound to be physically and emotionally healthy. Being connected to a group through the prey instinct is the basis of true sociability, as it assures the individual dog of an inviolate place. Confident in his place, he is free to expose himself to his group, thus developing in a positive social manner. Friendliness and submissiveness, as we shall see, are a generalized nervousness about *losing* a connection to the group. It is the friendly dog that can't handle the rigors and stresses of domestic life and is prone to breaking down altogether. What we call friendliness, tail wagging and face licking, is in truth an offshoot of defensiveness; it is a survival instinct.

It took millions of years for the wolf to evolve, and thousands of years for the modern dog to emerge. When we select breeding partners based on how they trot around a show ring, or on friendliness, the balance of temperament is left entirely to chance; a few ill-conceived crosses, inbred or not, and the balance quickly crumbles. The mind weakens, the body atrophies, and the dog is disconnected from his nature, becoming defensive toward life. We end up with nervousness and a preponderance of survival instincts.

The prey faculty is how the dog perceives the rhythm of his world and matches his pace to it. It is how he follows the call of the wild. When a dog through this faculty shares a common wavelength with another being, be it a dog, another animal, or a person, they dance together to the song of nature. A dog engaged in his hunting mood, is fully in tune with all living things around him that are acting in conformance with his prey instinct; he is complete. If a rabbit runs, he'll chase after it; if another dog wants to play, he'll be receptive; if a child approaches to stroke him, the touch will heighten the dog's good feeling. What fogs this clear picture of life for a dog is when the waters are muddied by stress of the survival instincts.

A dog is purely reactive; he doesn't lead the dance, he only strives to keep in step. In this day and age man calls the tune, and man represents an awesome force in nature of which all animals are instinctively aware. And, fascinatingly, they are attracted to man as well. Man alone, through the force of human intellect, is able to act on the world, and it is up to man to bear the burden of understanding when it comes to ensuring the safety of the animals within his stewardship.

I hope, after reading this book, the dog owner will learn to lead his pet to a safe expression of his prey instinct. Someday, our industrial and technological society may find a way to lead the wolf to a safe place in nature. We owe the wolf, after all—he gave us our friend the dog.

3

The Prey Instinct

EARLY ONE DAY, I was walking our dogs with my daughter Cara. The morning dew was fresh and cool and the dogs began to wallow and rub their backs in it. Soon they were excitedly chasing, biting, and flipping each other back down onto the grass with lots of growling, baring of teeth, and carrying on. Cara became alarmed and asked, "Daddy, why are they fighting?" They weren't fighting, they were only playing, I reassured her. She asked, "Why do they bite when they play?" Frustrated by not being able to convey more, I feebly responded, "That's how dogs play." But she posed an interesting question: Why *do* dogs bite when they play?

A dog uses his jaws for everything, from sport to serious combat, because his perceptions, manner of learning, means of experiencing, moods and sensitivities to the outside world, are precisely fitted to the life of a predator. Every action a dog performs is connected with every other along a continuum, the common denominator being the *prey instinct*. I admit that this connection, which envelops all behavior, is difficult to see, but continuity and unity is a pervasive theme in nature and it will be fruitful for us to search for it in a dog's nature as well.

A scientific definition of the prey instinct won't give us any inkling as to its larger function as overseer. In the biological context, the prey instinct is defined rather narrowly as the reflex to chase and bite something that is moving. While this definition is certainly correct, it speaks only of the prey instinct in its purest form, neglecting the full range of its many other variations. As a beam of white light will pass through a prism and reveal that it contains a whole rainbow of colors, the prey instinct refracts within each individual's temperament to produce the complete spectrum of behaviors, no matter how dissimilar they may at first appear. One of the reasons this instinct is hard to pin down is because it operates on all levels of canine behavior, in the emotional balance within an individual, in the balance worked out among members of the group, and in the balance of nature established between prey and predator. It also triggers behaviors not to be released until after long blocks of time, and so it gets called by a lot of names, but when not properly framed in terms of the larger context, these terms are meaningless.

Before we get specific about how the prey instinct affects behavior at the individual, group, and species level, I can still imagine that it might be hard to see the prey instinct in your household pet. After all, who hunts with his dog anymore? To confirm this instinct's presence in our dogs, we can't expect to find deposited on the back step for our inspection the eviscerated body of a mouse, as a cat would provide. In dogs, the prey instinct is much more complex and subtle than that, although it wouldn't be out of character for a dog to drag home the carcass of a deer. But let me assure you that even if your dog doesn't so much as look twice at chipmunks, if he walks and breathes, the prey instinct is very much alive in his heart. Over the next pages we'll see that the ways in which a dog uses his body, how he expresses emotion, and how he learns, is a function of this instinct.

The simplest way to discover what your dog views as prey is to ask yourself what turns your dog on.

To a dog, when you throw a ball or a stick, it is as if a bird fluttered from your hand, landing wounded and trying to escape, every hop, skip, and bounce increasing the drama. Perhaps your puppy has a yearning for your socks, which he fetches from the closet every time you're not watching. Or the prey might have nothing to do with you: A dog's prey may be a deer in the woods, the neighbor's cat, or a rabbit at the fringe of the yard. For other dogs, the prey instinct may be aroused by something moving on the horizon, perhaps a jogger bobbing down the road, a child pedaling hard on his bike, or a mailman making his rounds and swinging his pouch.

Cars bring out a lot of interesting prey-making scenarios for dogs. The high-pitched whines and whirrs of a car's gears and engine can interrupt a dog's snooze on a porch and instantly call him to the chase as the squeak of a mouse surely arouses a wolf to chase it. I've noticed the percussive sounds of Volkswagens, trucks, or motorcycles are particularly alluring for some dogs. Many owners have described to me how their dogs take up position in the back of the family station wagon to snap at traffic or looming road signs that whiz by. Under the influence of the prey instinct, motion breathes life into the dog's view of the world, thereby kindling his urge to seize things with his jaws. I know of one dog who was such a frustrated road warrior that he grabbed and punctured the spare tire mounted on the car's interior sidewall as a car sped past. Most dogs aren't that compulsive and are content merely to lean out a window and grab a turbo-charged nasal impression of their hunting grounds. But whether a dog storms about inside the car or calmly watches from his chauffeur-driven vantage point, we can see that not only does the prey instinct mean an unrestricted flow of emotional energy outward into the external world, it also means a heightened flow of sensory input as well. So even if your dog is quiet as a church mouse in the car, if he likes car rides, by hopping in he's saddling up for a hunt.

Vision is the most powerful sense relative to the prey instinct. In effect, a dog feels and experiences the essence of a stimulus with his eyes, which is why his eyesight is primarily tuned to moving things rather than to a three-dimensional perspective. A body in motion reveals for a dog the potential for pleasure, while three-dimensional facets of an object are of little value. A dog becomes consumed and intoxicated by the prey's "essence," revealed to him by the twitches beneath the surface of a bulbous shape or rounded form, its rhythmic or squirming motion. The thrashing action of a rake is strongly evocative to many dogs, especially puppies. Immersion in this essence is what the prey instinct is after, for when attained, the dog is left feeling satisfied as the prey instinct hits the "stop" signal. Otherwise, the poor animal stays perpetually charged, a state of existence for many terriers, with their constantly upright and tautly wired tails. They're like a live wire in need of constant grounding, both figuratively and literally speaking. The same drive to penetrate to the essence is why puppies relentlessly rip apart a stuffed toy for its fluffy innards or persist in tormenting a screeching vacuum cleaner to the consternation of someone trying to use it.

All the senses are in a rarefied state of heightened acuity when a dog is engorged with this instinct. To the sense of smell, the essence is a glandular odor, blood, urine, saliva, feces, any bodily product secreted or eliminated. The musky smell of a patch of freshly disturbed earth is also revealing to the keen nose of a dog.

When charged, a dog virtually touches things when he smells them, as we humans would probe with our fingertips to assess an object's texture or hardness, or how we might study something by balancing it in our palm. Smelling is how a dog tunes in, how he probes for a point of access, as when a dog snuffles a cat intensely, alternately licking and whining in his mounting frustration.

Absorbing through the jaws is the preferred manner of gaining fulfillment, and a dog is sensitive in this organ even when he appears to be biting with careless abandon. While crunching he is feeling in great detail every degree of resistance to penetration he is encountering. His teeth, hard as ivory, nonetheless feel with exquisite delicateness.

I've known many dogs mesmerized by water. Most of these water aficianados are of the garden-hose variety. Or, they may reserve their fetish for splashes at poolside, or a game of tag with waves at the beach. One Doberman pinscher in particular would plunge into ponds and snap at the waves his front paws created as he paddled. The undulating ripples in front of his snout were as magnetically attractive to him as the wiggles made in the fur of a raccoon's body as it rummages along. Once, this Doberman swam out to the middle of the Central Park Reservoir; aimlessly and recklessly he circled, growing more and more tired, swallowing more and more water, his head sinking lower and lower. Alarmed, his owner had to swim out to rescue him, no doubt a curious spectacle even by New York standards.

It is fascinating to note that as a dog becomes highly attuned to a specific kind of prey-making activity, his interest in other areas is dampened. One dog may become very intense about chasing motorcycles, while his interest in regular traffic subsides. Another dog might be fixated on trucks or buses and not care about motorcycles. A dog may chase squirrels but not cats, and some dogs will fight other dogs, or bark at deer, and by the same token be extremely passive toward people. How a dog distinguishes and becomes attuned to the unique sound of his owner's car from all others is due to this phenomenon as well. In the peculiarities of your dog's learning process you'll find this instinct's ever-present imprint. A dog's likes and dislikes aren't actually quirks of his personality; they demonstrate instead that the prey instinct influences learning in a way that promotes differentiation and specialization—vital contributions to the hunt.

The entire body of a dog develops to be tuned to its prey; in rough group play the role of the jaws can be displaced, yet the prey instinct can still find satisfaction. For this reason, the sense of touch is particularly arousing to a dog, and he absorbs great amounts of pleasure through a topline that extends from his head, down his neck, along his shoulders and spine, and culminates at the base of his tail. The topline is an "orgasmic organ" switched on when a dog seeks contact with the world through his prey instinct. A crisp dawn or a fresh snow could set your dog rolling about on his back in complete ecstasy, as if he were wallowing amid the guts and blood of a recent kill. Unfortunately, a dog is equally happy to roll in horse manure or adequately aged carcasses (I think several weeks of decay is the preferred minimum) so as to immerse himself in smells that only a dog, or wolf, could love.

This "immersion effect" tells us a lot about whether the dog feels connected to his group or not, and how self-confident and happy he feels in that moment. When I met my wife Agi, she owned Justin, a German shepherd dog. Every time she would return home he would get excited, as all dogs do. Then, as his greeting ritual escalated in emotional intensity, he would start rubbing against the furniture until finally she would have to restrain him before couches were rearranged into the next room. Conversely, when a dog doesn't feel connected to a group, as when a nervous dog encounters a stranger, the topline can become polarized in the opposite manner. His hackles stand up on edge and his head area bristles as he emits a low growl or bark.

Examples of the immersion effect abound. It is why water dogs love the water; the colder the better, as it means more stimulus, a higher state of arousal. For the same reason, a terrier loves the compression of a tunnel; he doesn't feel cornered but rather engulfed in the essence of his prey. A herding dog needs to be surrounded by the flock for his dose of pleasurable connection to the group. Similarly, an occasional kick or trampling won't have a lasting or debilitating effect either; when a dog is immersed in prey his tolerance for pain is extremely high. My father once owned a German shepherd named Rommel who was a prolific hunter on his farm. One summer, he took to molesting the underground nests of yellow jackets. Despite their incessant stings, he'd roll about in total rapture, as if his belly were getting a good rub. At the peak of their attack, his reverie was at its highest. Prey making is a marvelous opiate and every bit as addictive.

When the individual is fully involved with his prey, or immersed in an active phase of the hunt, everything he hears will deepen his commitment, even the nerve-shattering blast of a 12-gauge shotgun. Yet when this same dog is at rest, he might display an inordinate nervousness toward strange noises. If your dog should display noise sensitivity, or should you want to ensure that your puppy will grow to be immune to fireworks and backfires, get him excited in prey and then expose him gradually to potentially offensive sounds. Thereafter, loud bangs will either be neutral in his mind or can actually pleasantly remind him of his connection to his group.

The prey instinct not only quickens the senses and steeps the individual in pleasure but is responsible for the more complex aspects of learning and memory as well. The gun dog's ability to mark where several birds have fallen and then unerringly retrieve the day's catch is one example. But this kind of mental dexterity is small potatoes relative to the larger function of learning housed within the prey instinct's "mainframe," a Rosetta stone against which the body language of all life can be deciphered. A dog recognizes a good or a bad intention in a person or an animal, not through the mental comprehension of either trust or threat, but as to how their movements conform to the uniform code of this instinct. If the motion is fluid and rhythmic, then the stimulus is positive and predictable and the green light is on. If the motion is stiff, sharp, or irregular, the cautionary or red-light signal is given and the being is to be dealt with warily or avoided altogether.

The trait of curiosity itself is nothing more than the drive to find something interesting to bite; a tireless search through the catalog of life, shopping for interesting objects of prey. To fill the void created by the prey instinct, puppies are compelled to explore their world and are inquisitive about what they can stuff into their jaws.

The reason the prey instinct stands behind all behavior is because everything a dog does is emotional. And the first task of the prey instinct is to generate the emotion that drives action. Whether we're talking about such simple behaviors as the pricking of an ear, the cocking of an eye, or placing one paw before another—or whether we're talking about something as overt as rough-and-tumble play or all-out fighting, the emotional energy that stands behind any action has been summoned forth by the prey instinct.

What isn't understood about emotion is that it is monolithic; there aren't many emotions, *there is only one*. Emotion is a dull but ever-present force, like gravity. Once refined by the temperament. It can be described as a magnetic attraction to the essence of a prey.

The dog's senses are "hard wired" to be able to recognize its presence in a stimuli, and all the examples I have given so far occur when the dog is able to "tune in" to this frequency. Puppies are most uninhibited in this regard and in recognition of their need, they quickly sprout needle-sharp teeth for maximum crunching capability and maximum protection for their tender jaws. So armed, they can bite, slash, and tear to their heart's content. Whenever you see a puppy or dog pouncing, running, looking longingly at an owner, or becoming excited when being spoken to in a soft and rising inflection, you know his prey instinct is positively engaged. *The basis of any attraction, no matter what the context, is biting!*

This might sound radical, but bear in mind that the motivation to bite has nothing to do with the intention to hurt. The dog is only looking to get emotional energy out of his internal system, where it can then be consumated by physical activity. When this is happening smoothly, the dog is rewarded and assured by a sensation of pleasure, and his ability to learn is at its peak. Therefore, anytime a dog becomes excited, emotional energy needs to be burned off through physical reflexes affiliated with the prey instinct. The most direct expressions involve the jaws; slightly less direct expressions incorporate the topline, and then finally, the legs and paws, as when a dog runs or digs. Only under specific conditions does the emotional energy find its release through a pure biting reflex. Most of the time the reflex is of a highly constrained and limited nature, a social behavior. We'll explore why in the next chapter.

Unfortunately, excited activity in a dog is usually misinterpreted as a dog being out of control, rather than as a chance for heightened learning. When this opportunity is passed by out of a determined concern to squash the dog's exuberance, the groundwork for disaster is being laid. When emotion can't be expressed, it is converted into and stored as stress.

Stress, like death and taxes, has an inevitability about it, because it is nature's way of implementing an immutable plan for our pets. But the full scope of the plan makes it one we can't live with since it reduces a dog's nervous system to a state of wildness no matter how flexible and resilient his temperament might be, how masked his nervousness might be by "friendliness." When stress is dosed out by an owner as a first step in solving training problems, it only serves to create bigger ones.

In nature's way, stress is destined to be the dog's master; the canine mind is a sponge designed to soak it up. Stress activates the survival instincts, which shepherd stress along, transmitting its effects from adult to juvenile, superior to inferior, predator to prey. However, it is possible not only to use the prey instinct to relieve stress in our dogs and to break this chain of enslavement, but to turn stress around to our advantage. That will be the scope of the developmental and training sections of this book.

Stress exists in all shapes and sizes: Sexuality, defensiveness, frustration, friendliness, dominance, submission, and territoriality are some of the ways it comes packaged and, I might add, mislabeled. For convenience's sake, since everybody recognizes these terms and they are handy for quick categorization, I do use them, but later I will show why there actually isn't a defensive, territorial, submissive, or dominance drive in the manner in which these terms are generally used. These many forms of stress contribute to the vast diversity of behavior of which a dog is capable.

Stress is a pressure from which the dog needs to find relief, like a balloon filled with air to the bursting point. When the behavior selected to bring relief approaches the pure form of the prey instinct, the experience is pleasurable. Chasing, gripping, and sexual behaviors come to mind. The farther the instinct strays from the clear, unobstructed channel, the more the dog will act in a nervous way, engaging in the survival instincts of dominance, defensiveness, and submission. In these kinds of behaviors, more stress is being generated than is being relieved. The individual is being pushed into a corner with escape only being possible through an explosive overload that keeps the transmission of stress rolling along.

Seeing stress as being linked to the prey instinct, the wide variance in a dog's behavior can start to take on a crystal clarity. Pure emotion, refined by stress, gives to the dog a richness in his social behavior far beyond the simple reflexes of running, pouncing, and trying to bite each other. Canines are capable of the most delicate maneuvers such as licking an earlobe or probing an owner with searching eyes. Author Lois Crisler once wrote that an adult wolf she had raised from puppyhood actually nibbled on her eyelid and delicately opened it in the most tender fashion as she lay on the floor napping. The prey instinct indirectly causes such exquisite actions by allowing the simple emotional attraction of biting (the keystone of puppyhood development) to connect the individual to the group. Out of this linkage a bond grows. The bond is always savored by a dog with some sort of ingestive reflex: mouthing, licking, smelling, suckling, nibbling, snuffling, etc. Through group life, the emotional raw material becomes sharpened and focused, producing the vast and complex range of feelings we recognize and love in our dogs.

So, to repeat, there is only the one emotion, exhibited by the drive to penetrate to the essence of a stimuli, and this is why dogs bite. When biting isn't possible, the secondary need to be connected to the group comes to the surface. As the drive to bite is combined with the need to be connected, the raw material is distilled and filtered out into a vast range of complex feelings. Each feeling has a differing impact on a dog's body and he then acts to bring relief to the affected body part. While to an observer piddling submission may look diametrically different from bellicose dominance, and face licking may seem to come from a source other than defensive nipping, they are all connected by the same thread of the prey instinct.

I believe that any feelings the dog has, man shares as well. The difference, however, is that man *thinks* about his feelings (often incorrectly), while the dog *is* his feelings; he never stops to ponder them. Needless to say, there is an advantage to thinking: For one, it allows man to see things from many different points of view and with the power of hindsight or foresight—should he choose to do so. Nevertheless, it is exhilarating to look at the world through the dog's eyes, because they reveal an incredible vista over the natural order, an order a dog's emotions are infallibly in tune with, as he is never wrong about his feelings. To insist on seeing an intellect and the capacity to reason in a dog's behavior is a trivialization of his nature. It certainly isn't seeing the dog for the marvel he truly is, and it isn't taking advantage of the dog as an opportunity to see how emotion and nature are structured.

A subtle characteristic of canine emotion is that it can only be positive. This can be a difficult point to grasp, because so often we see dogs behaving negatively, sometimes running in abject fear. How could an aggressive or flight instinct be based on a positive attraction?

Negative feelings such as defensiveness, aggression, or flight are caused when an attraction (always positive) is dashed because the prey instinct couldn't be applied. When we see a dog acting negatively, it is incorrect to think that the dog has a bad intention in mind. Dogs don't have intentions—they have motivations that are rooted in instinct, and an instinct can only be involved with something concrete, solid, something holding a positive emotional value.

Rather than say that a stimulus holds a negative emotional value for a dog, the correct way to put the behavior into context is to say that the dog is unsure over his *access* to something positive. In fact, the intensity of the dog's original attraction determines how shocking the experience will be for the dog if he is to be denied. For example, a young dog may run enthusiastically to greet a stranger he spots at a distance. As he gets closer, the stranger grows larger and larger, until finally, the dog can't perceive any way to make contact with such an overwhelming being. The stranger up close is no longer in harmony with the puppy's prey instinct. He's no longer small, he's not moving away, and quite probably, he's making eye contact with the puppy; therefore, he doesn't evoke a derivative group mood. The pup finds himself in over his head, gushing with emotional energy but with no way to discharge it. His initial attraction suddenly converts to fear and he woofs or runs away. Whereas had their encounter been carefully managed, the pup could have easily made contact and played.

Negative feelings are learned and once learned are never forgotten! This is a vital point to bear in mind in raising a dog, and it profoundly impacts on training. In order to motivate a dog to do something, we must generate emotion, and that means that the dog's prey instinct has to be positively involved. But if we arouse a dog emotionally without satisfying his prey instinct, he is destined to have a bad experience. When you see a dog tuck his tail, it is a dramatic illustration of this kind of electrical short circuit in the flow of his emotions. It is as if he's trying to stem a gush of emotional energy from draining out of his system by covering up his anal and genital areas. An even more obvious indicator of this dynamic is when the burden grows too great and the dog is prevented from flight; he'll urinate, defecate, or void his anal glands. An external physical reflex always mirrors an inner emotional balance, in this case the emotional collapse of a mood of attraction.

The biggest problem I face in training dogs is trying to overcome fears that have accumulated in their character due to the inverse relationship between emotional attraction and stress. By most standards, fearful dogs haven't been abused by their owners. Any discipline administered is routinely advocated by breeders, training books, and behaviorists alike. But when we raise a dog without regard to his prey instinct, the dog's body will not be aligned in harmony with his group because the most important part has been left out of the formula.

If I may borrow a term from author Dr. Deepak Choprak, the prey instinct reveals a profound *body-mind* connection. Like the string that connects the marionette to the puppeteer's guiding hands, this instinctual cord weaves its way through every muscle fiber, nerve cell, and body tissue, massaging, tickling, and prodding the dog's spirit into the dance of life. The motivation of a dog in any given moment is merely to bring relief to a body part or organ energized by the prey instinct. Affected in this way, a series of reflexes tumbles out over which the dog has no control, the grand design of which he can't possibly comprehend. So the next time a dog mouths your arm, or rubs his shoulder and rump up against your leg, or jumps up and splatters you with his front feet, it may be of interest for you to note the wild genesis for this expression of attraction and to consider carefully how to deal with this behavior. The training section will provide you with some interesting alternatives to the ones that may seem logically appealing and reasonable on a surface level, but that inevitably nudge the dog farther down the path to wildness.

In studying the canine drive to hunt, one becomes aware of a powerful force in nature. I call it the "synergistic effect," and it is a significant element of the social bonds. A dog willingly subscribes to the group ethic not because he is altruistically inclined but because he is participating in and absorbing a higher and purer level of emotional energy than he could otherwise experience. Practically speaking, we need to understand this dynamic, because it is the glue of cooperative action, but it can be appreciated at a philosophical level as well. What is so clear in nature is how specialization and differentiation when combined properly yield a whole greater than the sum of the parts. A thin sheet of laminated plywood with its layers of grain running at cross angles can bear a weight that would snap a thicker beam. Male and female, two different kinds of sexual energy, for example, complement each other and tap into a greater source of creative power, new life. The wolf in its social structure represents a quantum leap upward on the evolutionary scale from the prey species below it, particularly in his specialized style of hunting, as we have discussed. Beyond the practical necessity of procuring food, I believe that the organization of the social life of the wolf speaks of a higher level of group energy, *the possibility that group living can be based on harmony rather than competitiveness.*

The synergistic effect is the release of energy to the group when they share a common purpose, thereby allowing them to be in harmony with each other. This purpose is made clear to each individual through the prey instinct, which assigns a focus in the hunt. Group coordination and alignment only occur under this effect, and as a dividend the reservoirs of accumulated stress are completely drained. We can analyze behavior in terms of hormonal chemistry, or we can look at learning in terms of schedules of reinforcement, but if this high energy of group life isn't understood, nothing will add up. Hormones and internal chemistry do not cause complex social behavior, they merely set the stage; they tone, they are catalysts, perhaps even putting the organism into tune with the long-range rhythms of the earth's cycles.

No matter how much rich data on instinct and behavior may have been mined from the scientific lode, unless the group dynamic is understood, and the raw power of synergistic attunement is tapped, we're going to keep on making the same mistakes. In truth, from what I see, we haven't come very far from the rolled-up-newspaper era. Try as one might to shape his dog's behavior for the better, unless the body-mind is tuned in accord with the prey instinct, success will be limited.

The phenomenon of group synergism is inherent in all dogs, but there are more dramatic displays in this measure from breed to breed. For instance, the synergistic effect in herding dogs makes them highly responsive to the sheepherder's commands even when they are deeply involved with their work and at a great distance from their master. When properly trained, they've learned that the herder is their pathway to their prey and they'll do anything to stay in harmony with him, including resisting the ever-present urge to bite what to them are clearly their prey.

Synergism is most graphically (and noisily) embodied in the hound breeds of dogs. When they're hot on the scent of their quarry they sing the song of the prey instinct with a melodious bellow intermingled with their bark. Beagles "bugle" to the same rhapsody, and sled dogs are another excellent example of this phenomenon. They howl and whine excitedly before a run as their handler prepares the sled and leather. When in harness these dogs are deliriously happy and run tirelessly, the distance of the journey and the weight of their burden being a minor encumbrance relative to their lust for group action.

The synergistic effect of the prey instinct is of utmost interest to dog owners, because it melts away the resistance inherent in doing something difficult, converting what is normally a negative into a positive. The resultant emotional high keeps physical fatigue at bay. Bolstered by this flux of energy released through the prey instinct, a dog can be motivated and sustained by a simple word of encouragement. Any dog well trained has been influenced by this principle even if his trainer isn't consciously aware of it. He is happy in his work, because he is in harmony with his group and his emotions are flowing. He is free.

Synergy in canines is released through a synchronization of moods, and I believe this is why wolves howl. Each wolf holds fast to his own specific note of the song, and the chorus resonates with the power of their combined voices. According to experts, six wolves can sound like twenty.

Syncronization drives the group forward like gears meshing to propel a car. This principle was illustrated for me in dramatic fashion. I had just let my female shepherd out the back door, and she was off the deck and onto the lawn as my male shepherd was making his own way through the slider. At this point, the female spotted a squirrel and barreled into action. Instantly, my male, simply by seeing her take off, was emotionally peaked and deep into the chase. I was so fascinated, I let the drama roll to the edge of the woods. It was just as if an electrical charge was transmitted from the squirrel to the female and then finally to the male; *and yet the male had never laid eyes on the squirrel*. In virtually the same instant, the male was galvanized and on target without hesitation. Such rapport was analagous, strangely, to neurotransmitters leaping across a synaptic gap between nerve cells. For the male, no analysis was needed; in that instant, male and female were joined together in the same mind.

Call it synchronization, harmony, cooperation, or intelligence, the bottom line in any discussion about dogs is their emotions. What they feel is what they do, and there is a physics, if you will, as to how canine emotions flow. Dogs have to "fit" together emotionally before they can fit together physically. When the prey instinct is at work, the fit is custom tailored.

Emotion is part of a master plan for the canine species that inevitably leads to the hunt. Seeing all emotion as being linked, we find that the prey instinct is to dog behavior what a blueprint is to an architect. In a building, each two-by-four that forms a partition, each block that makes up a wall, and every girder that supports the structure is placed according to this overall plan. The same precision and careful design holds true for the highly organized life of a dog.

Each and every action a dog may take, or subtlety of emotion he may express, is no more capricious or random than the music of a Beethoven masterpiece. In concert, the audience's mood builds, holds, falls, and soars in a deliberate ebb and flow, according to the master's artistic intentions. There isn't a note left dangling out of place to disjoint the listener's ear.

4

The Harmonic Pathways
of Learning

THE PLEASURE PRINCIPLE

SCATTERED WIDELY ACROSS an open range of wilderness one observes a number of wolves moving freely and purposefully. One of the wolves might spot a field mouse, and the group deftly converges to cut it off from escape. Or they might all pause in their places to watch an elk climb a distant ridge. Another might catch the scent of a deer on a faint breeze; his comrades are quickly organized behind him on a common line of pursuit. Wolves do *everything* in a coordinated manner, from where they lie to the order they file down a forest path to the spot on a prey's body they will attempt to bite. How do they know what they are all individually up to, how do they coordinate their actions? Are they communicating, and if so, what are their signals?

These are good questions, but they are only of relevance to the human mind. We watch such a group of wolves and think of them as being separated by distance, needing to communicate over that span. But among wolves, as long as they can see each other, and are tuned to the same deep-seated impulse to bite, an inner frequency of prey making, there is no gap between them to contend with or to overcome. They are not separate. They are directly experiencing one another's moods along a common wavelength, a harmonic pathway that will cause them to learn the cooperative spirit, ironically enough, *through the drive to bite!*

Now since most of the time dogs and wolves aren't to be observed biting, how can biting be of such an overwhelming influence on learning? The entire answer will be forthcoming through the course of this chapter, but our starting point is my observation that the canine prey instinct and the pursuit of pleasure are inextricably linked.

The experience of pleasure is a twofold process with an intake and an output component to it: Nothing can go in—*food or sensation*—if something isn't going out—*physical action*. Through action, emotion is expressed into external reflexes. In exchange, and as a direct result, sensory information is absorbed either through seeing, smelling, touching, or most important, biting. Through all of these mediums, the organism comes to feel good and is "filled up" on the biological level through the flow of nutrients, but, more important, on the emotional level through the flow of sensation. This is a mindless process completely beyond each individual's comprehension, but it is a condition well known to them through the uninhibited phase puppies spent early in life immersed in its programming. For an infant, pleasure at first meant nursing. Once mobile as a young pup, pleasure meant stalking, pouncing, and gripping. Once coordinated as an adolescent, pleasure came into its most developed and focused expression—the crackling, crunching sensation of something soft and furry squished in the jaws. All of these are uninhibited manifestations of the simple drive to bite.

The sixties axiom "If it feels good, do it" is apropos to our discussion here. A dog or wolf can't learn right from wrong in the moral or intellectual sense; he learns by whether he feels either pleasure or discomfort. A dog lives for the feeling of pleasure through a body that is an "orgasmic" device designed to crave contact with the earth, the water, the wind, and the animals around him. A dog feels through the pads on his feet, his shoulders, his genitals. He feels with his loins, whiskers, and teeth. Biting, feeding, eliminating, scratching, rubbing, rolling, and sexual contact are the sensual highlights to a dog's day. If something feels good, he does it—again and again. And then, if something makes a dog feel bad, he will quickly learn to leave it alone—forever. So there isn't anything complicated about how a dog "knows" what to do. The feelings of pleasure and stress (the opposite of pleasure), are the agents that modify behavior.

By grasping that pleasure in canines is defined in terms of the prey instinct and is the means by which a canine can learn, we realize that it isn't a whimsical or casual state of being in the natural scheme of things. The pursuit of pleasure isn't an act of hedonism or of creative indulgence on the part of the individual, nor does it have much to do with trial and error. It only flows in accord with a pulse inherent in the instinct to bite. It follows a specific rhythm that is timeworn and deeply grooved by the genetic imprint the prey instinct has etched in every canine's temperament.

If our hypothetical wolves cruising over a mountainside all have the same thing on their minds, then there is really only *one* mind to be considered here. There is no need to look for and then consider many points of view, which narrows our search as to how they are so cooperatively coordinated. The only thing that a group of canines can all hold commonly in mind at the same time is pleasure, the simple predatory impulse to bite. This creates a singular focus, so that all trails will ultimately lead to the same common destination. All spokes radiate from the group's center, the hub of the wheel, a large prey animal. On the other hand, the influence of stress destroys such a singular focus and reduces the one group mind to many individually varied points of view. The group dynamic intrinsic to the pursuit of pleasure is incredibly important to us as dog owners, for it is the basis of the canine's ability to learn to cooperate.

In this chapter we're going to be further redefining canine social behavior in terms of the prey instinct, and to keep the discussion most clear in the reader's mind I would like to introduce two different means by which to categorize social behaviors. Those actions indicating stress can be put under the heading of *pack behaviors;* these are the survival instincts. Those actions that show a dog full of spirit and yet in harmony with those dogs or people with whom he is bonded could be called *group behaviors.*

The prey instinct, like any other natural or mechanical force, creates a field of influence that all canines are sensitive to and are completely affected by. When aroused through the simple drive to bite, they align themselves within this field of emotion like iron filings distributed through the magnetic field of a bar magnet. The more uninhibited the urge to bite, the more easily the individual is deflected into coordinated group activity.

Out of this field of influence emerges an order with each individual occupying one of its polarities; it is quite like a compass. The group fans out to its far corners as if sensors are being deployed, and if one detects prey or is simply the most confident (behaviorally speaking, these are both the same state of being), he becomes charged, and the others react to him as if he were the needle pointing to the north pole. He becomes the pathway; if the group is in sync with him and redirects its own path of investigation onto his, it enjoys access to the prey. And for as long as he is that channel, he is the group's leader.

The group, when of one mind, is like a spider's web whose filaments, spun from the silken threads of emotional attraction, are stretched from one polarity or coordinate on the compass to the other. We're no longer talking about several nervous systems; there is only one, integrated so that a virtual sieve blankets the hillside. As long as they can see one another, each member internally feels what the others in the web are experiencing. When the prey tugs at the cord by activating one of the sensors, either through the whiff of a scent, the snap of a twig, or the flash of motion, the synergistic force of the predatory spider picks its way across the quivering strands to collect the group's treasure.

These lines of force, the harmonic pathways, are known to the individual not through an ability to reason but through the above-mentioned sensation of pleasure.

The prey instinct, as I've alluded—and not surprisingly—has a direct impact on the nervous system. Before being able to bite, an individual needs permission from his nerves, if you will, and this license to strike is dependent on what biologists call a releaser. The predator has to be in sync with his prey, with the nervous system implementing the rules of engagement in this process. An article by the scientist and author Robert Jastrow related an experiment in which a frog would starve before he would eat a dead fly. However, when the fly was dangled on a string to mimic its flight, the frog would readily gobble it up, the movement of the fly being needed to fire off the reflex to strike at it.

A releaser is the key that slips into the lock—the lock for canines being their prey instinct—the means by which they perceive and then navigate through the natural ordering of their world. In terms of their simple prey instinct, without motion, emotion stays bottled up within the organism. Specific movements, either something moving away or from side to side, are required to release the purest forms of the ingestive reflexes.

However, in dogs and wolves there are other and more elaborate releasers that permit action than are to be found in frogs and perhaps any other species of predator, save man. For example, the form of a body, with a bulbous shape and a horizontal backline rather than a vertical line, attracts the drive to bite. And then finally, in the canine species there is available an additional class of emotional releasers that through domestication have been emphasized even further in the modern dog. Without these, which we'll consider below, the wolf and the dog would be much less flexible in their range of responses to the outside world.

When canines are emotionally attracted to one of their own kind but there is no releaser of motion to permit biting, they nevertheless remain attracted. The attraction doesn't just dissipate on its own. As they go forward through the impulse to bite and encounter resistance because the object of their ardor isn't acting like prey, an amazing phenomenon occurs in two stages.

In the first phase the resistance they experience is converted into stress and internalized as a sense of pressure. The possibility now looms that the individual will experience this as a violent interruption to his flow of pleasure. This reveals the most important characteristic of the simple prey instinct. When in sync and turned on to bite, the individual is uninhibited but by the same token is completely *vulnerable*. The deepest aspect of the temperament while being expressed is also nakedly exposed to the outside elements. In fact, the individual has been regressed to the emotional status of a young puppy, limited in its ability to deal with stress. Given this built-in governor on biting, when dogs or wolves are fully immersed in the drive to bite, their nerves have become so integrated with their victim's that they are completely under the prey's control, were only the prey able to take advantage. Interestingly, many cats do learn to exploit this canine Achilles' heel so that a well-timed spit, hiss, and arched back will shock a marauding dog right out of his drive. While we may be observing a grown dog or wolf residing in a mature body and equipped with an adult nervous system, the inner core of his temperament changes not a whit from the first day of life onward. It resurfaces in all its newborn glory whenever the organism is deeply moved to bite. Like a puppy, once committed emotionally, the dog or wolf is easily deflected into the second phase.

Right after the charge to bite is internalized and right before it has the chance to shock the individual out of his biting impulse, the same charge can also serve to arouse the individual *sexually*. As a result, emotional energy is diverted away from the jaws and radiates into the body, arousing it particularly, of course, in the genital area.

Therefore, two canines interacting socially will become vulnerable through the drive to bite and thereby become sexually sensitive. Their bodies grow "polarized" so that they will position and realign themselves in response to this more complex urge, quite like stacking batteries positive to negative ends in a flashlight. When so polarized, dogs studiously smell each other from top to bottom, trying to ascertain where and how to "plug in." A sexual attraction is a latent charge to bite, internalized and stored when the flow of raw emotion is deflected into social activity. This in turn produces all the leg lifting, nasal investigation, and sexual posturing to be observed within the wolfpack and between dogs.

The sexual mechanism is the way the simple urge to bite is turned into the drive to make contact—the complex prey instinct.

Often when puppies play and are observed mounting and thrusting with a pronounced pelvic action, it is interpreted in the Pack Theory as being a reflex occurring out of sequence in the normal adult context. It is recognized as a hallmark of immaturity. Presumably, the puppy is working the kinks out of his instincts, and when he's an adult he supposedly learns to put the sexual reflex into its proper place in his repertoire. But the reason puppies vigorously mount well before they are able to breed is precisely because sexuality is directly linked to the prey instinct. They are responding automatically to this alternative and more complex means of prey making. When they go toward something to bite and meet with a degree of resistance—their partner doesn't act like prey—puppies will become sexually aroused as their nervous systems, being highly stimulated by the prey instinct, trip on the sexual circuitry. This reflects that the simple urge to bite is being channeled into a new avenue of pleasure so that the original mood of attraction doesn't collapse. Should the other individual be of the same mind, he will be receptive to becoming the prey, and a play session will develop.

Sexuality in canines is primarily concerned with alignment for the purposes of hunting; only secondarily does it have to do with procreation. Its most important function is to process resistance encountered in simple prey making into group and pack behaviors, the complex aspect of the prey instinct. That the prey instinct has a sexual component to it, and that the prey instinct was amplified through domestication, is why, in my view, modern breeds of dogs are so much more sexual than the wolf. Wolves breed once a year and in general are not sexually active until about two years of age. Sometimes they even mate for life. Dogs, on the other hand, will breed promiscuously; they can breed when as young as six months and females come into season twice a year. Sexuality in the domestic dog is quite detached from the natural rhythm of the earth's cycles, as it is more attuned to the magnetic attraction between animals inherent in the simple prey instinct. The emotions of dogs are more weighted toward the active aspects of prey making, searching, chasing, and biting. The wolf's nervous system remains more attuned to the seasons of the earth and to the migratory patterns of the prey species, which themselves are responding to the earth's magnetic field and influences of the sun, moon, and, perhaps, stars.

I often feel sorry for the domestic dog, since there is so much information from nature he is no longer tuned into. If we could experimentally graft a puppy into a wolf litter, from even a breed as detached as the Bichon Frise, might he not grow up to leap at a moose's fetlocks or to circle and press a herd of musk-ox alongside his brethren? How much genetic information lies untapped, undernourished by the emotional climate of modern domestic life?

Traditionally, sexual behaviors have been misinterpreted as a drive to dominate, or to submit, or to claim territory, and have been seen as causative and the means by which a pack is formed. But that is far off the mark. The alignment of the group into the structured order of the pack is due to the influence that the simple prey instinct has on the nervous system and temperament of the individual. When the individual is deeply aroused to bite, he is vulnerable and uninhibited. If in sync through the prey instinct, he is freed from stress and able to align. Cooperation and order aren't created, as the Pack Theory has suggested, through a dominance hierarchy, but rather through attunement to the pleasure principle inherent in the harmonic pathways of learning.

THE DISCORDANT PATHWAYS OF LEARNING

Dominance does not create structure, nor is it ever an intention in the mind of a dog or wolf. It is only a manifestation of tension when emotion isn't flowing through the prey instinct. There is no drive to make oneself superior. There is only the drive for wholeness, expressed in the reflexes of up and down, active and reactive, that positions each individual on the path that sooner or later leads them to the prey. The pathways to wholeness are revealed to the individual directly through the sensation of pleasure and then indirectly through the relief of stress, the discordant pathways of learning.

When overloaded by stress, the need to be connected temporarily displaces the desire to bite. Now the issue becomes how to handle the intense burden of stress. The discordant pathways are the means by which the individual learns to balance his nerves with the rest of the pack in order to remain connected. Such a balance is a short-term solution that lacks stability, since the pack instinct doesn't stand on its own. It is a derivation of the master prey instinct and cannot channel a pure flow of pleasure. The cohesiveness found in group life is not derived from such balances, it is derived from the flow regularly experienced through alignment, hunting. Were it not for group life, there would be no need for pack living.

When one puppy mounts another and a fight erupts, it isn't because there is a drive to dominate. It is because they aren't of the same mind, and they both become stressed by the interruption of flow. At that moment, they are not sharing the same focus and by being forced within the same mood (order) when not aligned, sparks are destined to fly. Canines get into tiffs over this matter the same way hawks rising on the same thermal updraft will shriek at each other when they converge too close on an upward spiral. The discordant note is sounded over the loss of flow, not because of a dispute over rank. In canines, these disputes limit each individual in a unique way so that each member becomes sensitive to its own specific niche in the overall prey instinct. They segregate according to temperamental inclinations. When the group works in harmony, pleasure returns to flow at a high rate. In contrast, when the group is discordantly polarized, the wheel has to slog through a slurry of social resistance, with stress bogging down the ability to align.

My belief is that an up and a down position is worked out in canine interactions only because each temperament reacts to resistance slightly differently, some preferring the active sexual role (up) and some the reactive position (down). The individual on the bottom is not trying to show submission to the stronger one any more than a predator crouches low before an advancing prey to show it his respect. The posturing of the stronger individual is not based on a need to be dominant, but comes instead from a desperate need to connect with the prostrate puppy so that he can restabilize his own nerves. The one on top is often times more stressed than the one on the bottom. In a flash his victim, which a second before was but a blob of essence about to be skewered, gains a *being* with whom he now needs to be connected; the sexual circuitry provides the means.

Since each individual has a different sensitivity to prey making, we observe the emergence of order—the creation of a group and a pack—evolving out of what was chaos. To repeat: This is all due to the simple drive to bite with its attendant effects on nervous systems and temperament. The sexual instincts that are misinterpreted as the drive to dominate within a pack reflect instead the processing of resistance into more complex modifications of the simple prey instinct.

This brings us to a critical question: What is the point to the pack if it isn't to create order, or friendliness, or a chain of command and lines of communication? Its real function, in my view, is not to produce social behaviors but to inject *stress* into each individual's life. What we call friendliness is really characterized by nervous submissive behaviors, where true sociability is free-flowing. In the pack, each individual is constantly being aroused to bite as they are emotionally attracted to one another and this impulse has to be constantly repressed, with stress being the resulting by-product. Within the pack balances are worked out among members merely as a means of managing the stress; these are the ritualistic displays. They fall far short of a full-fledged sensation of pleasure, and everyone ends up pointing in different directions, one facing front, one to the rear, one up, one down. In the short term, nothing collective can get done; they aren't aligned toward a central focus.

As the pup is initiated into the rigors of the pack, stress comes to stand as a block between the individual and his access to the inner code of prey making within his temperament. By taking on stress, eventually a puppy's uninhibited access to the simple impulse to bite is completely muted and obscured and can only be released by certain conditions. Namely, the form and motion of a large prey animal as it now becomes the only target that can absorb the combined and uninhibited predatory impulses of the group, thereby allowing them to align with one another as they so readily could do as pups.

Once again, we find that every subtle nuance of canine behavior has to do with hunting. When a social being is repressed, he becomes especially aroused to bite a formidable prey animal that he has no hope of killing on his own. In the same breath, he has become dependent on his oppressors so that when charged by the prey, he will feel incomplete and need to be connected with them. This is why if a dog is trained through stress, he will develop two seemingly contradictory behaviors. On the one hand, he will be very dependent on his owner; on the other hand, he will have a pronounced need to be disobedient because he will need to escape the stressful confines of the pack his owner has created. The disobedience becomes a manifestation of nervousness from a hunt denied.

THE GROUP DYNAMIC

Since members depend on one another for access to their inner temperament and this same urge allows them to align with each other sexually for a full experience of flow, *being in harmony is the exact same condition as the experience of pleasure*. In other words, a dog or wolf can't feel right if he's acting out of rhythm with his fellow group members; synchronization is the only way that emotion can flow through his prey instinct. Harmony and making prey are one and the same!

Every wolf or dog moves in a way and is elaborately marked and colored to release and heighten the effect the prey instinct exerts on the nervous system and emotions. We can visualize the group dynamic on the nervous system as being like a rheostat that controls the flow of electrons through a light bulb. When the switch is turned all the way up, the light glows brightly, the group equivalent to ecstasy. When the light is dimmed, the flow of electrons is reduced, and the emotional circuitry of the pack is commensurately squeezed. Whether the switch is open or closed depends on the group's focus. In hunting, if the central focus is a large prey animal, one that can absorb their collective predatory energies, the pathway is cleared all the way back to the simple prey instinct heretofore buried under mounds of stress. And in play, if the group is aligned on a harmonic pathway, pleasure that had to date been repressed can be consummated.

Once the group is coordinated along the harmonic pathways, members may act in ways that look to us like communication, hindsight, and foresight. In fact, each individual is merely following the rhythm of the prey instinct precisely in the manner his temperament is uniquely sensitive to. Whenever one of the wolves on our mountainside is charged by the sight or smell of a prey animal, and since they're bonded through hunting onto a common wavelength so that distance isn't an issue, the same dose of energy ripples through the others at the speed of light. They will act in conformance to the simple prey instinct and then to its complex nuances, known to them through their position within its order. Were group members not to align themselves, then the emotional juices would stop flowing, thereby injecting stress into the members' mood, threatening its collapse. It is in their mutual best interests and not due to an allegiance to a superior to align in deference to an overall order. Now, while all of a sudden the group's activity seems to have become highly complex, it is still in fact a simple alignment for the pursuit of pleasure. Intelligence is not to be found within the individual; it exists externally in the gaps between them. Intelligence is manifested in the group's relationships as woven by the prey instinct.

All relationships—between the group and its prey, among group members, and between mother and puppies—can be explained in terms of the prey instinct. The rule being: If an individual is in possession of a prey object such as a bone, or in control of his own body, even if he is the most inferior—*or the prey*—he controls whoever is attracted to that "preyful aspect." A female in heat is the focal point of the group due to her estrous secretions and her body mannerisms, and she will breed as she alone sees fit. The pups with their fuzzy movements and roly-poly bodies, and any group member infused with prey-making energy are in control of all who are attracted to them; their nerves have interfaced through early programming like a network of computers.

A submissive-acting inferior is in fact acting "preyful," not submissive, lowering his height, increasing his body vibrations (tail wagging and lip licking), and is secreting his essence (submissive urination). The more preylike he can make himself, the more surely he can unnerve an aggressor. Likewise, when the puppies yelp or whine, this discordancy penetrates right to the quick of an adult's nervous system, granting the pups complete license within the group while they are young and preyful.

ONENESS

The harmonic pathways of learning, whereby every member is aligned on parallel lines of flow, aren't abstract or only to be found on the tundra plains. Dog owners are quite familiar with them in the everyday things their pets do. They are observable as mimicry when dogs feign left, then right, and seemingly invite us to join them in a game of chase. And we've all known times when our dogs have sensed and responded in kind to either a buoyant or a depressed mood that we may be in. These are examples of the dog's nervous system, and therefore his feelings, becoming grafted onto the body language of his owner's so that his own emotions ebb and flow in resonance with the group that dog and owner make up. The dog *feels* your body language. How your emotions and nervous system move your body move an emotional charge inside his body as well. It *is* possible to reach inside a dog's mind and body and touch his soul. We perform this miracle every day with a soft touch of affection and a warm word of praise.

At all times a dog needs to be in tune with his owner so that his nerves are in balance, or in the best-case scenario, become mutually entangled in a harmonic pathway of pleasure. *A canine cannot experience a pure flow of pleasure unless he is neurologically in sync with his group. His nervous system is mirrored in each group member; it does not stand on its own.*

A harmonic pathway is created when individuals are on a common wavelength with a common purpose. Uninhibited play among dogs is a very pure example. The muscles are soft not stiff, tails are high and freely waving, and eyes are bright and alive. Emotional juices flow fast, leaving the participants happily exhausted at play's end. In one moment, one playmate will be the prey and the other the predator; the next moment, roles are reversed. The focus shifting the charge from one to another drives the emotional frenzy higher and higher. This rapid shifting is a sexual stimulation in and of itself. They'll clash teeth, grip the nape of the neck, tumble to the ground, and orgasmically writhe in the dirt. Often the pelvic thrust erupts when the "prey" on the ground lies still. Should one of them press the flesh too hard and elicit a growl or a yelp, that shrill note of discordancy penetrates to the nerve in both partners, crashing their joy into a heap. After the shock dissipates, the game is renewed with a wary caution toward closing in on that danger threshold, each dog self-modifying his behavior—as he does in hunting—to keep the game afloat. These dogs aren't learning how to play by learning not to bite; *through* biting they are learning *how* to play. When they are highly attracted to bite, and then elicit a squeal of pain, they are shocking *themselves* by biting too hard.

The critical point here is that they learn to self-limit their behavior through the expression of the urge to bite. By holding back a wee bit due to their vulnerability, they can constantly adjust their alignment to keep flow rolling along, garnering a sexual charge to boot, and so they quickly learn temperance as they are one with their prey. Discipline isn't being imposed on the individual from without, from the fear of retaliation. It arises from within, in the deep urge to keep on experiencing pleasure in rhythm with the prey instinct. Order, and a group leader, is created from this dynamic, not the other way around.

I've noticed that when it comes to car rides, all owners are awesome group leaders to their dogs. There the owner sits in the position of first place, the position of direct access, gripping the wheel, and sweeping it with an arc of commanding body language. Every decisive flick of the signal lever and tap of the brakes (or shouted expletive) adds to the luster of his position (since here the sensory stimulus associated with the authoritative body language is what makes the body language attractive—otherwise it would be threatening) the world swooshing by in a delectable flow of sensory delights. The rhythm of the car's vibrations and swayings accentuates the good feeling of being in phase with the dynamic virility of the owner's body language. The owner parks the car and gets out and upon his return finds his seat cozily warmed. Dogs crave the position of direct access to flow.

The harmonic pathways are the highest point of the prey instinct involving an unrestricted flow of energy from one individual to another. When the harmonic pathways are skillfully worked with (requiring far less effort than struggling with the dog anyway), the intermediary stage of stress can be bypassed as needed or greatly reduced or, even better, put to a higher use. The dog is put into a cooperative mood and becomes highly bonded to us as leader, eager to work to obtain whatever object on which we choose to focus the group. Even more important, the reflexes to sit, stay, heel, down, and come quickly—to be in alignment—are already on the "harmonic inner tape" held deep within the temperament, ready to pop right out given the proper excitation and releaser. When the dog is trained on a harmonic pathway, he learns from the inside out, with the specific intention of any obedience exercise being precisely translated into instinctive code. This rapport makes him extremely self-confident, since he moves in harmony with the leader, his access channel to the prey. Along the harmonic pathways an individual experiences an emotional confluence greater than anything possible by individual action alone, and so cooperation, affection, and loyalty become deeply impressed.

What we most need to glean from this discussion is that as hunting is the end purpose of the wolf's life, it is therefore a dog's, even though he may seem to prefer resting on the sofa for the better part of his day. We arouse the dog's drive to hunt without knowing it. Whenever we get him excited, or create the potential for relieving stress, or define a collective purpose, all of these being done by the simple act of opening a door to let him outside, we are inviting him to the hunt. The only question now becomes: Are we going to use this mechanism to be in tune with his prey instinct and train him how to behave or are we going to fight him over his evolved behaviors, causing him to tune us out?

Hunting transcends even reproduction in the grand design of nature. The bonds forged here can yield for us very handsome dividends for our effort in understanding it. When a canine becomes bonded to another, this member's body becomes *his* body, and he needs to connect with it in order to experience pleasure. I am not using the term *oneness* here in a vague way; I mean a visceral welding of the many into the one.

The irony in hunting is that despite its violence in the wild and its potential for nervousness in the home, it really is an attunement to others, and then an alignment with all the living beings in the situation, group members and prey animals alike. Symbiosis can't adequately convey how intimately linked the predator is to his prey and how they are mutually attracted to each other. Along the harmonic pathways, the emotional charge is passed from group member to member, converted into stress, and then volleyed over the thin line that separates hunter from hunted. Communion rather than communication is the best way to describe the flow of life in nature.

5

Myths About Learning

LEARNING EQUALS BONDING

Wolves don't learn directly how to cooperate with one another or to target vulnerable prey animals through random trial and error, not even through the consequences of their efforts. In reality, learning has been carefully pre-scripted along the harmonic pathways.

The catalyst to a harmonic pathway could be the smell of a fresh track, some droppings, an airborne scent, a flutter of motion, or the shape of a form. These stimuli release individuals from the veil of stress and put them instantly into sync with their fellows. If necessary, a group of wolves might need to tune in to one another through a visual or scent cue to deepen their connection back to the simple prey instinct. Wolves have been observed to scent a moose, assemble to touch noses with tails wagging, and then proceed toward the animal to test it. Once aligned on a common focus, either on a particular direction of travel or in the targeting of a prey animal, the synergistic weight of the group shifts toward this new center. The point that I have been developing throughout this book is that the perceptive faculty with which an individual wolf tunes in to and then aligns with the moods of his fellow group members is the same ability to detect which prey animal is weak and available for killing. Through the prey instinct, the wolf is able to tune in to the nervous system of its prey and read its innermost emotional balance, since it mirrors his own.

The wolf can "feel" who is ready to die by the subtleties in its mannerisms. In the graceful mechanics of a healthy prey-animal's body, there is a perfect symmetry. The movement and pace set by the animal's gait provide the key that fits into the inner temperament and unlocks the prey instinct, granting direct access to the code within. This arouses the drive to bite in the temperament's eternal quest for flow. When the prey's movements are distorted by injury, deformity, or age, the sexual desire to *fight* is turned on in the predator. At the moment of the strike, these simple and complex urges work together to regress the individual back to a mood of uninhibited biting, the final sequence in the chain of hunting reflexes.

As we look at all the growth and development a puppy goes through to prepare him for complex social living and an advanced style of hunting, there really is nothing *new* to be learned. Experiences are required not for practice, but to reawaken a memory of uninhibited biting already tucked away within the temperament that is only accessible through outside contacts. Since the full code resides within each member, once charged by a prey's stimulus, each nervous system in the group becomes synchronized with the rest. So while practice may be necessary, and although puppies do appear to be learning how to make prey by grappling with each other, and the mother does seem to be leading her brood off to learn how to hunt together, it isn't because the wolves or dogs need to learn how to make prey. What is happening here over the course of the litter's social development is that the need to be connected is being upgraded into a bond through a common pursuit in hunting. What we call learning is actually the process of bonding, and this is the force that spins the group wheel faster and faster, with the distinctions of individuality and separateness merging into oneness. At the pinnacle of unity, the complete prey instinct emerges, and fulfillment is at hand.

MYTHS

It's commonly held that dogs learn by association, communication, repetition, demonstration, rationalization, observation, trial and error, habituation, or imitation. Now, while some of these have something to do with the learning process, some of them absolutely do not. Even those that are relevant to learning are not fundamental. When they are seen as such, they serve to perpetuate many myths. We end up with a body of traditional beliefs and notions that reduce such terms as *intelligence* and *instinct* to buzzwords. An owner of a Border collie asks why his dog chases cars, and he's told it is because of a herding instinct. Because an Irish setter can open doors, his owner believes it is due to his superior intelligence. These fables are appealing, as they conveniently provide handy explanations for the diverse and complex things that dogs can do, but they are an intellectual dead end preventing us from becoming fascinated with the true mystery of behavior. We end up missing valuable clues as to how the canine mind actually works. The easy answers are seemingly satisfactory until you realize that we've only categorized data rather than explained it.

My premise, as I've stated, is that dogs learn through the expression of emotion into action, or to rephrase it so that we can have a term of more relevance to training, they learn through the "flow of drive." Drive is different from emotion in the sense that it is emotion under pressure; it is emotion contained within order, an order derived from the prey instinct. The pressure caused by containment gives drive a high degree of penetrating impact necessary to overcome a large prey. It is different from pleasure in that it has a definite focus toward which the organism won't feel satisfied until it is either attained or made contact with.

The manner by which drive flows through the dog's mind and body into the outside world determines and then reinforces his behavior. When drive flows *a dog experiences pleasure, and he's learning that what he is doing is good.*

A dog, awash in the mood in which he swims, can only appreciate his own immediate point of view. He can never entertain any other perspective, not even a familiar point of view that he may have experienced in the past, or one he is about to revisit in the immediate future. In any given moment he is completely immersed in the state of drive at hand. How emotional energy flows through the mood sensitizes the body in a particular way, with the dog becoming motivated to bring relief to whatever body part is affected. These sensations are how the dog "knows" how to act, and they guide and coordinate his behavior so that he complements his peers.

When drive flows, things that were once separate become connected in the dog's emotional impression of a situation even should they appear to us to be greatly different and the opposite to this rule holds true as well. When drive is blocked, what to humans may appear to be connected appears to the dog as distinct and separate. The prey instinct, when engaged, settles over these variables and brings them within its order. At this point of unity the dog's behavior takes on a clear focus, and his actions come to have a strong, coherent direction, as if he were aware of the consequences to his actions over the span of time and how his behavior might be affecting others.

Now let us examine some of the popular myths concerning how dogs are supposed to learn.

DOGS LEARN BY OBSERVATION AND IMITATION

A dog's emotions are primarily activated by his senses, particularly vision, as that sense best serves the active reflexes of the prey instinct—chasing, striking, biting, and fighting. When dog A is watching dog B, B influences what A is going to learn only through the effect of energizing him. By moving animatedly, dog B is exuding his "preylike" essence, thereby arousing the observing dog into a similar mood of drive. The more frenzied the first dog acts, the more excited the second one will grow. Emotional energy is being directly transmitted from one to the other; nothing of a mental nature is being communicated. Since all dogs carry the primal prey instinct as the basic software for their behavior, both dogs once put into the same emotional state of drive are likely to end up acting with roughly the same reflexes.

It may appear that the observing dog noted the first dog's behavior and then imitated him, but that isn't what happened. If high drive is being transmitted, high drive will be received, and the two dogs will act in unison within the prey instinct. The same goes for medium and low drive as well. Therefore, the two dogs inevitably will operate on parallel wavelengths even though neither of them is aware of the other's point of view. This is not in any way a cognitive capability; it is simply a "mirror effect" of the prey instinct that causes synchronization within the group. There will, however, remain variations between the two dogs' behavior based on temperamental differences, which allows for specialization if they have to work as a group.

Another example frequently cited to demonstrate learning by observation or imitation are those occasions when a young dog seemingly learns to bark at strangers by watching an older dog. In such cases, the knock on the door unnerves the older dog, and his discordant actions of barking or growling similarly unnerve the younger dog so that they are now both in the same mood. Defensive responses to stress are again part of the universal software of the prey instinct and so here, too, the younger dog appears to be learning by observation and imitation, when in fact, he is merely conforming to the master code operating within his temperament. He hasn't learned from the older dog's experience; he has simply learned from his own experience.

DOGS LEARN BY TRIAL AND ERROR

This myth presumes that there is a great element of randomness in nature, that things aren't connected, that it is random exploration and a mental ability of the dog to link elements together through his experiences that gives his behavior coherency. Dogs are presumed to explore one avenue of approach to a situation and then record the consequence as to whether they were successful or not. Then it is assumed that in a similar situation they can recall their experience and opt for a different approach if they're looking for a higher dividend. This theory presupposes that dogs, like humans, have the ability to deduce and make choices and that they can project even a millisecond into the future to predict a possible outcome based on a previous experience.

Dogs perceive their slice of the pie through their prey instinct. A dog can only respond to stimuli that are of relevance to this instinct. Therefore, problem solving for him has to do with ascertaining whether something is pertinent to this means of perceiving and experiencing. This basic information is what dogs are after when they smell, and that its function is so central to their lives is why they are so studious and assiduous about nasal activity. There is much in man's world that dogs have to deal with that is not at all straightforward in terms of the prey instinct, and there are many complex stimuli that only indirectly connect with or have a marginal impact on the prey instinct. Trying to come to terms emotionally with these and tie them together into a unified order is the main scope of the dog's learning process in our world. The stronger the attraction, the more direct the dog's response is going to be, and the more relevant his response to the problem in question.

When we see a dog trying several different approaches before taking a successful one or giving up altogether, it isn't that he's practicing. In his first impressions of a situation, he perceives several variables that aren't connected, and this dilutes his ability to solve the problem. If drive gets high enough, the variables merge into one coherent entity, an order, and a reflex relevant to the prey instinct will become available to him so that he can persist. By contrast, a dog that fails is exhibiting low drive in that moment, not being able to perceive an avenue of access. Instead of having one problem to solve, he has many problems to deal with; the variables never get tied together into one order. He tries, and then he stops, and then starts over anew without making any real progress, because he's faced with a new problem on each attempt. Each time his emotional reserves are drained lower.

No matter what dog we're talking about, the rhythm of the prey instinct as sensed through the temperament gives the individual an immediate feedback as to whether he's experiencing pleasure and relieving stress, or whether emotion is being internalized and stress is mounting ever higher. In each second the dog is being informed, via the prey instinct's influence on his nervous system, whether he's on the right track or not. The issue is whether the variables are tied together in the same order, thereby granting him access to his inner temperament. The individual isn't mentally rating his performance, nor need he wait for a result to be obtained in order to catalog his experiences. In each successive moment, his nerves are either in phase with the appropriate sequence of the prey instinct or they aren't. He reacts based on that immediate sensation and his actions are very often effective simply because he's responding to the way nature is organized, his instinctive reflexes mirroring this same organization. On the other hand, if the situation is completely foreign and irrelevant to the prey instinct, no amount of practice will allow the dog to benefit from his experiences.

DOGS LEARN BY DOMINANCE/SUBMISSION

This is an anthropomorphic theory that appeals to our intellectual sense of logic and the way nature appears to be ordered from the point of view of the human ego. Supposedly, dogs can learn to respect another individual through dominance. This presupposes that they can perceive another being's point of view. Humans can indeed entertain others' points of view, yet we know that no one learns to work effectively through the dominance/submissive model. No matter how much employees respect their boss or how submissive they may act around him, they expect to be paid fairly. Not enough pay and the attraction turns to resentment and a poor work-

ing attitude. Since humans reject and resist such an approach whenever they experience it, how can we expect the dog, with his more
limited view, to work on this basis?

Not only does dominating a dog make him resistant to cooperation, but dominance has nothing to do with the smooth operation of
wolf society. While it may appear that the leader is the most dominant in a pack of wolves, and that the inferiors have a profound
respect for this "alpha" wolf because he is so dominant, that is a
surface misreading of their lives. Supposedly this dominant individual teaches the other members of the pack what their lesser stations
are, bringing order and stability into the group. However, the reason this individual is superior is because, within the group mood,
he is endowed with the most uninhibited temperament and perceives order when the others sense disorder. This produces an
emotional balance—a self-confidence level—that makes him active
and direct in his behavior when the others are reactive and indirect. This confidence is then broadcast through his body language and probably through an internal chemistry revealed when
he eliminates.

Given the pack leader's internal balance, he will experience the
least amount of stress when passing on to less familiar ground, as
negatives are smaller in his sense of order. Furthermore, the pack
leader will feel the strongest compulsion to be first on any path that
leads outward to the hunt as he acts in the most straightforward
manner. The inferiors will depend on the pack leader's enthusiasm
to draw them across a threshold that may have a stronger inhibiting
effect on them. An individual doesn't become superior by being
dominant; the leader, to feel complete, needs the group behind
him, just as they need him at the fore. Only by leading the hunt
does one become a leader.

DOGS LEARN BY COMMUNICATION

If a dog could appreciate another being's perspective, he might
try to communicate, but then he would need a whole host of physical adaptations to his throat and neck structure. Not only is the
physical capability missing, but the mental hard wiring for communication isn't available either. More important, communication isn't
necessary to account for the way dogs learn.

There are two sources of this myth. First of all, if one talks to a dog, the dog responds. That's because our voice reveals our emotional balance; a rising inflection is attractive and a lowering inflection is repulsive, as it is with babies, for that matter. The same emotional energy that motivates a dog is also within man, so it is not surprising that a dog's temperament is charged by the energy transmitted as we talk to him. Of even more impact than our voice is our body language, which of course accompanies our speech and deepens its emotional content. When we talk softly or sweetly our body language is equally inviting; when we're loud and harsh our stance is similarly aggressive. Body posture and vocal projection go hand in hand, and this is foremost in the dog's ability to interpret our emotional moods.

Given the group dynamic in behavior, the dog will respond to the tone or inflection in our words by adjusting to us, thereby strengthening the myth that the dog understands what we're trying to communicate. That the rest of the time our words fail to have any beneficial impact serves to reinforce other myths (stubbornness, stupidity, etc.), instead of the simple observation that dogs are energized and not informed by our speech.

The second source of this misinterpretation is the biological interpretation of wolf behavior. Wolves attack animals much larger than themselves—reportedly, they may even drive their prey into an ambush—and therefore it is presumed that communication among group members needs to be sophisticated. The ability in wolves to yip, growl, squeak, bark, and howl is seen as an indication of communication relative to hunting. It is easy to see that this isn't so, because hunting is a *silent*, intense affair more like a dance. There is nothing to be gained by making noise. The prey looks inviting, the wolf "asks" the prey by advancing on him, and the prey choreographs the sequence of moves from there. There's no need to communicate, because all the wolves are born knowing the steps.

In truth, vocalizations in canines are an expression of resistance to the flow of drive when the body becomes polarized by stress. Vocal expressions and body language allow the others to react instinctually so they can all fit into the same mood. A mood is each member's sensations interconnected; it is the prey instinct's order.

There is, however, a vast amount of information flowing from one individual to another, especially through eye contact, but that still isn't communication in the human sense. Eye contact reveals the innermost balance of the nervous system. When canines are on the same frequency of prey making, they are of the same mind, and focusing on each other reaffirms the connection. And then when they're not, direct eye contact is extremely unsettling. When a wolf or dog is intently staring at a prey or another social being, he isn't so much looking outward as he is peering *into his own temperament:* the outside world being required to connect with the inner realm. All external stimuli are but mirror images of inner emotional balances.

DOGS LEARN BY ASSOCIATION

While dogs form associations, they don't directly learn by forming them. First they learn through the flow of drive and *then* they associate the level of pleasure or stress they experienced with the situation.

In the human mind an association is the linkage between thoughts, ideas, feelings, or sensations. These linkages form concepts that the human mind can then carry around and apply in novel, abstract ways and in new situations. A concept is a complex intellectual feat based on events that transpired over a span of time, and it also acknowledges that there may be other perspectives on the experience. In order to articulate something this complex, man requires an intricate language to communicate the vast range of possibilities created by intertwining the perspectives of many beings through the infinite dimension of time.

A dog, not having an intellect, can't range through time, nor can he entertain any other possible perspectives on an event. He only knows his own point of view in any one particular moment. A dog can't carry a lesson around with him as an internal concept—A caused B caused C, therefore A leads to C—that can guide and shape his behavior. He needs an external event in his immediate surroundings to awaken any internal memories, and its storage and retrieval have to be in terms relevant to the prey instinct. For example, a dog can't think of a bone he has buried unless he returns to the area and then familiar releasers rekindle the memory so that he can unearth it.

He forms an association in terms of drive, and this learning is then only valid in the place learned or for a preyful aspect focused on. If you trained your dog to sit by your side, every time you say *Sit* he will first have to come to your side. He never learned the concept of sitting upon command; the command is relevant if he's by your side. If you train your dog to heel, then everywhere you take your dog he can heel properly as your stimulus is right in front of him. But you can't just turn him over to a stranger and necessarily expect the dog to heel. For most dogs, this represents a brand-new order, since the variables have shifted widely and so the command to heel no longer has any meaning.

Huge mistakes in dog training occur when it's thought that a dog can form even the most rudimentary of concepts. For example, an owner scolds his dog for chewing on a rug and the dog stops chewing. To the owner it appears that the dog is forming an association about the rug and the owner's desire for the dog not to chew it. What the dog actually learned was that the rug delivers intense pleasure, pure drive flow, and that the owner is stressful. The dog avoids the owner by stopping his chewing and increasing his distance from the owner (or, with some temperaments, to be nervously—submissively—attracted to the owner). As the dog leaves the rug, his attraction to the rug remains and tugs at him, actually building in intensity like a rubber band being pulled away. When the owner isn't present the stress that dampened his nerves is absent, so the dog is drawn back to the rug even more powerfully; now the pure pleasure of chewing is coupled with the need to reduce stress. Interestingly, alternately shaking one's finger at the dog and then back to the rug in question makes the dog *need* to chew it to relieve the stress generated by the owner.

DOG OWNERS ARE INCONSISTENT

Poor dog behavior is often blamed on inconsistent dog owners. There is some merit to this, but this hardly means that all an owner has to do for success is to become consistent. In fact, all dog owners whom I've met, no matter how organized or how haphazard their approach in training might be, have one thing in common: They confront their dog over his behavior when his actions upset them. Whether the style of confrontation is old-fashioned, with an icy glare, a rolled-up newspaper, banishment, or a swat on the rump or high-tech, with an alpha wolf rollover, a cuff under the chin, or a shake by the scruff of the neck, from the dog's point of view they are all variations on the same theme.

Ironically, even if an owner is very progressive and humane, following appropriate positive reinforcement schedules or a love-at-any-cost approach, the dog will be compelled by instinct to seek out confrontations with the owner to satisfy the prey instinct. When a dog's prey instinct isn't exercised to drain the mind of social tension, the dog's fighting instinct becomes attracted to that very tension so as to purge the system of pent-up emotion. This is why the most pampered of pooches tend to be snippy even to the hand that feeds them.

Not only are dog owners incredibly consistent, but most places a dog may find himself, be it the city or the country, are pretty much alike to him as well. Because the prey instinct is all too infrequently utilized in a dog's training and development, most environments just offer different kinds of frustrations. So given a high degree of instinctual frustration and an inordinate amount of confrontation, from the dog's point of view, all dogs owners are consistently confusing.

Outside of extreme abuse, which in my view is rare, what distinguishes one home from another to a dog would be the degree of trauma that the dog's prey instinct experiences, either from frustration or direct confrontation. When the prey instinct is denied the dog experiences it as a shock. This is why so many dogs with sensitive temperaments act as if they have been beaten when they probably have not.

DOGS LEARN BY REPETITION

At a quick glance, it seems that a dog takes many repetitions to grasp a lesson. According to dogma, a dog has to practice a behavior many times until the lesson seeps into his limited mind. Then, once a lesson is mastered, it becomes so ingrained in the dog's brain that it becomes a habit. That dogs require repetition to learn from an experience is particularly noticeable when we are trying to train the dog to do something that isn't natural for him, such as walking nicely on a lead in an area full of interesting sights, sounds, and smells. It would seem that this exercise is difficult for a dog to learn and would require many practice sessions for it to become a reliable habit. Therefore, traditional thinking holds that it's best to start practicing the lesson with puppies before they might have the opportunity to practice the undesirable habit of pulling hard on the lead and also while they're small and easy to outmuscle.

A clue that repetition, while part of learning, isn't fundamental to learning is revealed by other observations that people commonly make that contradict this traditional premise. For example, we don't think of ball playing as something mastered through repetition. It looks like the dog is having fun, and that seems sufficient explanation. The first time the owner attracted his dog's attention to the ball and rolled it away, the dog immediately chased it, grabbed it, and then carried it around proudly. The lesson took one repetition and had a permanent effect for the rest of the dog's life.

This pure example of learning shows us the formula at the core of the process. If an activity is natural, the dog gets it immediately without the need for repetition. And, since the most natural activities involve the prey instinct, we find the best examples of quick learning in this regard. In ball playing, what determines each individual dog's enthusiasm and rate of progress is how much prey value he invests in the ball. That some dogs may take longer to build an attraction to the ball is not due to a need for repetition, but because the prey instinct isn't yet turned on. Through repetition, as the dog grabs the ball, his sensitivity to its novelty or his owner's influence starts to relax until drive starts to flow into prey making. Once uninhibited, the ball no longer has a being to which the dog needs to appeal for access, which initially thwarted his drive to chase and bite it.

A habit is like a riverbed: The stronger the flow that courses through it, the deeper the bed is carved, and the more water it will be able to channel. When the full current rushes through the organism, a completely mature behavior emerges as if learned. In truth, the lesson was gained in the first instant of making contact through the prey instinct, no matter how feeble the first trickle. It just took time for the pathway to be scoured deeply enough in the brain and body to handle the full load of drive.

DOGS LEARN BY WANTING TO PLEASE

The bedrock of most approaches in dog training is to appeal to this faculty, the desire to please, which is supposedly at the core of the domestic dog's character. According to this thinking, all an owner needs to do is to gain his dog's respect and then his dog instinctively will want to please him. Then when the owner makes clear what he expects from his dog, the dog will learn to do his bidding posthaste.

The simple truth is that a dog is attracted to his owner through his instincts. If the owner is highly positive to the dog's prey instinct, the dog will appear to be highly motivated to please, but it is really the drive to be in harmony through the prey instinct. By the same token, if the owner is abrasive to this faculty, the dog seemingly won't want to please and will appear to be stubborn. That there could be an intellectual point to the dog's attraction to his owner, that he should want to do something to please his owner, is beyond the dog's comprehension. A dog can never aspire to please anyone because he can never have the faintest idea what anyone else might possibly require to be happy.

DOGS LEARN THROUGH A FACULTY OF INTELLIGENCE

Most of what people interpret as intelligence is actually sensitivity. In humans, sensitivity facilitates intelligence, because it is a first step to perceiving another's point of view. But when a dog is sensitive, he is only being made more acutely aware of his own point of view. He is being sensitized to the barriers that prevent drive from flowing and that keep him from participating in the group mind. On the other hand, when a dog becomes high in drive, he will appear to be at his least sensitive even though he has integrated his nervous system into another's. This doesn't mean that he can appreciate another's point of view; high in drive while along a harmonic pathway, there is only the one group point of view.

In any discussion of intelligence it is mandatory to consider breed differences. From the dog's point of view, a main aspect of any problem involves bending the flow of drive in order to get around a barrier. When a dog successfully solves a problem, it's because his prey instinct channeled his emotional energy into a productive avenue, a harmonic pathway. Each breed is but a magnification of a particular harmonic pathway that stereotypes how he copes with barriers and how stress influences his temperament. A bird dog will appear to be smarter in terms of hunting birds, but this only reflects a behavioral manifestation of one aspect to the master prey instinct. A bird dog's drive is readily deflected, like a puppy's fluid adaptability to any new group, which is why these dogs are so social and why they can be so easily trained that the hunter is their access channel to the prey. A hound dog, on the

other hand, will appear to have more intelligence in hunting rac-
coons. This critter's preyful ways rather than the hunter's way is the
access channel in this case. A herding dog will seem to be more
intelligent if the problem at hand involves herding sheep. Such differences in performance among breeds reflect that variations in behaviors are but specializations within the grand theme of channeling
drive.

Since the human concept of intelligence isn't relevant to training, most professionals and breeders talk about drive, instinct, and
trainability when they compare breeds to breeds or individuals to
individuals, rather than discussing performance in terms of smartness. My own definition of trainability is a dog's ability to change
moods rapidly and yet still sustain a singular focus.

Because the dog is such an intense reflection of his surroundings,
and because the group dynamic means that his intelligent behavior
is catalyzed by his relationships with those he lives with, if one is
searching for their dog's mind in that mass of gray matter wedged
between his ears, one must look further, as it is not to be found
there. The dog's mind belongs wholeheartedly to the group mind,
it exists disembodied in the web of social ties as woven by the prey
instinct. When we ask if our dogs are smart or are willing, the question is a self-examination. Ultimately, we have only ourselves to account for. There is no sense getting mad, disappointed, or frustrated
by a dog's behavior and then looking askance at him for his supposed
deficiencies. A dog mirrors his owner.

6

Conflict of Interests: Dogs Versus Owners

SO FAR, WE'VE BEEN LOOKING AT things from the dog's natural point of view. We've seen that a dog lives to hunt and bite, but a dog doesn't live in nature. He lives in man's world, and he's not free to bite and run as he pleases. We have to consider how to reconcile the dog's drive with his owner's needs, because clearly something has to give. The degree to which a compromise isn't worked out to everyone's mutual satisfaction will be the degree to which the relationship will be tense and the dog will become disobedient or neurotic.

What does the owner want and need from his pet so they can live together in harmony? Most dog owners I've met aren't looking for a fancy show dog that can do exotic things; they just want the dog to be mannerly and to listen to them when it's really important. They also need the dog to be predictable. An unstable dog puts himself or others in danger, not to mention the legal liability in these litigious times. The dog owner needs to know how the dog is going to respond in all situations. My father put it well when he said, "A dog should be a maximum of joy and a minimum of anxiety." Dog owners want the simple pleasures of companionship and, mostly, they want their dogs to love them. Let me assure the reader that everything he is looking for in the relationship is simple, reasonable, and easy to obtain.

Meanwhile, all a dog is looking for is to be connected to a group so that he can make prey. Anyone who has ever driven home with a new fuzzy puppy snuggled in his lap readily understands this basic need of the dog for warm, emotional contact. But it won't be long before the puppy discovers that the laundry basket is home to a "covey" of socks, fit to seize and race about the house with. Those socks are as instinctually scrumptious and squeezably soft as any quail.

A dog has a happy attitude in life when his need to be connected and his desire to bite are in harmony so that he feels complete. *This harmony is the only way the dog can recognize and absorb his owner's love.*

Bonding with one's dog by satisfying his need to hunt is as easy as it is vital; however, it has been my sad experience to find that most owners unwittingly are working very hard to short-circuit their best intentions. They will read things into their dogs that aren't there, and in so doing, they will miss what's really going on, as well as the opportunity to take advantage of their dogs' cooperative nature. At best, they end up with a pet that is merely dependent on them. This propensity in dog owners is almost involuntary, because it will flow from very deep emotional aspects of the owner's relationship with his pet. No matter how much intelligent data the owner may hear or read about the true nature of his dog, until he gives up certain ideas that are rooted in these deeply held personal beliefs, he won't be able to implement any of the useful knowledge he may have gleaned.

This chapter will explore these ideas and impressions and show how they're corrosive to the relationship between dog and owner because neither party ends up getting what he wants or needs.

A THEORY OF BEHAVIOR

As the relationship with a dog deepens, the owner loses his ability to make calm and objective training decisions. He will assume that his dog's needs flow from the relationship, as the owner's needs do. He will develop a theory for his dog's behavior predicated on their relationship. Such a bias will make him unaware of his dog's true nature, and then a large part of the dog's temperament will be left unsatisfied. The dog will start to develop problems, and instead of seeing the problem's natural cause, the dog owner will either gloss over it or define it in terms of a problem with their relationship.

Due to this thinking, the dog is interpreted and dealt with as if he were a moral and intellectual being, knowing the difference between right and wrong. Eventually, within this broad view of dogs, the owner will further develop a specialized theory to explain what makes his own particular pet tick. Then as issues come up that need to be solved, such as the rules of the household, these conceptual and moral guidelines for human relationships are transposed to the dog in order to establish behavioral guidelines. Since it's assumed that the dog realizes the impact of his behavior on the relationship, this course of action seems logical and reasonable to the human mind, which can conceptualize without any effort.

If a dog owner ever finds himself using the term *shouldn't,* as in, "Scruffy shouldn't do that," to categorize his dog's behavior, his theory has morality imbued in it. Whenever a dog owner uses the term *knows,* as in, "Scruffy knows how to do that," his theory has assigned an intellect to the dog's mind. If we boil this kind of theorizing down to its central premise, we have to admit that we think of a dog as *a furry little person who just can't talk!*

Even though such an idea clearly isn't supportable, it is constantly perpetuated, because dogs will display submissive and evasive instincts when their owners get upset. These instincts are associated with such human moral standards as guilt, jealousy, spite, etc., and are then seen as proof that the theory is correct.

When the dog is caught on the couch and is reprimanded, he acts submissive and looks like he's "sorry." Later, when the owner walks into the room, the dog hops off the couch without being told. Now he appears to be feeling "guilty." If a dog could talk, he presumably would be able to say, "I know I'm wrong to do this because dogs shouldn't be on furniture as it makes their owners upset when they find out." These submissive and avoidance instincts are misinterpreted as demonstrating a moral and intellectual capacity in the dog, rather than as simple evidence that a dog can feel his owner's anger at that moment and is reacting in an instinctive way to maximize his chances of surviving the encounter.

Whenever Scruffy hears, "Scruffy, don't you *know* you *should* never, ever, do that?" Scruffy runs for his life.

Actually, one of the main reasons we think about a dog in moral terms is not out of concern for the dog's welfare, but because if we as dog owners occupy high moral ground, we can feel better about ourselves no matter what course of action or inaction we might choose to take. The bottom line here is that a theory about a pet's behavior that is intertwined with the emotional aspects of the relationship has absolutely nothing to do with getting to a desired objective. This is why in so many cases a deteriorating pattern of behavior doesn't threaten the theory until the owner's safety comes into the formula, or until the dog goes clearly out of control, in which case the dog's welfare may finally be taken into account. I think this is why when the owners of problem dogs finally come to me for help, they appear emotionally spent and exasperated; this issue has touched them so very deeply.

The other reason for developing a behavioral theory based on the relationship is to validate the kinds of intellectual methods that we humans are most comfortable with. Human beings are communicators, and it takes two intellects to enjoy a dialogue. Therefore, it's handy if the dog is assigned an intellect so that he can be addressed and informed of the concepts that we think he needs to know. This means that the owner is going to do a lot of demonstrating and talking. Once again, such an approach has nothing to do with dog training.

I find that in the informational marketplace this tendency gets a lot of reinforcement, as trying to communicate with animals is currently the height of fashion. In books, articles, and on television, the average dog owner will find an endless accounting of the drive to communicate in the animal kingdom. Many times the canine species is held up as a prime example of this capability. Seeing wolves howling and dogs barking as forms of communication encourages the owner to invest his energy in talking through a situation, trying to show the dog what he means, instead of understanding and working with his instincts.

It is an unfortunate trend; rather than looking for what is manlike in animals, it's more revealing to look for what is animallike in man. That's where we'll find our common linkage.

Below are some of the philosophies and doctrines I've found people use to deal with their pets—theories that arise from the view of the dog as a moral and intellectual being.

The Fairness Doctrine

"You, my dog, are my buddy, my friend. I will treat you the way I want you to treat me." The problem here is that this puts the dog's mind into chaos. A dog needs to know his place, and he needs to sense a clear structure in the group in order to find his place. When you try to be a friend to your dog, he will become confused, as it's being left up to him to figure out where his place is. Not only does this lead to friction and occasional tragedy, but at best the dog will be confined to a world of nervousness because he has no peace in any of his endeavors.

In this attitude, all influence over the dog is gauged by a "humane" standard that is actually a *human* standard, or how the owner would feel if he were in that position. In order for a dog to know where he belongs in his owner's life, his instincts need to find expression, and he needs to be approached and dealt with as a dog, not as a furry little person.

If geese tried to migrate using the fairness principle, they would have to fly abreast in a straight line and they wouldn't get far. There is no such thing as fairness in nature, and it's futile to try to cultivate a trait in a dog that can't possibly take root. A dog needs order, and that means subordinance to the purpose of the group, which only the owner is in a position to know.

The Love Doctrine

Some people see dogs as "love cushions." In this system, love is dished out lavishly and then withheld when the dog doesn't conform to the owner's expectation. Unstructured affection is the quickest way to alienate a dog, as it creates the canine equivalent of contempt. Love is an inaccurate term to use here, because it isn't love from the dog's point of view; he is not being accepted as a dog.

Ironically, if attention and love are the dog's only means of feeling connected to his owner, he will become very anxious. He no longer is in control of his own emotions, so he'll constantly be treading a thin line between dependency and panic.

The Permissive Doctrine

This is the attitude that to control a dog is like caging a lion; it's considered immoral and bad for the dog's spirit. Once again, this will confuse a dog because there is no such thing as freedom in nature. An animal is born wild, a slave to his instincts. Every animal in the forest is in a daily struggle to survive, and there is no time or capability for idle or creative musing. All live through their instincts, and only in those fleeting moments when instincts are fully expressed and fulfilled do the animals feel "free." It is a short-lived sensation, for in the next moment the weight of survival reasserts itself.

Training doesn't damage character. By shaping instincts into a sense of place, the dog becomes strengthened. Training is a responsibility inseparable from dog ownership.

The Domination Doctrine

Some people have very strong personalities and deal with the dog from this perspective. Others read about wolves and try to be the pack leader through the dominance behaviors that the alpha wolf displays in the natural setting. This confuses the dog because it is only teaching him that he has *no* place. As we've discussed, in nature there actually isn't a dominance or submissive thought in the mind of the wolf or dog. The overriding motivation is to get the group working smoothly, as the group brings about the highest level of individual satisfaction. All the members of the pack learn their place through working together, through the hunt and the killing of prey, and our job here is to develop an alternative means of achieving the same high ends.

The Dog as a Wacko

Whenever the dog's behavior won't fit into the prevailing theory, a term is introduced to cover the irregularity. These special terms are then put under the heading of *personality*. But dogs don't have a personality, they have a temperament. When the temperament is ignored by the theory, dogs develop defensive strategies that the owner then misinterprets as his personality. Personality quirks fill voids in the theory; the dog is called crazy, hyper, dumb, stubborn, or said to have a mind of his own (whose mind can it be?), and the like. Once the behavior is labeled, whenever it crops up again we can say, "That Scruffy, he's nuts."

Emotional theories and doctrinaire approaches toward dogs bind both parties into a self-sustaining and negative feedback loop, because it gives the dog the chance to experience, even if for only the briefest of moments, the difference between man's way and nature's way. Naturally, the dog will always choose the latter as it represents the path of highest pleasure. And in the little snippet of freedom the dog is allowed while the owner wastes time by reacting and trying to communicate, the dog will taste the sweet fruit of the wild life and thereafter calmness, when the owner wants control, will become more and more difficult.

Finally, the situation will hit rock bottom and the owner, in total exasperation, will resort to confrontation. This puts the dog deeper and deeper into defensive strategies in response to such intense pressure. Such an overload injects a huge dose of tension into the social life of the dog and this starts a new chain of learning, whereby the dog will *need* to be disobedient.

SOCIAL RESISTANCE

A dog confused by the moral and abstract dimensions of life in a household becomes defensive toward his owner in order to get back to the business of being a dog. Tension between dog and owner is "social resistance" that is a generalized nervousness inherent in the wild pack life of the wolf. It's like a mighty spring coiled back, storing potential energy that's reserved for eruptions about group disputes (the discordant pathways) and also propels the group out into the field on hunting forays. Around the home, when social resistance finally explodes, it will never find a domestically acceptable form. Subsequently, there are two general types of characters that the dog can develop.

The first type is what I call Bleached Character. This is the dog that has been given too much latitude for whatever reason. The dog's drive has leeched out into the environment and is naturally channeled by free-ranging activities with neighborhood dogs or through chasing squirrels. On a surface reading this type of dog appears to be calm and stable, since on the average his character isn't pent up with stored drive. However, whenever the owner has to put a demand on his behavior, the dog becomes hyper or panics. A little burden becomes a big overload. His character is actually brittle, like the handle of a shovel that's left out in the rain and the sun. One goes to pry a rock out of the garden with it and it snaps in two.

The second type I call Bruised Character. This is the kind of dog that has learned that whenever he is excited by something—the garbage, a squirrel, another dog—he gets into trouble. He is hit, yelled at, or bullied out of his drive activity. Such a dog learns to anticipate an impending battle by familiar circumstances, like clouds forming on the horizon, and he will become preemptive to protect himself. Unlike the bleached-out dog, he isn't given the chance to get far from the stressful conditions, since he's mostly indoors, tied up, or territorial by nature. As he can't maintain the distance needed for his comfort level, he doesn't appear as "calm" as the bleached-out dog. His nervousness is on the surface and he acts more hyper.

Social resistance acts like a battery in that it stores emotional energy, holding it pent up until a releasing instinct becomes available. It is the means by which the dog keeps score of his wins and losses; it is the dog's social *memory*. A dog owner can win a thousand straight battles with a puppy, then, years later, lose the war.

When a dog is burdened with social resistance, he will be oppositely polarized by whatever the owner does. There are hundreds of manifestations. If the owner wants to go through a door, the dog will need to bull through first. Then when the owner wants the dog to come in, the dog will balk. Trying to put a collar on will prompt the dog to wiggle away or lower his head to the ground. When asked to sit, the dog will comply slowly, or will increase his distance from his handler or hook his paw on his lead. In training classes, I find that these dogs are unwilling to point in the same direction as their handler or to sit still for more than two seconds. Basically, whatever the owner wants the dog to do, the dog perceives as negative, and whatever the owner doesn't want the dog to do is perceived as a positive. The world is turned upside down.

In effect, the owner has become a catalyst for confusion and conflict and his attention and praise to the dog become perverted. Ideally, praise should make a dog feel good about being with us, to be an effective reward for doing something that may have been difficult and unnatural for the dog. However, when a dog is bleached or bruised he evaluates all data in terms of their survival value, rather than as catalysts for a harmonic pathway. Ironically, with submissive dogs the problem can be masked because the dog becomes even more unrelentingly friendly.

Unfortunately, when burdened with social resistance, the owner's attention to the dog actually reinforces his feeling of incompleteness.

THE ANSWER: SCRUFFY, MEET YOUR MASTER

When I ask people to reexamine their ideas about their dogs and how they need to be handled, a lot of them ask, "Why own a dog if I can't treat him as a child, or as my friend?" Maybe I'm idealistic, but why can't we love the dog just for what he is? Why does he have to reflect positively on our ego or compensate for our needs? Parents love their infant before the baby can know how to please or obey them, before he can return their love or manifest any of the virtues we assign to dogs. Babies are limited and yet they are loved unconditionally for what they are and for the incredible mystery and beauty of love and life they reveal to us. To force a dog into a role to serve one's misconceptions is to deny its nature and the beauty to be found in nature.

Letting go of these old ideas and ideals of dogs may be hard at first, but I can promise the reader that a new view is not at all limiting. One can love a dog as a dog, instead of trying to re-create a human kind of relationship. Besides, the panoramic vista afforded by being sensitive to the dog as a vital part of nature is breathtaking.

A dog isn't looking for a best friend; he doesn't want to be "part of the family"; he's not looking for a litter mate or a substitute for his mother. He doesn't want hugs and kisses, to be dominated, or to have a partner in life's journey. All he wants or needs is for his owner to be his master.

When one is a master, one has an objective knowledge of what the dog truly is, so the dog's welfare can then come above the emotional attachment to the pet. That is a genuine love for the dog. I shudder to think of all the dogs I've known that have been "loved" in the old way of thinking, quite literally to their death.

Mastery of a dog doesn't mean a master–slave relationship. It's a much deeper concept such as what a child craves from a parent and an apprentice looks for in a mentor. To the dog, the owner is all, the owner controls all, the world works through the owner's mastery of it. A dog becomes complete and thereby bonded to, rather than dependent on, his master. Man is the most awesome creature in nature; all animals feel this power and an owner must live up to that instinctive expectation in his dog. Man is the big negative, the whole enchilada, and this touches a dog at his very core. So go ahead and be human, but use human intellect to become sensitive to an animal's conciousness as opposed to rationalizing an emotional bias.

A master cannot be arbitrary, so an owner must be governed by two skills: sensitivity and decisiveness.

To be a master an owner must be sensitive to the needs, the desires, and the limitations of his dog, which is why we have spent so much time discussing how the prey instinct modifies behavior and controls learning.

To master a dog, we must be *decisive* and control everything the dog learns so the dog will have no opportunity but to learn what we want him to learn. When a dog owner approaches his dog from the emotional and doctrinaire points that we've talked about, the owner's judgment is immobilized by guilt, anxiety, and anger. We need to be fully in control of our emotions, because they are our primary training tools. We attract our dog's instincts, which then become available for training, through the emotional energy that we generate.

A dog sees his master as the answer to the confusion of the domestic world and not the source of it. Without a master, a dog is beleaguered with social resistance, and he learns to keep his "dirty little drive secrets" tucked away deep in his temperament, his character no longer expressing drive directly. He waits for his owner to be away from him or inattentive before he feels free enough to express himself instinctively. The rest of the time he covers up what is deep in his heart with his "personality." Let's release the dog from moralistic expectations that mislead us into giving the dog freedom as a kind of test, thinking that the dog has mastered a concept or a moral standard of conduct. This only leads to disappointment. Instead, everything should be managed: The dog has absolutely no unsupervised freedom; we obtain positive results according to an objective criterion; and the dog can enjoy a life of participation in the family. A dog is happy to be a dog; all we have to do is learn how to treat him as one and give him what he needs.

DEVELOPING WORKING CHARACTER

As I've defined bleached and bruised characters as possibilities we want to avoid, I'll spend a brief moment here talking about our objective: working character. This means that the dog brings his drive to his owner in order to gain satisfaction. The owner can then select an instinct that both fulfills the dog and brings him into balance with the owner's life-style. We'll get into the specifics of this kind of dog in the developmental and training sections, but take heart that in the matter of the dog's feeding, you have probably already mastered the necessary principles. When your dog was a puppy you recognized his limits and his desires and you kept the feed bag securely locked away. The pup wasn't free to feed himself; through such decisiveness on his owner's part, he learned he needed you if he was to eat. When he's grown, whenever he's hungry, he comes looking for you. The more excited he is about eating, the harder he'll look to find you. We're about to find this same learning can be applied to every issue, from coming when called to lying down, and staying put. He can be trained so that the more he may want to do something, like chase a cat, the harder he'll work to be in harmony with you. Uninhibited drive and calm control are not mutually exclusive. All that is required of an owner to effect this cooperative spirit is sensitivity and decisiveness.

7

"Kiss with a Touch"

SOMETIMES YOU LOVE your dog so much, or he looks so irresistibly cuddly, or he's done something so incredibly good, that you want to bend over and plant a big kiss smack dab on his schnozz. But if you ever watch a dog's reaction to being smothered with a kiss, you can clearly see that the worst way to transmit your affection is via a kiss. From the dog's point of view, if a human head is put toward his, it is a form of aggression toward him. Just because he loves you doesn't mean he likes smooching. So don't kiss a dog with a kiss, kiss him with a touch. Touching, body contact, the physical compression of the group immersed in their mutual good spirits is how a dog comes to feel connected and loved.

The great thing about working with dogs is that each one presents a new opportunity in the adventure of learning. I've been around dogs all my life and yet I learned one of the most important lessons from a young girl hired to care for the dogs boarded in our kennel. She was emigrating to this country and couldn't speak any English. She was extremely gentle and sensitive, almost timid, and fittingly, her name was Timy.

Initially, I didn't envision her handling any of the aggressive dogs in the kennel. Yet, I soon noted that she not only could walk into the most aggressive dog's kennel but could calm the most fearful kind of dog as well. I observed her technique and was struck by the profound effect she had on one dog.

A pampered little dachshund had been admitted to the kennel for boarding. After settling in to his new domain, he wouldn't let anyone touch him and launched himself into a frenzy whenever approached. I cautiously looped a lead over his head and found him a quiet place in the cattery, away from the hubbub of the daily kennel activities that had so unsettled him. Later I intended to instruct the other workers on how to handle this dog. But an hour later I noticed that Timy was carrying the dog back to his cubicle. She had taken him out on her own initiative and I assumed that he must have simply adjusted. I approached his gate and to my surprise he erupted into his regular display.

Later that afternoon, Timy came to get him again and I watched carefully. He carried on aggressively as she approached, but she didn't react at all. She didn't look at him or slow down or speed up. Calmly and gently, she approached and opened his gate, seemingly at a pace that put her in sync with this dog. As the gate opened, the dachshund retreated to the far corner. She cooed to him softly and extended her hand closer to him, but far enough away so as not to be provocative. She let her fingers dangle limply with her palm held down in a totally passive position. After several long moments the dog's snarls and growls tapered off and he tentatively sniffed her fingers. As he continued to smell, she slowly escalated her verbal reassurances. Slowly, as he became a little animated, she turned her palm face up and brought her other palm alongside, and the dog hopped aboard, apparently eager for a ride like a young child atop his father's shoulders.

Upon reflection, I realized that Timy's style was so passive and sensitive that it calmed the dog. She gave him the chance to tune in to her, and he could align with her at a pace his nerves required. When the first fragile physical connection was made, all the resistance that provoked his defensiveness immediately melted away. By working so slowly and sensitively, she became a mirror to the dog's aggression, doing absolutely nothing to reinforce it. Once turned on itself, the dog's aggressive drive quelled itself and the group dynamic, which stands behind every ounce of a dog's emotional drive, was able to express itself.

Having made this connection with Timy, after a few days the dog's demeanor changed toward everyone else. Soon the dog grew happy and eager to make contact with any of the other workers who were patient enough to go at his speed.

Along these lines, I want to tell a story about Penfield, a German shepherd husky cross. In the office when the owner was registering the dog for boarding, the dog lunged at me and clearly had biting in mind. I was able to safely secure him by the lead and when the owner left the dog became more tolerant of me, as his focus was now diverted. I took him to his kennel and set him loose, but from there on out, whenever anyone walked by, the dog would explode violently against his gate. On this first visit I didn't have any time to attempt to befriend him, and my policy at this point was just to ignore a dog that didn't want to socialize. When the owner returned I had him go to the dog's kennel to retrieve him. On the dog's next visit several months later, I resolved to defuse his aggression and put Timy's technique to a more rigorous test. The more the dog would bark and lunge at me, the greater my praise of his virtues would grow. Then I would slide his food bowl into his kennel and leave the gate slightly ajar, trickling food into the pan. There I would sit, casually repeating my high opinion of his good character as he fed. In a short while his tail would hint of a wag. When I saw this sign I left my hand limply exposed at the gate's seam so he could sniff me if he felt so inclined. He smelled cautiously, and I was careful not to make any eye contact with him, as I could see he was expecting some kind of trickery from me. After several repetitions I was able to walk in, and by the next day I was able to give the dog a good petting and a rub-a-dub all over his backside. Amazingly, after only a few days he would melt like butter as soon as he saw me approaching, even though he hadn't softened or relaxed his vigilance toward the rest of the staff. When the owner returned, I nonchalantly walked the dog to the office, talking to my good buddy Penfield.

Not until a year later did the dog board with us again, and he arrived while I was out. My manager gave me an anxious rundown of a dog that had to be put by his owner into a holding kennel and now wouldn't let anyone near. When I heard it was Penfield I groaned; I didn't feel like going through the orientation process all over again, and it was too bad I had missed the opening bell when my chances would have been greatest. I ventured out to resume my acquaintance with Penfield fearing the worst, but to my complete amazement the dog, upon seeing me for the first time in over a year and from a distance at that, instantly dissolved into bubbling effervescence. He hadn't forgotten our rapport and was just as intensely social toward me as he was the day he had left. The permanence of the trust that is generated through the avenue of touch is truly startling.

Touching is the way to calm a nervous dog that has learned everything on the discordant pathways. If gentle and passive, it melts resistance, and it only takes a moment or two as a first measure to help stimulate a dog to go your way instead of nature's way.

8

One Problem to Solve: An Introduction to Training

WERE WE ABLE TO ask a dog how he felt about living in man's civilized world, and if he could put his feelings into our human language, he would say, "Every time I get excited or nervous, I get into trouble. What am I supposed to do with my drive?"

Dogs see the world in their own way, and they solve problems in their own manner. For them dog training represents a lot of unnatural obstacles to overcome. When we humans think of dog training, we think about our dog learning all kinds of skills, such as heeling by our side, listening to commands, doing this, or not doing that. We think in terms of teaching the dog a wide variety of rules and regulations. It appears to us that the dog has dozens and dozens of things to learn, but at the deepest level, the dog only has the one issue of drive in his heart. So no matter how different one situation may look from another to us humans, to the dog, it all involves the same question: *What is he to do with his drive?*

The matter of drive and its flow must therefore be foremost in our approach to training, for no matter how well we may think we have taught our dog to heel or sit, and no matter what the rules of the house are, if we haven't addressed this fundamental concern of the dog, he will never be 100 percent reliable. In fact, the likelihood is that he will never have learned how to be under control in the first place, and that a great degree of resistance between dog and owner will lie unresolved and crop up again in future encounters or nervous outbursts.

The term that best describes what should be going on when one trains one's dog, a term that I first heard from the eminent German dog trainer Helmut Raiser, is *channeling*. In training a dog we are channeling his drive from instinctive, wild behavior into domestically acceptable behavior. Furthermore, understanding the dog's natural learning mechanism is mandatory, or otherwise we will need to rely on mere force, and the effects of such training would lack permanence and have only a weak influence when the dog is away from his handler. For a trained behavior to be of a lasting duration and impregnable to distractions, it must be learned by the dog on a harmonic pathway, from the inside out, and therefore we have to consider how the training exercises appear to the dog's point of view.

On the other hand, a dog not trained with the principles of channeling in mind might very well listen to its owner when it doesn't matter; however, in a critical moment, dog and owner are destined to be dreadfully out of sync. So instead of trying to solve a thousand little problems without regard to an overall balance (which would be like building a house without consulting a blueprint), I suggest that we break down each problem to its most fundamental element as it pertains to the flow of drive. In this approach we'll find at the core of every problem the same central element. By taking heed of this standard, every area of our training will be in balance with every other area. Each step will dovetail neatly into the next step on a smooth and steady progression, with social resistance melting away not only in the exercise at hand, but most gratifyingly in other areas of the dog's life.

A big advantage here is that when we arouse the dog's drive and then channel it appropriately, the dog is put into a mood of calmness that is the only condition in which he is ready and able to learn what a command means. Another way of saying this is that when we frame a problem for the dog in terms of his drive, we are giving him the answer before exposing him to the problem. Before he will ever experience any correction for misbehavior, his drive will have first been programmed to flow in the appropriate direction. Once this flow is strongly imprinted, all corrections will then be perceived by the dog as stimulants of a deepened attraction to his handler, and the obedience exercises as a means of being connected to the group.

I am reminded here of how parents teach children to speak, read, and reason—exactly in this natural way. In fact, we make sure the child knows the answer before we burden her with the question, pretending all the while that she came up with it on her own. For example, we might ask a child what two and two equals only after having first taught her how to count to ten on her fingers. And as we wait for her response, we'll display four fingers prominently, perhaps simultaneously, using an exaggerated facial expression to convey the word *four*. If that's not enough, the sound of the first consonant somehow slips past our lips as if by accident. Needless to say, in order for the child to even be able to discern these cues, she must first be in the mood to learn, in other words, attracted to us and appreciative of the attention.

Now, in order for a dog owner to give his pet the answer, he must present the information to him in terms that he can understand, because it is a futile exercise to try to communicate objectives through the human techniques of communication. This means arousing the dog's drive, in other words, his feelings, which are nothing more than the simple urge to bite blended together with the need to be connected. And the dog finds this information embodied in our body language—for example, how the handler positions the food, the ball, or the overall expressiveness of his body movements—which, in the instinctive sense, is translated into the visual imagery of access to prey. Therefore, the bulk of training time should be allocated to improving the degree and purity of excitement that we can evoke from our dog. Only when we get the dog excited and high in drive so that he learns to associate us with this happy state of affairs, are we in a position to take the raw emotional power that fuels behavior and sharpen and refine its focus so that the dog is resolutely fixated on the harmonic pathway, with his owner at its center.

Putting the dog into the proper mood, one of attraction to his handler, is therefore the most important fundamental in channeling. The traditional way of commanding the dog and then trying to show him what the command means is the wrong way to train one's dog. It causes the dog to associate the command with the shock or discomfort of having been made to change moods, especially without any instinctive gear shifting to soften the shock. Before being commanded to heel, for instance, the dog may have been in the mood for examining buttercups or inspecting grasshoppers. Arbitrarily changing the dog's mood without providing a good enough instinctual reason grates on his nervous system, precluding his ability to learn in a positive manner. The dog is being stressed, being presented with a problem, and yet the answer we want him to grasp is not readily before him. By bellowing a command, we're not acting in an attractive manner, and neither is the dog being motivated to be receptive to our help. The dog, by being commanded out of context with the mood he is in, is being pushed along a discordant pathway of learning.

If we want performance from a dog, we first must inspire the appropriate mood that will then evoke the desired behavior. Behavior flows from a mood, so we must first use the flow of drive to create the desired mood. Remember, the dog is reactive; his behavior flows out of either a group or pack mood, it doesn't just pop out on its own. Create the mood (arouse drive), provide the releaser (a harmonic pathway of access to the desired target), and the behavior we want to cultivate will follow. Take note that every action that we want the dog to perform, be it heeling, sitting, laying down, coming when called, and staying out of the garbage or off of the sofa is already on file within the dog's temperament. The dog already "knows" what to do, he just needs to be put into the proper mood. So forget the idea that you must teach him how to sit, how to lie down, and so on. He already knows how to do these things, he comes from the factory fully equipped, there is not any knowledge that we need to cram down his throat. Notice that the infant puppy is born knowing how to search and respond to his mother. He innately knows what is good or bad for his survival and development so that he unerringly seeks warmth and nourishment. He knows how to align with his littermates to gain access to his mother's teat, and he knows to be calm and content once he's found what he needs, just as he knows to be anxious when deprived of his lifeblood. In training, all we ever need to do is inspire or rekindle this inner knowledge in the dog through the arousal of his drive. Once drive is elicited, a mood of attraction is established, and ultimately the desired behavior will come forth. Now the dog is ready to have the relevant verbal command associated with the desired behavior. Channeling drive through this sequence ensures that at the end of the training program the command will instantly evoke a cooperative response from our pupil. The experience of flow is the natural mechanism by which mimicry and alignment can occur for a dog.

In all training exercises, we're looking for straightforward expressions of drive so that the dog works in a straight line, parallel to that of his handler. When drive flows directly, his behavior is pure, and he works with a happy attitude; these are the moods we want our commands to evoke.

Thus, training must always be approached from the issue of drive and its flow, not dominance and submission, reward and correct, or command and demand. If we fail to work with the fundamentals of drive, we create within our dog's temperament a block, one that prevents him from aligning with us on a harmonic pathway, and that is a recurring obstacle in any new situation. It continually sets up a field of resistance between dog and man, and so whenever any critical moment crops up, it serves as an additional impediment to calm learning. A dog so impaired ends up acting crooked—submissive, dominant, nervous, in short, confused.

In dog training we need to answer these questions: If we want to train the dog to our command, how are we first going to attract his drive? And, if the dog's drive is already aroused, how are we going to permit the dog to find relief?

There are also those situations that are so unnatural that an evolved instinct isn't available to handle the flow of drive. A stranger knocking at the front door is a highly charged event, and the social instincts of many dogs are not designed to easily plug in such a scenario so that drive can be calmly fulfilled. Excitement in a dog turns to nervousness if a course of action—a pathway to the target—isn't clear while high in drive. The dog just can't be told not to have drive—"Quiet! Calm down! Stop jumping! Go to your place! ¢ &!!#*%!"—he's stuck with it, like a car approaching a curve at high speed. What is such a dog to do with his drive? In the matter of a stranger being welcomed into the home, the owner needs to deepen the group mood through praise and constructive obedience work so that drive will flow into calm resolution.

First, understand that everything we want the dog to do is unnatural from his instinctive perspective, and that the process of learning is a matter of drive flowing from a mood into a reflex of action. Therefore, we can see the need to develop the harmonic-pathways instinct to deflect drive, without any loss in its "velocity," i.e., straightforwardness, in the unnatural direction the handler wishes.

The first step is for the handler to be able to attract his dog's drive, not just part or the majority of it, but *all* of it. A simple test is to try to get your dog enthusiastic about you or something you have when in a new place or around strange dogs. If you succeed, next, observe the length of time the dog can sustain an active form of interest. The longer the period of interest, the greater the flow, and the greater the dog's ability to resist something that is perhaps more naturally appealing, such as another dog or a cat, especially when then the dog is at a distance from his master. Many dogs considered trained fail this test miserably.

Dogs don't *choose* to ignore their owners, they are *forced* to because they have been trained to relate to their owners via their pack instincts. A pack instinct is designed to store stress and to set overload thresholds, not to conduct drive in a calm manner. After a life of being constantly rebuffed when excited, the dog learns that he can't "plug into" or be with his owner whenever he's high in drive. He learns that his drive can only be expressed through distorted pack behaviors, as his mind and body are clouded by the survival instincts. This precludes control in a critical moment: If the owner is a source of nervousness, how can the dog be attentive to him? And if the dog is nervous, how can he learn to be controlled? Unless the dog is in a group mood, he can't be both attentive to his handler and direct about dealing with all the chaos inherent in the modern household. Even those dogs that are extremely outgoing and merely become hyperfriendly when confused are still a discomfiting source of anxiety, annoyance, or embarrassment. And many the friendly dog who has darted across a street to be killed by a car. Dog training is like insurance, it deals with absolutes and worst-case scenarios, and so no temperament gets a pass.

At first glance, one might be tempted to substitute the terms *distraction* and *shaping* for "channeling," but that would so narrow the discussion as to render it meaningless. We have to think on a larger scale than just saying, "I'm going to distract my dog," or "I'm going to gradually shape his behavior toward the desired goal," as these only describe in a pale way some parts of the channeling process. In channeling, drive flows into the path of highest resistance—the dog is working, doing something unnatural, whereas a distraction just presents an alternative path of simple pleasure. A dog induced to follow the simple path of pleasure isn't being built up to follow the highest path of resistance, which is what domestication always requires. Besides, a squirrel or a strange dog is infinitely more attractive than a tidbit or a pull toy can ever be made to be for most dogs; an approach based on distractions won't get one very far. In channeling, one does not give the dog any choice over what the number one variable in any mood is going to be; the handler is the group leader who always keeps himself and the dog on a straight line together.

The term *shaping* is misleading, because in channeling, the dog gets the lesson on the first occurrence, repetition being required not to deepen understanding, but simply to strengthen the harmonic pathway's ability to carry more drive. It takes time to generate a strong flow in an unnatural direction, away from an attraction that is compellingly "magnetic." Just as it is hard work for water to flow uphill, it is difficult for dogs not to chase cats and for kids to do their homework on a sunny afternoon. In the beginning, flow might start with a trickle, starting and stopping, given the tentativeness of the connection, but like a frozen pipe starting to thaw out, every spurt through the channel erodes a portion of the block and a torrent eventually ensues.

Channeling is a comprehensive process predicated on fulfillment through the prey and the subsequent group instincts. When a dog's drive is channeled, he learns to comply happily with our wishes because his drive, while not flowing in the natural direction, is nonetheless flowing in a *normal manner;* we're using an instinctive process of learning millions of years old. Eventually, since he's learning in a way which leaves him feeling satisfied, the newly trained behavior will feel completely natural to the dog.

The best dividend to be realized through the channeling phenomenon is that all of the emotional energy that usually pulls our dogs away from us can actually be rerouted right back into the owner. The more powerful the distraction, the more attracted the dog becomes to his handler. It is quite like the strength of a proper knot increasing its binding power no matter how hard the rope is pulled. What would normally be expected to pull the dog away binds him more closely by the very strength of its attraction.

As I mentioned in the Prey Instinct chapter, dog owners tend to equate a dog's excitement and his natural behaviors with the problem. They set out to repress drive, perhaps believing that the dog has a choice about whether he can be excited. This then sets up a lot of misguided training. Equating excitement with disobedience causes an owner to wait until a moment of misbehavior before training is felt necessary and is attempted. Of course, the worst time to start training is when a dog is misbehaving. Now when the owner issues his command, the dog is being conditioned to associate the owner's command with the mood that is producing the problem behaviors. "Scruffy, come back here," is instinctively translated into "Scruffy, go faster, I'm catching up."

There are also those people who recognize the need for training at the outset but nevertheless make their dog perform his obedience work in low drive. They use stress to dampen the dog's nervous system should he bristle at a stranger or a strange dog, or, in the case of our friendly Scruffy, be unable to keep still as he wags his rump in anticipation of a frolic with a doggie friend. Thus, tentativeness, working slowly, and submission are rewarded as enthusiasm is discouraged. Exercises that require inaction such as lying down and staying are frequently emphasized. Once again, this is consistent with the view that natural behaviors are the source of trouble.

But what is the dog actually learning when he's being repressed? In many instances, the owner appears to be gaining ground with the dog that is seemingly learning the prescribed obedience exercises. The owner commands the dog to sit, the dog doesn't sit and is corrected for his error, and then the dog sits. How could it be that the dog isn't learning how to behave in conformance with his owner's wishes?

In reality, the dog is being trained to resist his owner with every training exercise if the flow of drive isn't being taken into account. Look closely. Is the dog sitting on the first command, is he sitting quickly, enthusiastically, coming closer to the handler as he sits? Are dog and owner facing in the same direction? If the dog were outdoors or off lead, would there be any likelihood of compliance? Would the dog obey if there was a powerful distraction nearby? What the dog is actually learning is *to avoid* his owner by sitting!

Since the owner isn't training with drive flow in mind, he is inadvertently stressing his dog. The dog then associates stress with the command; to relieve the stress generated by his owner, he sits. Every time the owner picks up the lead and collar, the dog becomes properly subdued. It seems that the dog is getting the idea, when in truth he's learning something far different from what was intended by the owner.

A related problem is that the dog quickly learns that the owner stresses him through the lead. The stress that clouds the learning process, that the dog has to drag around as excess emotional baggage, making him either sluggish or nervously active, is a general lesson that was never truly intended and will corrode their relationship. Had the dog been trained with high drive and its pure flow in mind, he could have become so intensely focused that he would be oblivious to everything outside his narrowed scope. When high in drive, even if the owner should correct him while in full view of the dog, the dog will not attribute the correction to the owner. Instead, it will incredibly serve to heighten and strengthen his focus on the owner. Since our Scruffy is never encouraged to be high in drive toward his owner, he is destined to remain sensitive to leads and distances between himself and his owner, precisely because of the high stress level used to reinforce his learning. All in all the dog is only learning that his owner is the source of stress and resistance whenever he becomes excited. This condition can become so acute that whenever the dog is with his owner and there is something naturally attractive nearby, the dog will become nervous and need to be disobedient. Take the lead away, or add distance between the dog and owner, or add an excitement level above the stress level used to subdue the dog (for example, by encountering a strange dog), and you end up with a state of disobedience worse than had the dog never been trained in the first place!

In the more progressive approach, where the dog is taught how to sit before any corrections are made, we still have the original question of drive flow before us. A dog doesn't perform an action to avoid a correction or to gain praise from his owner, he performs to *heighten his state of drive flow*. Was the dog trained to sit by being aroused into that action? If not, then obedience doesn't progress past the relief of stress formula.

In any approach be it correct and reward, or teach, reward, and correct, what isn't the dog learning? Foremost, *when he's excited*, the dog isn't learning *how* to pay attention to his owner. If we think about it, it's only on those few occasions when a dog gets really excited that we ever need control in the first place. That the dog may come when called indoors, or outdoors when he's already content to be hanging around, has absolutely nothing to do with the dog turning on a dime while hot on a chase. Most dogs are obedient indoors, but few are responsive when aroused to hunt. So if one has to deal with a runaway, teaching him to respond to his name by repeating it dozens and dozens of times when he's low in drive isn't accomplishing a thing. A dog doesn't learn to respond to his name or any command by repetition, only through the flow of drive!

A second thing a dog isn't learning is to view his owner as an access channel, a pathway to fulfillment, a leader. And to dredge up an old cliché, if the owner isn't the answer, then he must be the problem.

The most important thing a dog won't be learning when his drive is repressed is to be active about learning, to be eager for work. We want to make obedience training the highest form of drive flow the dog can experience. Then the dog will seize the initiative to learn something if a little opening is given him. In the handling techniques to be learned, we'll give the dog a little gap across which the spark of his drive can leap to make a strong connection with his handler in the course of learning how to heel, sit, and stay. For a fleeting moment, the dog transcends being a reactive animal held prisoner to instinct as he bonds with his human master.

In training the dog, we'll propel him to a high state of drive, and the dog, in this moment of opportunity and powered through the group ethic, will *choose* to perform along a path of high resistance. This means he's learning his work from the inside out, and such strong learning can compete with a previously learned bad lesson, or a primal instinct luring him back toward wildness.

9

Training Tools and Equipment

LEARNING HOW TO TRAIN a dog can be a little like learning how to play golf. To hit the ball well, the impulse to swagger up to the tee and mash it has to be restrained. The correct grip and a smooth swing, which at first feels unnatural, needs to be mastered. It is practice well spent, and soon a little bit of coordinated effort can send the ball a towering distance. As a hapless golfer, I can assure the reader that learning how to train a dog is easier than mastering the game of golf.

In the beginning of this chapter, I start with a group of concepts with which we need to be familiar. They may not at first seem to fit into a chapter on equipment, but the most important tools a trainer brings onto the field are his attitude and his short- and long-term goals. The concepts discussed below will put the trainer into the proper frame of mind and will help to focus efforts so that our training program is consistent with the dog's learning process. While these concepts may seem illogical, please persevere, for once understood, a little bit of coordinated effort in training will yield a dog eager to learn and happy to work. At the end of the chapter the reader will find that traditional tools such as leads and collars are covered.

On the one hand, these tools get across to the dog a very specific point in terms of his instincts and how they are to be expressed. But even more important, they come to release the synergistic power of the prey instinct bonding dog to owner. Through this bond, the dog will become so motivated as to arrive at an emotionally "free" state of experience. Once in this mood he is able to learn that our praise is synonymous with a harmonic pathway, at which point we no longer need any training aids. The dog will work tirelessly for a simple word of encouragement.

CALMNESS

This is a subject that is very much misunderstood. *Calmness* means the appropriate response in any given situation, and it is a quality we must completely understand.

A dog gains calmness by focusing on an objective and then attaining it through action. A dog can't think his way to calmness nor can he learn it through the example of another. A dog learns to be calm by doing. If a dog's action leads him to fulfillment, patience becomes a learned skill, at least relative to that particular course of action. And if a dog gets enough practice in a variety of endeavors, he can develop an overall character trait of calmness.

The biggest mistake is made by attempting to calm a dog by trying to train him to be still. This kind of training is typically confrontational, seeking to calm the dog through a policy of denial. Whether the handler yells, slaps, pleads, nags, grabs the dog in some way, or stares, he is only going to make the dog nervous, and I need not recount again here the litany of woes that flow from the condition of nervousness. The irony here is that the most effective way to train a dog to be patient and focused is through the most active of his instincts: the prey instinct. A poised state of balance during the stalk, an internal composure before the strike—in other words, calmness and patience in the face of denial—are built into the prey instinct. Through the prey instinct the dog can learn that a condition of denial is not only temporary but is *positive*, as it is a *predictor* of eventual success. Then the clever trainer can expand the dog's definition of temporary from a few seconds to a few minutes, hours, and finally to the normal course of doing business.

CORRECTION: WHY DO WE CORRECT A DOG?

What are we trying to accomplish when we correct a dog? Do we want to make the dog submissive to us? Are we trying to show the dog that we're displeased with his behavior? Do we want the dog to feel guilty or ashamed over what he has done or how he is behaving? I think not. When we strip away all of the emotional considerations involved in any incident where we feel the dog deserves a correction, whether it be anger, disappointment, a sense of betrayal, or embarrassment, we want him to stop doing something that isn't appropriate. The owner wants the dog to settle down. Unfortunately, this kind of thinking, while justifiable in most cases, simply won't work because dogs can't learn *not* to do things; they can only learn *to do* things. Now, I'm not suggesting that a dog can't learn to be still; my point is that a dog can learn to be still only by learning how to be calm. So, while we may think that we want inaction from our dog to accomplish our aim of settling the dog down, we really need action.

What gets dogs into trouble with their human companions are the canine's natural tendencies and inclinations, their wild instincts. These instincts would be completely appropriate and normal if the dog were living in the wild, and so it is to be expected that dogs become excited at the arrival of strangers or at the return of their owners. It is natural behavior for a dog to be destructive when left alone, or to pull rambunctiously when walked on a lead. When dogs do these things the problem isn't that our pets are acting abnormally and that we're bad dog owners: These behaviors are inborn traits. The real problem is how we perceive a dog's behavior and then how that perception influences the way we present training problems to our dogs.

Rather than saying to the dog, "Don't pull on your lead," we need to speak in terms of an instinctual message: "Be attracted to me even though there are powerful distractions about." Rather than commanding a dog not to jump on strangers, we need to train him *how* to make contact with strangers. We can't tell a dog not to bark, or to cease being a pest, but we can train him to have an unswerving focus on an objective. Through such a focus, a dog can be commanded to settle down. Ultimately, the dog can develop so much patience that whenever he wants something, calmness rather than nervousness will be his habit for success. If we analyze what we're trying to accomplish in those everyday situations that require manners from our dog, we'll find that we actually want to train our dog to do things. Therefore, our correction should have the effect of *stimulating* the dog toward whatever action we want him to perform. This may at first seem contradictory, but once again ask yourself: If we have to correct a friend, a child, or a coworker, what is the best possible outcome of such an interaction? Do we want the person who is criticized to have a defensive reaction toward us and thereby become subdued? Or is it not much better to leave him feeling powerfully motivated to adopt our suggested course of action? The answer is obvious: In the final analysis, we truly desire to see the one just criticized become *excited*, so completely enthusiastic about doing things our way that he holds nothing back. On the other hand, the degree to which the person, or dog, were to become defensive may prove to be the degree of unreliability we can expect from them when we're not around.

DISASSOCIATION

We've established that when we correct a dog, more than simply changing his behavior, we want him to become excited about doing something that we need him to do. In this way the change adopted is more likely to become permanent. However, what prevents such a willing response is if the dog associates the correction *with* his owner. When this occurs, the dog will, through a process I call *attribution*, respond with a survival instinct (flight or pack). Needless to say, this kind of stress isn't the attitude we're looking for. I'll briefly describe the process of attribution below; however, the long and the short of it is that the dog needs someone (or some being) to blame for anything negative that he experiences, because it is a resolution of the negative that determines access to the prey and hence is the bedrock to any instinct.

Attribution occurs whenever a dog perceives resistance, a disturbance, to the flow of his drive. At this point it becomes necessary for the dog to identify a living being as the source of such resistance or disturbance so that a social instinct can be brought to bear on the situation. Attribution is the instinctive mechanism for "finding fault," so to speak, and it serves the productive purpose of bringing order from chaos.

Suppose a dog is walking along and a branch falls out of a tree and crashes to the ground next to him. The dog isn't able to think, "Whew, that was a close one. I guess I'm lucky to have survived this accident." The canine mind can't reason that the wind blew a limb from a tree and that its fall was a random event, and then continue on along his way. In the first instant, the dog will attribute the shock to the branch; as there aren't any pack cues associated with its sudden appearance, there is disorder, and he will take flight. The next step after the shock subsides (which it will, as the branch isn't going to continue its "attack") is very enlightening; the dog will approach the branch to smell it. Why, we might ask, would a dog want to go up and smell something that just scared the living daylights out of him? The answer is that smell is the dog's most fundamental social sense, and to complete the process of attribution and bring the branch within the realm of his experience, the branch must be categorized in terms of the pack instinct. Were the dog able to identify it as a social inferior or superior, he would then be able to relieve the stress of having just been shocked through some type of social interaction, submission or aggression, for instance.

Attribution happens whenever a mood is destroyed or when prey making hits resistance. This attribution process is a very basic behavioral mechanism in all social animals, including man. Perhaps this is the instinctive root as to why people need to find fault when there is an accident, and if no one is available to be blamed, we are prone to feel guilty; we blame ourselves. Good examples of attribution are easy to find with young children. I know that if I'm too convincing with a puppet monster, my youngest daughter Sondra can be made genuinely afraid of it. Part of her—her emerging intellect—knows I control it, but her instinctive nature attributes her fear to the puppet, which takes on a life of its own. It not only becomes a living being in her eyes, but, indeed, a "monster"; then she pleads with me to make *it* stop *its* menacing behavior. A child may take a tumble that shocks him, but the fall on its own isn't enough to cause him to cry. Then an adult rushes up to help during that pregnant moment in which the child is evaluating just how shocked he is. By getting to the rescue during such a moment, the adult will attract the child's instinctive process of attribution, and we'll get a bucket of tears. From an instinctive point of view, which isn't at all interested in the rationality of the situation, the adult *is* the negative in the situation. It isn't that the child thinks the adult is to blame; it is that the child *feels* the adult is the negative. Such an irrational formula for behavior does, indeed, make sense, as crying out to a social superior is an effective strategy for survival. On the other hand, if the adult acted as if nothing was wrong when the child fell, and distracted the child by pointing out a creepy crawly bug nearby, the scrape would have been forgotten.

The point in all of this is that if we're going to correct the dog and then show him that we're the source of the correction, we're only going to get panicky, stressed, or muted rather than excited responses out of him. When corrected or punished in the traditional manner the dog is only going to try to fit in with us—assuming he is on a lead or is indoors or is very young and therefore has no other choice—and he'll feel he has to be the opposite of what we are. If he sees us as acting superior, he'll be compelled to act inferior, and vice versa. If we're active, he'll become reactive. If we're forceful, he'll become tentative. In all of these behaviors, the dog is holding back and not expressing his full drive. So rather than try to emphasize our superiority in training through confrontation, we should make every effort to disassociate ourselves from the correction. When the dog doesn't associate his handler with the correction, he can learn that he's not the source of the problem; he's the answer to the problem. Now the negative is reduced to something specific: how to gain access to the food, ball, or contact with the owner.

Disassociation is effective. In my career, I have never been asked to train a dog to stop stealing food when it's being cooked on the stove. What is everyone doing right here? Obviously, the hot stove is correcting the dog, and it is a shock the dog can't attribute to his owner. Were he able to, he would most likely develop a social strategy to circumvent his owner, which is why I've had to deal with hundreds of food snatchers of every conceivable variety when it comes down to the owner trying to control his dog through discipline. This latter category of miscreants have been chastised, smacked, ostracized, and disciplined in a multitude of ways, but still their pilfering continues. The difference is that they have associated the correction with their handler, whereas when they approach the hot stove, their urge to eat causes the correction and they can easily learn to forget about it. In fact, they learn this lesson so well that the food on the stove comes to hold a neutral value. Even when the dog is hungry he won't drool no matter how delectable a steak may be sizzling!

Disassociation is not at all hard to do. Simply by keeping the dog high in drive before, during, and after a correction, the attribution process doesn't occur. Since he's not going to be blaming his handler, the dog will associate the correction with whatever instinct he was engaged in at that moment. Now he can easily choose to discard an instinct that is so nonproductive and unfulfilling. And if he's high in drive and the correction leads to success in a direction his owner supplies, the correction will excite him toward the desired objective beyond its normally attractive value.

I'm often asked if a puppy or dog should be hit. I cannot state emphatically enough how wrong it is to hit a dog either with one's hand, a rolled-up paper, or a switch. Such violence excites his survival and fighting instincts magnifying the negative energy that he senses in his owner. Obviously, it undermines the disassociation process, so no matter how frustrated you may be by your dog, don't hit him!

Disassociation is something people try to do intuitively when they deal with other people. Parents say such things to children as "This will hurt me more than you," or "If *you* don't eat your vegetables, *you* won't get dessert"—you will cause yourself to lose dessert rather than I will deny you your dessert. A good conman or salesman knows that if he gains your confidence by developing a warm, friendly rapport and by casting a rosy tint on his proposals, a negative downside to a scheme or purchase will be hard for his customer to perceive. Once a person attributes a negative outcome to another person's advice, everything subsequently suggested to him will seem disingenuous. If a boss has to correct an employee, he'll seek to avoid the attribution process by pointing out that it is *her* performance that invokes the disciplinary measure, not *his* desire to hurt or punish her. If he's skillful, he can show her that she is punishing herself, since she is the one not adhering to company standards.

Between people, disassociation is relatively easy to accomplish; we can communicate about causes and effects—which may span long periods of time—because we are bestowed with the gifts of human intellect and language. Language allows us to share our different points of view. In a conversation, I can see how things look to you and you can see how I view the world. Human beings, through the power of intellect, have the opportunity to choose to see another person's perspective. In dog training, disassociation requires a different set of skills apart from the human desire and ability to communicate, because no matter how much we talk at him, the dog can never appreciate our point of view.

This retraining can be difficult to learn, despite its incredible simplicity, because it is human nature to try to correct or punish the dog for all of the reasons we have so far discussed.

We'll be covering the necessary techniques at length in the training chapters later in the book, but in general, by keeping the dog attracted to a toy, ball, food, or his handler, the dog forgets the correction as if it never happened. He doesn't waste time or energy with the attribution process and instead puts all of his effort into being in harmony with his handler. He is able to flip-flop fluidly from one behavior to the next, every change heightening the pleasurable sensation affiliated with the flow of emotions. And it isn't that there are two differing points of view that need to be compared and reconciled with each other. When we get the dog high in drive there is only one point of view that both dog and owner participate in. Isn't this the ultimate objective behind the boss's correction of his employee? Even if he is the boss or the owner of the company, there is a group ethic, a group way, that is bigger than the employer's or employee's self-interests. It is simply that the boss is most intimate and responsible for this ethic and therefore it is his job to express and enforce this group standard. And if the employee becomes excited about the company's way, the correction will be converted to a pay or benefits increase.

SHOCK

I use the term *correction* when I'm talking to people about training because it is such a widely accepted term. It conveys the general idea that we want to change the dog's behavior because he's doing something inappropriate. But because I intend to stimulate, rather than to inhibit, through a correction, I find that the term is quite inaccurate and misleading. Furthermore, it is too broad. I don't want to correct the whole dog, I only want to influence one specific instinct that is in the dog's mind in one particular and probably very brief moment. If I correct the whole dog, the dog just shuts down and doesn't want to do anything, and this is exactly the approach I want to get the dog owner away from. Discouraging the dog from chasing a cat, for example, is only the first step in changing his behavior. The most important step is redirecting the dog's drive. This is a motivational process. Since the term *correction* so inadequately describes why we correct a dog, we won't be using it in the training or developmental sections of this book.

It is much more accurate to say that the jerk on the lead and collar should have a shocking rather than a corrective effect on the dog. This shock is transitory, soon to be converted into something positive.

Now I'm not talking here about shock in the electrical sense, although that could easily be worked into this discussion. Since an electrical device isn't necessary for family dog training, I'm not going to bother with it here. Our technique in training will be a simple jerk, delivered in lightning fashion, on the dog's lead and collar.

Some people may like to think that one may train a dog without administering a shock of any kind. But bear in mind that anytime one interrupts the flow of a dog's drive, no matter what the method of interruption may be, either by a sharp word, a clap of the hands, a swat on the rump, a jerk on a lead, or an electrical device, from the dog's point of view these methods are all shocks. They vary from one another only in matter of degree and, in fact, a sharp word is much more traumatic to a fearful dog than is an electrical shock when properly administered to a self-confident dog. The all-important factor is the question of how the dog *perceives* an interruption to his drive.

Let's consider the term *shock* in a natural context and discover just how malleable a canine's perceptions can be in this regard. Suppose a dog was in full gallop after a white-tailed buck. Just as he was closing in for the strike, the buck whirled around and lowered his antlers against his pursuer. What would the likely canine reaction be to this sudden turn of events? I would predict that the dog's high drive toward the deer would be violently shocked and that he would experience a sudden rush of fear. He would feel and act almost as if he had just been jolted by an electrical collar activated by remote control. In other words, all the emotional energy generated by the deer running away is suddenly converted to stress when the deer turns to fight his pursuer. Here we have a natural instance of a shock being attributed to the predatory aspect—the eyes, the horns, and the motionless, steadfast form of the deer ready to fight—of what was just earlier a fleeing prey animal.

Now imagine another scenario, wherein the dog does indeed close the gap and strikes into the deer, clamping on to his neck or hindquarters with a firm grip of his jaws. In this instance, should the deer struggle and fight for its life by thrashing or kicking, the dog in this phase of the prey instinct won't perceive such combative actions as shocks. Instead, the struggle of the deer will heighten the pleasure he is experiencing and his commitment to the kill. In the first instance the deer's aggressive actions are shocks, but in the second scenario the same sort of changes in the deer's behavior are positive stimulations for the dog. The difference in the dog's behavior is how the dog perceives the shock. Timing is everything, as the dog's perception hinges on which phase of the prey instinct his drive is engaged in. Just because we are going to shock a dog doesn't at all mean the dog has to experience it as something negative.

Using the prey instinct, it is easy to convert a shock into a stimulation, building slowly with the young dog until the dog is able to experience a full jolt. A training program isn't successful by avoiding shocks; it is vital to expose the dog to them so he can learn what they are. Shocks are information when contrasted with high drive. Therefore, it is necessary to build the dog all the way up to a powerful shock so that it will serve as a permanent insulator between his emotion and an inappropriate instinct. Only then will he be 100 percent reliable off lead and fully focused on his owner no matter what conditions may bring.

TIMING

Good timing is critical to success. When we wait and then react to a dog's behavior, we are always going to be behind the eight ball. On the other hand, influencing a dog's emotional process *before* he acts is an incredibly efficient manner in which to train him. When timing is correct nervousness is inhibited and drive is reinforced. Also, since we're affecting the internal emotional process, the dog in effect "chooses" to be calm rather than being forced to be under control. A dog so trained will be mannerly or mindful of domestic restraints even when his handler isn't near.

The key to proper timing is not quickness, although that is a valuable asset. Rather, the key is anticipation. The handler should always be thinking ahead and anticipating what the dog might do next. It is a skill easily acquired if one becomes disciplined enough to pay constant attention to the dog. Without good timing, training degenerates into a question of strength.

By being relentlessly focused on the dog, the handler will start to sense the dog's rhythm of actions and be able to anticipate what the dog is about to do. Then, before the dog acts, the handler can already be in gear taking steps to predetermine what the dog will do next. The dog will be choosing to obey; however, since we're controlling his instinctive emotional process, there won't really be any choice involved.

For example, if I'm training a dog to heel I watch his head very closely. When I sense he is about to shift his attention away from me I make a shock on the collar and begin to praise the dog at the same time. Additionally, I pick up my pace, and to complete the process, I throw a ball for him to chase or give him a food treat. In this sequence of events, I'm not correcting the dog for being disobedient, I'm shocking the nervousness that I feel is about to influence the dog's behavior and disrupt his focus on me. The praise, food, and the ball then serve to convert the shock to a stimulation. Since I'm the source of the excitement, the dog's calm focus on me from which he was about to stray is renewed and reinforced.

I like to emphasize my point about timing with the following analogy. Suppose you were a therapist assigned to help a heavy drinker recover from alcoholism. When would be the best time to influence this person's pattern of behavior—before, or after he decided to gulp down a drink? The very same question is before the dog trainer: Is it best to react to a dog's behavior or is it better to take the initiative and ensure that the dog always performs appropriately? Why wait for a negative behavior to express itself?

DISCIPLINE

The dictionary defines discipline in several ways. I favor the following: "Discipline is a branch of knowledge or of teaching." I interpret this to mean that when an individual is motivated, he becomes self-disciplined by virtue of what he learns. It is an internal phenomenon. A musician isn't controlled by the conductor; his passion for music is channeled and orchestrated. The musician controls himself, as does an artist or a football player or anyone dedicated to his field. In martial arts training, if the student doesn't display the correct attitude in his training the *sensei* ignores him. When the student shows spirit and dedication the *sensei* will seek to shape him in the discipline of the art. Whatever the art form, discipline is more the responsibility of the teacher to know his subject, and to be able to teach, than it is something to be imposed on the student.

This subtle aspect of discipline is even more true in dog training because, unlike with a human student, the motivation behind the dog's desire to learn is wholly dependent on the trainer. To motivate a dog, we need to know how he perceives, how he feels, and how he learns; it is the dog owner who requires discipline so as to inhibit the impulse to lash out in anger or to be discouraged by failure or immobilized by guilt. A problem must always be approached from the dog's point of view. When we ask, "How much discipline does my dog or puppy need?" remember that the question is moot. Discipline isn't like a vitamin that needs to be dosed out periodically. Dogs are disciplined by their instincts and they don't need more.

There is, however, a lesser definition of discipline that has some value in dog training. To quote the dictionary, "Discipline is a systematic method to obtain obedience. A state of order based upon submission to rules and authority. Punishment intended to correct or train." While I am about to explain that there are times where this more limited view is necessary, I wish to reaffirm that the higher definition should be foremost in our minds and at the foundation of our training program. The usual way discipline is discussed in dogdom is relevant far less than 1 percent of the time.

But there are those times when I will correct an extremely nervous dog—ideally with the lead and collar and in a training context—in such a way that he associates the correction with me. By acting confrontational, I can calm such a dog. My specific purpose is to have the dog attribute the shock to me so that his nervous system is dampened. It is quite analogous to grasping a tuning fork to quell its vibrations. Once dampened, and depending on the dog's temperament, I will immediately try to put the dog back on the path of pure drive and happy motivation.

But I must reemphasize that most dogs considered hyper are only that way because they have been trained through confrontation and denial. Or their prey instinct has been allowed to find gratification at its own level, away from the owner. Whenever domination is required, we should immediately redirect the dog into a positive, instinctive pathway for success. Of course, with a nervous dog positive results will take time to cultivate; nevertheless, cultivating a harmonic pathway immediately becomes my objective. Because domination may have helped this dog, it doesn't mean that dominance was the missing link in the dog's development. A dog that is nervous lacks focus, and a permanent cure will only happen when the dog grows to be self-motivated through positive experiences.

PATIENCE

We needn't develop the virtue of patience for its own sake. There is nothing to be gained by being patient with a dog headed in the wrong direction; what's needed then is quick and decisive action. On the other hand, when the owner is guided by knowledge and understanding it's so easy to be patient that we can't even call it a virtue. When I'm traveling the highway to Boston I don't need patience; in fact the longer I drive, the less I need. The map says the road leads to Boston, and so, the longer I drive, the closer I am. The dog owner only has to see that his dog's drive is flowing; with such evidence plainly before him, he's confident of his inevitable success in the dog's training. The real virtue in dog training isn't patience, it is faith—faith in your dog, a perfect animal that is genetically programmed to be in harmony with you. No matter how botched up his training may have been until now, you can fix it. That is the message that dogs bring to us.

PLEASURE

If we want our dogs to do things for us, we need to know how to make them feel good. Below is a discussion of the positive induce-ments that can win the heart of any dog.

Food

For a puppy, feeding is like breathing: It is life itself. Filling a belly does more than merely nourish; it displaces the nervousness caused by the pangs of hunger. The warm glow that comes from a plump tummy assures the puppy that he is securely connected to his group. Therefore, we shouldn't hesitate to use food in training.

Since eating is so basic with a pup, it is easy to excite him with a tidbit. If in his rush to grab the food, he snaps at your hand very hard, don't correct the dog. Just take the time to calm him by giving him a steady flow of food so that he is reassured that he is going to get all the food he wants. As the pup becomes satiated, his drive to grab the food will start to subside and he'll be ready to learn how to take the food gently from your hand.

Food is very effective with adult dogs as well. It clearly indicates to the dog that he has an instinctive advantage in doing what his trainer wants. Also, food can be used to relax an adult dog's nervous system by washing away social resistance. Using food to soften a hardened dog's negative attitude is like bathing the joints of a rusty tool in oil. Remember that although our pet seems domesticated, his instincts are still wild and need to be calmed. Every dog that I train, eats his daily ration from my hand. If he won't, I fast him to wake the puppy within.

To learn if a dog's drive is flowing in my direction, I'll often take a dog that I'm training out for a walk on his lead. After he pulls and snorts around for a few moments, I'll whistle or cluck to him to attract his attention. When he nears I'll give him some food. There aren't any commands involved; the dog is simply learning how to be attracted to me. I'm developing a group instinct, which can chan-nel drive.

I'll often hear that the use of food in training is tantamount to bribery, but such an opinion is based on a moralistic and anthropomorphic view of canine behavior. In reality, food serves to mobilize a dog's drive. It gets drive to the surface and relaxes a dog so he can act and learn more freely. It relaxes his sense of vulnerability when in drive. And it gives the dog a simple focus as the first step in mastering a difficult exercise.

If we really think about it we'll find that underneath our suburban or urban veneers, we're all rather good behaviorists. If any one of us were to have a wounded wild animal to care for and befriend, we all would choose to use food to break the ice and to build a bond. We all recognize the way of the wild.

Using food in training is analogous to priming a pump. Once a dog starts to feed, his drive begins to flow and his enthusiasm starts to build. Little by little, as the dog's self-confidence about being in drive and working with his owner is built up, the role of food becomes a minor aspect to his work. As the dog gains confidence about being in drive, the handler can use attractive body language and verbal praise to heighten the dog's sense of participation with his group. Ultimately, drive flow becomes a reward unto itself, and many dogs lose interest in food in preference to the more exciting reward of being high in spirit and working with the group.

Every dog, as part of his wild nature, maintains a protective bubble around himself. It's that force that creates social and flight distances. Even very friendly dogs are sensitive to this field of resistence, which, when violated, makes them "vibrate" intensely, expressed in tail and rump wagging, nervous head motions, grinning, licking, and the like. Using food, a handler can train the dog to be free of this envelope of resistance so that he can be both with his handler and free to act in a straightforward manner. Food allows the dog to learn that his handler's touch means a deepening of the group's mood, as opposed to a disturbance of the pack's order. The first step in training a dog is to use food and touch to train him to sit down and to stay in a purely inducing manner.

First, one accustoms the dog to being touched while he feeds. I wear a bait pouch on my hip so that I have a steady flow of food available. Next, while touching the dog with the left hand, the right hand holds the food and lures him into a sit or down position. If hungry, the dog will happily perform actions over and over again. But the main objective is not to get the dog to obey, but to calm him through our touch. This is the foundation for a harmonic pathway, where dog and handler fused together through touch, leaving no gap between them. Also, bear in mind that even when a dog is doing everything correctly for a tidbit, in reality he is only halfway to being trained.

Practically speaking, use a soft, moist kind of treat such as cheese or hot dogs chopped into tiny pieces so that it can be swallowed without chewing. Or if you're going to use his kibble, presoak it so its a little mushy. Since we're going to be requiring action from the dog, we don't want him spending a lot of time chewing and then gagging because he's got either a lot of food or some dry morsel to swallow.

Ball

I prefer to use a tennis ball because its bounce is most easily controlled by the handler, but by and large, anything thrown represents the same prey instinct from the dog's point of view. A rope toy when thrown can have a particularly attractive flight rhythm to a dog's prey instinct. There is also a toy called a Kong that bounces unpredictably on every throw and really brings out the ratting instinct in a dog. But with a tennis ball I can run with my dog heeling beside me, bounce the ball as I make a lightning-sharp reverse of direction, snag the ball in midair, and keep the dog riveted on me despite the blur of the turn just completed. Because a dog's prey instinct is so aroused by the ball, it can be our most powerful training tool in converting a shock to a stimulation. I like to describe it as being analogous to a computer chip. In computers, the more powerful the chip, the faster the computer can work and the more *relevant* data it can handle. Likewise, in training a dog with a ball, the more powerful the dog's attraction to the ball, the faster he can learn how to obey his handler and the more *irrelevant* data (distractions) he can exclude from his attention. In later chapters we will discuss how to build a dog's drive to the ball and how to use it to gain complete obedience.

Contacting

When a dog is working he should have the desire to want to jump on you even if he has been trained not to. Such an attitude doesn't arise from force; you need to cultivate the desire within the dog. Even if in training the dog is rarely going to make contact, the desire should be ever-present. Many of my clients resist this suggestion, fearing they will be encouraging their dog to jump on strangers. Ironically, if the dog is confident about making contact when invited, he will not be a problem jumper.

All the behaviors the dog is going to learn in his obedience training are forms of the *drive to make contact*. The desire for contact may be fulfilled through some other behavior, such as sitting in front or heeling alongside. However, to make contact by jumping up is always just below the surface of an obedience behavior. All too frequently, and especially with puppies, dog owners spend great amounts of time trying to block and suppress that need. In reality, it only serves to make the dog nervous and neurotic about something completely fundamental to a dog's existence. This issue about training a dog not to jump is complex and will be explored at length in the chapters on puppy development and on jumping.

Body Language

By moving away from the dog, by shifting our weight from side to side, and by lowering our height, we make ourselves more attractive to a dog. The dog's drive to make contact with us becomes heightened through stimulating him with such body language.

Praise

Our dogs will work well for us if we can make them feel good by being with us. The sound of our voice, the touch and stroke of our hand, should be capable of raising our dog's spirits to a joyous state. When a dog is part of a group that heightens his drive, he becomes stimulated to maintain his good work. Praise must come from the heart and be deeply felt. However, it is OK to be a good actor about it because, after all, if we become good enough actors, we'll begin to feel the depth of emotion we're attempting to duplicate.

COLLARS

What collar to use in training is perhaps the most controversial subject in dogdom. There is a variety to choose from. There are flat collars, and there are choke collars made from leather, nylon, or chain. Finally, there is the pinch collar, also known as the prong or spiked collar. At first glance, it might seem that the most humane collar to use is the flat collar or one of the light choke collars. These look the least threatening and appear to be the most comfortable. However, if you really wanted to hurt a dog, the thinner the choke collar, the more damage to his throat and neck you could inflict. Also, with a choke collar the dog has an instinctive reflex at his disposal to deal with the sensation of something tightening a grip around his neck. He may misinterpret the correction on the choke collar as a stranglehold and unnecessarily become rebellious or afraid. So things are not always what they seem. For example, what kind of knife would a patient want his surgeon to operate with, a dull jackknife or a razor-sharp scalpel? Obviously the latter, even though its edge can send a shiver through us.

While I start every dog on a flat collar, it is only the first step on the training ladder. The next rung up is a choke collar and finally I work up to the pinch collar. Remember, we're not using the collar as an instrument of punishment or correction; its function is to shock an inappropriate instinct and then *arouse* or stimulate an appropriate instinct. When the dog learns to be positively motivated by a light tug on a flat collar and then a stronger tug on the choke collar, he will be introduced to a light jerk on the pinch collar.

Training a dog with a pinch collar is consistent with the way a surgeon uses his scalpel. The doctor wants to cut out the tumor or damaged tissue and by doing so he arouses the patient's healing powers. While the pinch collar may seem to be a menacing implement, when used properly it is very "clean" and therapeutic.

Finally, when a dog is shocked by the pinch collar in the correct manner he is aroused by the novelty of the sensation. It is a feeling he has never felt before, nor is there an instinct evolved to deal with it. It is a brand-new moment and the handler is free to train the dog how to deal with it. This new burst of energy can be converted into a synergistic surge of attunement.

LEADS

We'll need three kinds of leads. One is six foot long and is for training the dog in close on his obedience work. I prefer a light but high-quality leather lead for its comfort and also because it won't get twisted. Nevertheless, the features of the lead are irrelevant to the dog and his ability to learn. Also, we'll need a variety of long leads for when we work the dog at a distance. I like to use a fifty-foot nylon lead as it isn't going to rot when exposed to harsh elements. Finally, a tab lead is, as it suggests, a short length of rope or leather just long enough to dangle over the collar and be easy to grab. The dog can run freely with this lead without being able to trip himself.

10

Puppy Development

WHETHER WE KNOW IT OR NOT, we stimulate our puppy's instincts all the time, and in so doing we cast a template against which the rest of humanity is to be evaluated. Most of what a puppy learns about people, he absorbs from his owner, the first human he knows. If the two are aligned along a harmonic pathway, the dog will learn confident and calm responses to his world that are of overwhelming consequence to his character development.

The enemy that has to be overcome in the raising and training of a puppy isn't his natural instincts; it is the nervousness caused when these instincts can't find a harmonic expression. The reason owners run into so much trouble isn't that dog training is hard; it's that we spend so much time doing things that don't work. While dog training may be easy, fixing problems born from nervousness is indeed very hard.

Developing and training a dog is analogous to building a fire. One needs to ignite the flame of confidence and then nurture it with the dry kindling of little successes. Until the fire is blazing, too big a log can't be added, and neither can the flame be exposed to outside elements. Once the critical point is reached, any size chunk of wood can be handled and any gust of wind will serve to heighten its roar rather than snuff it. In our program, we're going to encourage and then gratify our puppy's instincts so that he learns confidence in his owner. Little by little this confidence will be burdened with the problems inherent in domestication, but always in a controlled setting. Then, and not until the dog displays a full expression of drive through the appropriate pathways we've created, will the dog be given unstructured freedom.

Every so often to maintain the fire of self-confidence and calm learning, one must add a log to the fire. Training is an ongoing process, and intermittent reinforcements are needed over the course of the dog's life.

11

What Are the Puppy's Limits?

A GROWING PUPPY learns about what is positive in his world through his prey instinct. He explores the world around him through the eyes of a predator until he runs into a dead end, a point that is unique for each puppy, given its temperament. It is exactly at this point of limitation that the pup has the opportunity to learn a response that's either fearful or social. And if the lesson is to be a social one, it will then fall along either a discordant or a harmonic pathway.

A puppy poised in such a delicate moment is about to learn a character trait as he has become vulnerable and sensitive in the most profound way. Therefore, how to handle the pup here is an issue of overwhelming importance. Since the pup is motivated by his prey instinct, he is about to do something inappropriate that will lead his owner to become confrontational. But a scolding or a smack here will only place him along a discordant pathway, and a golden opportunity for heightened learning will have been missed. Instead, the handler should engage him at his level so that by participating with the puppy in his deepest urge, both parties are on the same wavelength. Get in tune with his needs and decisively but sensitively redirect him into the right path.

Interestingly, all dog owners do this when it comes to such matters as the pup needing to eat or going outside to eliminate. The positive dividends in this approach are plain to see. When moved in this regard the puppy seeks out his owner as a source of relief. But even though this kind of attunement is so effective in simple areas of development, in all other aspects most owners get bogged down and resort to discipline and confrontation. To avoid the pitfalls, let's consider what is reasonable to expect from a puppy given his distinct limitations, the emotional point at which he becomes defensive or nervous. Also note that just because his nervous system and ability to learn will progress at a lightning pace, his emotional level lags far behind exactly because of these limits.

These limits are in effect with all puppies, and for our purposes the restraints they impose on his emotional capabilities can be overcome at around ten months of age. At this point we can expose the harmonic pathways we're going to be creating to the outside world. At around ten to twelve months the puppy is ready to learn the full consequences of his actions; he'll be exposed to stress and allowed to choose to return to the harmonic fold. Certain breeds mature later, so it's advisable to follow the breeder's guidance in this matter. It's also prudent to take these same limits into account whenever one is trying to train an adult dog to do something new.

The limits inherent in the prey instinct are so much at the heart of being canine that the dog can never fully escape them. He is indeed born wild. Genetically speaking, if one weak link is introduced into the pedigree of a well-bred line of dogs, the whole thing unravels and we can get spooky or nervous puppies even though the overwhelming majority of ancestors are sound. At the individual level of behavior, perhaps one has walked with a dog in the woods and come upon a piece of metal or an abandoned farm implement that completely spooked him; such fright is a wild vestige of what I'm talking about here. A manmade artifact jutting from the ground, with its harsh lines and shape, severely disrupts the limits in the natural patterning of the forest, thereby shocking the dog's drive. While most dogs are oblivious to something this subtle, their overall ability to adjust to change will be lessened if their emotional limits are continually ignored. If in a dog's upbringing he's chronically stressed when at his limit, he will grow to be overly fearful, nervous, or hyper toward any new thing that disrupts his mood, especially strange people. Once anything new falls within his perceptive field, his nervous system will regress toward a wildlike state.

Furthermore, a dog is faced with many unnatural stresses for which a wolf never had to evolve a response. As I mentioned earlier, we are going to require that our dogs learn to be alone. We are also going to take our dogs into unfamiliar territory and have them examined by strangers, such as at the veterinarian's clinic. We are going to invite strangers into our homes. All of these are a burden on the puppy's nervous system. In the wild, it's appropriate to become fearful whenever there's a discordancy perceived, since positive changes follow a predictable rhythm in terms of the prey instinct. If something's not positive, it is by definition negative, and up pops a survival instinct. Emotions are bruised when stretched out to a limit, and everyday domestic events can appear life-threatening. Our handling should offset these survival tendencies rather than promote them.

To get on the right track, go slow with a puppy; allow him his puppyhood without hurrying him through his training. Develop the prey instinct instead of repressing it so that you maximize its flexibility. With the flow of drive cooled by the prey instinct and shaped along a harmonic pathway, limits that normally make dogs nervous can instead be converted into positive stimuli to work. On the other hand, if the prey instinct is arbitrarily violated, the puppy is filled with dread and a sense of alienation, giving a host of undesirable behaviors a foothold in his temperament.

The limit is *inside* the dog; it need not be created or imposed from without. We just need to let the prey instinct tiptoe up to the danger line, and then get in tune with whatever is in the dog's heart—the focus of the drive to bite—so that we can smoothly redirect his attention our way. It could be something as gentle as a warm touch, or as active as rustling a stick along the ground and giving it a hearty throw. We want the dog to take action toward a new number one variable that we've created and that fulfills his desire to bite or his drive to make contact with us.

We're going to let a pup be a pup, but that doesn't mean we're going to let him explore his limits on his own. If one takes a cavalier approach to a puppy, one can violate his emotional limits just as easily as if one is intolerant. We have to decisively define the limits according to our standards, or the temperament will assign them according to instinctive standards. Temperament needs to "know" where the negative lies in the environment; otherwise instinct is without order and nerves are exposed like live wires. A dog raised in a permissive household feels that danger is everywhere. We must be active in this regard so that learning isn't left to chance. The puppy must be carefully managed or natural channeling and indiscriminate emotional bruising will be the result. By encouraging the prey instinct under controlled circumstances, a limit can be assigned to our liking. Then, once the bounds are carefully secured, the pup is free not only to make prey within them but to be in harmony with his family as well.

The most obvious limitation in puppies is their short attention span. When confronted with resistance, a pup is unable to blend two different emotional values (strengths of attraction) together to come up with one focused response. The simple prey instinct follows a simple rhythm in a natural way. Anything that is more complex—all of our training and domestic requirements—will cause the dog to divert his attention so that he doesn't have a negative experience. Not until he sexually matures and can process stress into social behaviors will he be able to handle such a complex undertaking. The most important thing is to recognize this limitation and not become upset with a puppy if he gives out when faced with a simple objective that is nonetheless taxing. The next time, make the problem easier. Problems in this regard reflect errors by the trainer, not learning deficiencies in the puppy.

Attention spans lengthen as instincts are strengthened through the flow of drive. Getting a puppy to perform a task is not as important as "hardening" his focus on a positive stimulation so that he learns to persevere. The trait of stamina gives the pup the confidence that an attitude of resolute focus always leads to success. *Success for the dog must be focused on gaining instinctive gratification rather than on avoiding a correction.*

Another obvious limitation in puppies is that they tire easily, both emotionally and physically. Being young, the prey instinct isn't synchronized with the outside world; the puppy can't pace himself. He'll go at full tilt toward whatever is interesting him until he's exhausted. Conversely, if something is upsetting him, he can't see a light at the end of the tunnel and he'll panic easily. When tired, a pup will only learn to be nervous rather than how to do an exercise.

Also, a puppy can't be expected to inhibit a natural impulse. Pups just want to have fun through the drive to bite; that is what millions of years of instinctual development are inviting and commanding them to do. They just want to follow the path of least resistance in the natural flow of instincts tumbling toward the hunt. For this reason, there is a chapter on avoiding negative training included on not exposing the young puppy to those situations that are just going to encourage him to be disobedient.

Another limitation in the puppy is that outside the scope of the simple prey instinct, he can't change direction or moods quickly. He gets into following the prey instinct along its natural path and can't get out of it until it reaches a natural conclusion or until he's exhausted. It would be like discovering an intriguing path in the forest and wanting to walk it to see where it leads. Puppies, like

children, need time to explore, and we have to guide them gently
through transitions of mood with an alternative attraction such as a
piece of food, a happy tone of voice, or a ball. A puppy needs a
good reason to change a mood.

Knowing and recognizing these limits is the sensitive aspect of
being a dog owner. It should now be easier to see how a puppy
could be overloaded and given a bad experience in a very subtle
way. For instance, you could be asking the pup to return the ball
to you when he's tiring and you've thrown it once too often. This
may seem a minor point, but to a pup, bad experiences have a cu-
mulative weight and their load never goes away. Instead, recognize
when your puppy has reached his limit so that an unreasonable demand isn't placed on his behavior. When you see his drive lose its
zip, stop. The next time, quit while you're ahead.

By working within temperamental limits, and by activating the
prey instinct, little by little the dog's level of performance can be
pushed out beyond the genetic parameters with which he's been
endowed. Then, when the dog encounters an unnatural stress it is
easy for him to learn a very specific and healthy lesson through attentiveness to his handler, instead of being overloaded and made to
feel defensive.

An important point must be made about being patient with a
puppy and understanding the world from his point of view. We've
been taught through the study of animal behavior that much of what
a dog does is a random charting of the world through the experience
of positive and negative reinforcements. This suggests that a positive
value is equal to a negative one. Nothing could be further from the
truth. Order in a dog's mind is comprised of a constellation of positives crystallizing around a single negative. When the dog is at the
height of drive's expression, the negative is defined most narrowly
in terms of access to the prey, a healthy harmonic pathway. The
negative is most broadly defined when drive loses its focus or none
is to be found; then the security of the order is itself shattered. All
of a sudden, the dog is in the midst of chaos as surely as if a predator
swooped into the den and was ravaging the litter. It is a shocking
experience that he is not able to cope with and for which a flurry
of subsequent positives can never compensate. Therefore, a correction is something that needs to be carefully administered at the appropriate time. It should guide and enhance focus rather than be
used as a means of inhibiting the individual.

Finally, we often hear the expression that a pup wants to test his limits, suggesting that he needs to be pushed back to be kept within them. A puppy has a drive to find a limit not because he wants to test them, but because flow can only happen within order. The limit defines the negative around which the positives can be arranged. At the same time, an individual is motivated to seek the highest and purest rate of flow; otherwise, canine behavior would be stagnant and lacking its dynamism. It may appear as if the puppy is testing his limits, but he's only trying to bring the highest rate of flow within the sphere of a defined negative. This doesn't mean that the pup is seeking to pit his strength of will against anyone else's, because his drive is no different in this respect than that of cows craning their necks through a fence to nibble on some sweet green grass. The farmer doesn't take offense; he just checks to ensure that his fencing is stout.

In one sense we should imitate the natural model: In the wild, puppies start life fully immersed in group living. They are granted a high degree of license and initially are free to bite without sanction. As long as puppies are within the group's realm, the negative is always narrowly defined as being connected to their mother, providing them with an uninhibited access to their inner temperament. If we take this formula to heart, a puppy raised properly can convert a negative, such as a correction, into a releaser for a harmonic pathway. The dog will grow in his self-confidence, which is a social phenomenon we can put to inestimable good in his training.

12

Developing Self-confidence

IN RAISING A PUPPY, we have two objectives. One is to train the dog to behave, but more important, we need to mold his character. These two aspects are intertwined so closely that you can't do one without the other.

The major mistake made in puppy development is only to think about training the puppy to behave. Serious thought is not given to his character development, because this area is not at all understood. In this chapter we're going to concentrate on the most important character trait in a dog: his level of self-confidence.

Self-confidence is the key element in getting the dog to give his drive to his owner, which is essential not only to our control, but to the dog's calmness as well. Confidence keeps a dominant dog from becoming sharp and aggressive, and it keeps a sensitive dog from becoming shy and fearful. It may be more work to think in terms of developing self-confidence, but training a self-confident dog is a lot less work.

Self-confidence means the predictability of success. I don't mean that the dog can look into the future and see what his chances are. It simply means the "feeling" of being in a "rhythm" or "groove" that in the immediate moment feels good and that ultimately leads the dog to the condition of feeling fulfilled.

An athlete knows this feeling well. A tennis player knows when he's hit the ball well off his racquet long before he sees where it lands. When he's hitting the ball crisply and surely, he's confident about his game. This is not in any way an intellectual experience; the sensation of impending success is strictly emotional. For a dog, feeling good means that a stimulus matches up smoothly with a prey or harmonic instinct.

The opposite is the sensation of nervousness: The dog can't sense a target or focus for his drive; and/or the rhythm of events is discordant and he's experiencing resistance to his drive.

An example of making a dog nervous in the first instance would be by wrestling too hard with the puppy. The pup gets aroused, but he's blocked from biting due to his need to stay connected. There isn't a way for his prey instinct to come to a successful resolution. One might observe a puppy start to scoot around madly, nip, bark, or growl in frustration. The owner may then compound the error by taking it personally and getting mad at the dog for following the rule of instinct in a game the owner started. What the puppy needs here is an acceptable fulfillment of his prey instinct before the resistance breaches his limit. One can feel free to start a vigorous game, but when it escalates above the comfort level, the owner could throw a ball or stick. The game shouldn't have been started without the owner having this alternative focus at hand.

In the second case, an example of giving a puppy too much resistance would be an overly intense game of tug-of-war. The toy or rag is the clear target in this case, but the owner's strength suggests to the dog that he's not going to win. He whines or growls, indicating his unsureness. In these kinds of games, which can indeed be very healthful when played properly, the pup must always win. Before he hits his frustration point, let him wrest the toy away, and praise him loudly as he trots about, cocksure of himself. As he gains in self-confidence, he will become that much easier to train in the rules of the game when this activity is incorporated into the obedience exercises.

What does self-confidence look like? A self-confident dog moves in a supple manner, with tail high and slightly waving. The eyes are clear and bright, and the facial expression is focused but without anxiety. When the dog encounters something novel, his hackles stay down and he is inquisitive yet relaxed. Self-confidence is not submissiveness, and neither is it dominance. Both of these are first cousins to nervousness. Some dogs are born with the ability to become self-confident more than others, but we can always be a positive influence on this trait as dog owners.

When we're training a dog we should visualize the outcome of the lesson in the body language of self-confidence as opposed to the tenseness of an animal afraid to make a mistake. In learning, a dog must make mistakes, and we need the dog to be stimulated by the learning or channeling process instead of reticent and afraid of working freely and independently.

I've often noticed that people may mistake a dog that is stressed or inhibited for one that is calm. The dog may prefer to lie down around people when first introduced, or be passive at the vet's office. This is especially a misinterpretation when a puppy is involved. A pure drive behavior is full of life and curiosity and is always looking for action, and in some eyes such a pup will be viewed as a troublemaker. In reality, he is healthy, only unchanneled. When a dog is lying down in a context that is normally exciting, it is because stress is overwhelming him.

Calmness doesn't mean a low-keyed or lethargic animal. Sometimes a dog may lie down when he's relaxed and there's nothing doing, and then, in another moment, he could be bounding about happily. It is the appropriate response for the situation. When I take my puppy to a shopping center or the vet's I want him to be straining at his lead, highly aroused by the swirl of activity going on around us. If he hangs back, I'll try to pump him up so he categorizes the moment as something positive. A healthy puppy should hardly ever lie down except when he's physically tired or emotionally spent from having fun.

In the old days, most breeds were directly of working stock. A golden retriever or an Irish setter used to have to bear up under the discharge of a 12-gauge shotgun. They used to have to accept a large burden on their drive around the prey and in the field. The same strong instincts, sound nerves, and flexible drive that made a good working dog are essential to self-confidence in home and everyday life. Sadly, today, especially with the popular breeds such as golden retrievers and German shepherds, many dogs are problematic because the genetic base has atrophied since breeders are selecting for show criteria rather than field, sport, or working merits. The modern dog owner is left with little margin for error and to improve our odds, I hope the consumer will become educated, demand higher quality from breeders, and expect to pay for it. Breeders who test, train, and work their stock expend an exponentially higher degree of effort, and they deserve to be rewarded and encouraged.

How does a dog learn self-confidence? There are three interrelated steps.

1. *Put the nerves on the positive setting*. This means simply that you want the puppy to be "up," highly active, and looking for fun. As a training dividend, the dog's drive can now be found right at the surface, accessible to channeling onto a harmonic pathway.

2. *Develop the instincts*. Instead of trying to repress the dog's instincts, which can be used to relieve drive, encourage their expression. When a dog's instincts are developed, nothing is held back, leaving nowhere for the seedling of a problem behavior to take root in his character.

3. *Channel the drive*. Once the pup has a positive outlook, his instincts are fired up and the drive is channeled into the handler so that he becomes the dog's connection to the target. The negative is therefore defined in terms of a harmonic pathway, with the owner being its focus.

When this formula is followed one is directly "wiring" how the dog's temperament is categorizing what people, animals, and places mean for him. You're showing the dog where his instincts belong in your life, which is the only way the dog can learn where he belongs. Having access to the first moments of the way a dog forms an impression is priceless and makes for the most reliable kind of pet.

An important point must be made for those people who own more than one puppy, or for those who have puppies living with adult dogs. Dogs are group pack animals and when left to their own devices, drive will end up being naturally channeled and divided with the owner in many situations falling outside the scope of a more narrowly defined harmonic pathway. In the wild channeling process, each animal will mature to be only a fraction of the whole. If there are five dogs in a pack, each one has one fifth of a character, so they can all fit together when naturally channeled. The mob effect means that they have been raised to be incomplete, and when in a critical moment—such as when the dog is exposed to something new and instinctively powerful—he will become nervous, control and predictability will be hard to come by. To be self-confident in man's world, a puppy must develop a complete character along a harmonic pathway, crystallizing around his master. Therefore, if one owns several dogs, each one must get individualized attention in critical moments, such as in greeting strangers at the door and in forays into the outside world. When one of a pack of dogs finds himself on his own, the inevitable unsureness can take on undesirable expressions.

13

Knocking Heads: The Politics of Confrontation

WHAT IS WRONG WITH THINKING ONLY IN TERMS OF CONTROLLING A PUPPY?

WHEN PEOPLE COME TO ME with their puppies for evaluation they usually have a pretty long list of his "offenses." Everything from raiding the garbage to chewing on shoes is generally on that list. The most troublesome offenses are those evolving during the dog's social development, i.e., jumping, nipping, and chewing. Given the pup's lengthy rap sheet, his owners are quite concerned that their dog is becoming a pest, perhaps even a danger.

If a puppy is healthy and has a good temperament, he has two directly related potentials. The important one is that he can grow up to be a self-confident and well-adjusted dog. By the same token, he will be capable of destroying a house in under half an hour, and he will likely be a social pest with his desire to gnaw on hands, shoes, and jumping up for attention.

At first glance, it would seem that these two potentials are opposed to each other rather than being compatible. It would be logical to assume that by making the puppy mannerly and controllable at an early age, we are in fact making him well-adjusted and he should grow in his self-confidence as he learns our rules. It seems reasonable that if we can purge his "destructive" tendencies, we are making his temperament better and more to our taste.

That line of reasoning has merit. However, since we are not dealing with a logical or rational animal, this approach doesn't work. It doesn't work because in order to get a puppy to be clean and mannerly right away you have to frighten him. When a dog is afraid, his "nervous process" is inhibited. That means the dog won't respond to naturally attractive things. In other words, the puppy won't do anything. One could say that the puppy doesn't chew or eliminate indoors anymore because he has learned that his owner doesn't want him to, but that would be self-delusion. The puppy is scared, plain and simple.

We could get into an elaborate proof of this statement, but it isn't necessary. We can easily see that the same dog is becoming defensive in other unrelated areas of his life. In fact, this fear is now bleeding through to other interactions with people or in the puppy's response to new situations, wherein he is either tentative, cowering, avoiding, piddling, hyperfriendly, displaying his hackles, or barking incessantly. If the dog became housebroken by grasping the owner's concept of housetraining, why should there be this negative transfer into other areas? The reason is quite simple: Fear is like an oil spill; it generalizes onto anything that is new to a dog.

Dogs that seem to learn their housebreaking through punishment become dependent on their owners for their sense of order. When left alone they're afraid, and eliminating and chewing to have fun aren't likely natural activities. The pup will prefer to remain hidden or inhibited, thereby minimizing his exposure to danger.

The above method of confrontation and discipline doesn't work at all with dogs that are less sensitive. They continue to soil and destroy the house, since the absence of the owner means the hunt is on. This is not "spite," because they have no idea what potential impact their behavior can have on their owner. Their nervous process is stimulated and they need relief. Relief for a dog is spelled g-a-r-b-a-g-e. The dog either needs to get into the garbage or turn the house into garbage.

With those dogs somewhere in the middle, their resilient temperaments will emerge from their shells eventually, and then they can take up housewrecking with a renewed vengeance. Their owners are chagrined; the dogs had seemed to get the rules early on.

Many dogs, no matter how they're trained, grow to be clean on their own once they mature beyond the chewing stage. But then we're still left with the long-term damage of defensiveness. As he grows older a dog's pack instinct becomes more discriminating—which humans are familiar in an intimate sense and which ones are more distant—and much of this defensiveness to the owner will become masked by nervous friendliness and transferred over to new humans. It is also possible that when the dog has to deal with a somewhat familiar human in a new situation the original defen-

siveness he learned from his owner will tumble right back out. I see
this all the time in my boarding kennel. The dog is reunited with
his vacationing family in the office. They understandably make a big
fuss and reach out for the dog. In the instant before his nerves plug
in, he may flinch, cower, or piddle. Then, suddenly, the nervousness will convert to hyperfriendliness. The greeting ritual is not
a pure drive behavior and the encounter is actually damaging his
character further as nervousness is growing more deeply ingrained.
Since nervousness is affiliated with survival, the dog does survive
the moment, and so each incident reinforces itself. Therefore, no
matter what we want the dog to learn, he only ends up learning
more about nervousness. Ironically, even if the owner should notice
the brief moment of shock in his dog, he'll misinterpret it as something to do with his stay away from the family at the kennel. In fact,
it was he who taught the dog to be stressed in such critical moments, and it is the reunion that is so stressful. Damage is permanent, but it's hard to see except in highly charged moments.

A dog who cannot sense the group's purpose in any new moment
develops an unsure character. His temperament is no longer
healthy, because he starts to analyze things not according to their
naturally attractive value but for its survival value. This inflicts un-
neccessary emotional stress. In my kennel, I see this graphically
illustrated all the time. On admission many dogs become depressed
and start to drool or retreat to a corner of their kennel. Logically,
we might think that they miss their owners. Really, it's because the
dog has experienced too much punishment for reasons he couldn't
comprehend. The newness of this moment at the kennel destroys
his sense of order, renewing the emotional pain of a violated limit.
And while he can in time be acclimated, each visit recycles stress
yet again.

The owner never intended to do this to his dog. In many cases
he was following what seemed like expert and logical advice. All he
wanted to do was to train his dog to behave. In the short term, he
thought he was seeing success. The dog became cleaner in the
house and less active around people. However, in the long run the
dog's character was being undermined.

I'm not suggesting that manners are bad for a dog. A dog does
indeed become less nervous when he conforms to the rules of the
household, but only if he absorbs the lesson in the manner by which
dogs learn. And only if the lesson is defined specifically in terms of
a harmonic pathway. When we attempt to modify a dog's behavior

with yelling, hitting, or any kind of physical discipline we are only training the dog to be defensive and nervous. Later, whenever he has to switch moods, the shifting of limits reminds him once again of the initial overload.

Confrontation distorts our message. When an owner "disciplines" his puppy physically or verbally he has changed the subject from what he was initially trying to get across. The puppy was in a prey instinct, which provoked the confrontation, and now the encounter with his owner has changed the mood into a defensive instinct. Before the outburst the puppy was thinking about the sock or the garbage and then hello: Now he's thinking about his owner. Whatever transpires next has nothing to do with the puppy's original error. All that's being accomplished is the brutalization of the puppy's nervous and emotional processes.

There are dozens of ways dogs can be trained to be defensive. One such destructive exercise is to teach a puppy to "go to a corner." A dog can't form a concept to go to an undefined place; he can only be motivated to go to a place where he has learned fulfillment. If the dog isn't being motivated to go to the corner with food or praise as the cornerstone to this exercise, he is going there for security. In other words, to be safe from his owner.

While normal puppies can be hellions when young, they also are displaying a perfect aptitude for "clean learning." The specific intention behind an exercise can become the releaser along a harmonic pathway for a reflex already on file, which will readily pop out either on command or automatically when the situation warrants it. The only thing that stands in our way is nervousness. Nervousness is as corrosive to a dog's character as acid is to metal.

14

Avoiding Negative Training

HOW NOT TO TRAIN A DOG TO BE DISOBEDIENT ON COMMAND

Channeling the prey instinct is impossible if the dog is going to be given a choice between doing what's natural and doing what's artificial. A puppy just wants to get into his hunting gear and go, and if given latitude, one is inadvertently encouraging disobedience.

Negative training is when we heighten the dog's drive to act wild. It can be unintentional or accidental, but it can only occur if the dog is given the opportunity to be wild even if we're talking in terms of bare split seconds. It generally occurs when the owner makes a handling decision based on guilt, convenience, or a misunderstanding or denial of the pup's inherent wildness.

Since coming when called is the central objective in this book, let us start with avoiding negative training in relation to this most important training exercise.

When our puppies are young they can only make prey within the first social order: the sense of being connected to the mother or others of the group. In most cases the sense of security is relative to a distance between them; they can only feel secure enough to have fun within this safety range. When they spot something attractive at a distance they follow their curiosity precisely to that threshold of connectedness and then scamper back should the group move away. In a puppy, this threshold at first is only a short running distance, but the hunting mood strengthens as mobility increases and every day the growing dog will be able to venture farther away. At some point, roughly between six to ten months for most dogs, the urge to hunt slowly starts to outweigh the need to be connected, especially when there is something of interest to lead them astray. It is at this critical juncture that most negative training relative to coming when called occurs. At first they aren't leaving the group: They are following their prey instinct.

Because a puppy so readily responds to his name, given his need to be connected, it's easy for an owner to get the mistaken impression that his pup has learned his name. This delusion primes him to fall into the trap of trying to call his pup when he's least likely to come, instead of reserving his name for those situations where he is always going to respond.

Up until the point when the puppy's prey instinct starts to penetrate beyond familiar territory, the puppy appeared to have learned his name. Every time his owner called, clapped, or whistled, the puppy came happily no matter what he was doing. But had the owner paid a little closer attention he would have seen that the puppy was hesitating longer as he got older. Also, the owner had to provide more and more attraction for an ever-diminishing return. Nevertheless, the pup always did end up coming to his owner even if he needed a little more "scolding" from time to time, so things seemed right on track.

What, in fact, was the puppy learning each time his owner called him? Let's consider a puppy straying into the neighbor's yard because he saw their cat stretching on the porch. The owner looks up from his yardwork and calls the dog just when the pup was perched on the threshold between the pack mood and the potential for a new hunting mood. The owner's tone of voice was severe enough to shock the dog out of his focus on the cat, which is the number one variable of the prey instinct. The dog became unsure at this place, so he ran from here to a new number one variable in his field of interest, his owner, as the puppy's need to be connected outweighs his desire to hunt. What the puppy learned was to leave the place of stress, a place that represented an interruption of his drive (shock) and go to the number one variable in a new mood.

After a few months, a new temperamental balance is emerging, with the hunting desire starting to outweigh the pack need in certain situations. He will be less limited, so he can sustain a focus on something of interest beyond the first social threshold, the den. This means that when called, he will start to hesitate; his curiosity toward the distraction is displacing his unsureness. Also, his owner is not so clearly the number one variable in the environment, because the pup's need to be connected has for the moment been displaced by the prey instinct. Unfortunately, the owner doesn't recognize this second of hesitation as an indicator of a deteriorating pattern. He still believes that the dog has learned to come when called, and that the dog was smart to learn that. He continues to expose the puppy to the distractions, thinking the puppy has mastered the exercise. Indoors the puppy always comes quickly when called, continuing the delusion. As performance deteriorates, the owner reasons that it must be a matter of defiance, so he'll correct the dog either verbally or physically. Once corrected, the puppy may display an increased submissive attraction to his owner, and the need to be connected will in the short term be increased. The dog may even improve from the point of view of responding, but his responses become less pure, less direct expressions of drive. Even though the owner remains the number one variable, social resistance is creating a bigger and bigger buffer zone between them, to which the dog becomes increasingly sensitive.

Finally, the puppy hits adolescence and gets stuck. He's not quite ready to run away, but he is so charged in prey that he can't respond submissively to his name anymore. It becomes too painful to resist the flow of drive when aroused. Sometimes out of this dilemma a "game" emerges, where the puppy runs around the owner, or barks, or comes close but not close enough. In this situation many owners do the worst thing possible and run after the dog, all the while calling his name. This results in a particularly neurotic pattern of learning so that the dog can feel connected to his owner by running away from him!

Some owners may break this impasse by finding an inducement such as a ball or food, but then they erase their good work by snagging the dog with a quick grab or locking him up indoors. Such a sudden reversal of flow trains the dog that even positives affiliated with his owner are negatives.

After being chased on a number of occasions, or when the hunting urge gets strong enough in and of itself, the space around the owner now becomes the place where the dog feels unsure. At this emotional level, only the simple prey instinct can define a number one variable for high drive, and it will be one that totally excludes the owner from the group. Now the dog *needs* to run away, and can always be put into this deviant mood when he hears his name or if a door or gate is left unsecured. The dog runs away, experiences hunting nirvana with his doggy pals, and from now on the owner is the big negative to be avoided at all costs whenever the dog is aroused to hunt.

Aside from this pattern of directly training a dog to be disobedient on command, there are indirect methods of negative training. For example, when the pup is young he is let out the door to run around the yard since he has seemingly learned its boundaries. A dog is turned loose and he's gone. He's crossed the road and he's off on a magnificent lark through the meadow or across the street to peruse some compelling garbage cans. When the owner finally catches up to him all the problems are generally repeated. Even if the owner just collects him or the dog returns home on his own, the dog is still being allowed to learn to hunt for himself, a negative lesson that erases and overwhelms any positive work one might tirelessly do.

Other forms of negative training flow from this bad beginning. Once the dog is deemed unreliable, he is tied out or put on a trolley. Perhaps it's thought that if the dog does time he'll repent and go back to the good ways he showed as a puppy. However, this has exactly the opposite effect; when you restrain a dog you frustrate him and increase his attraction to distractions. We all have seen the pitiful spectacle of an active dog tethered to his house with a path worn to outline his hunting domain. I can recall a German shepherd that tirelessly paced his rounds at the slightest hint of something attractive on the horizon. He was tied to a hickory tree that shed its juicy nuts each fall, luring squirrels daringly close. I doubt the dog ever caught one, but I realized that he never had to. The rush of adrenaline, the abbreviated charge, and the inevitable jolt at the end of the chain were tangible things for the dog. The flip he did at the end of a particularly close chase was for that dog the only physical consequence to his prey instinct and so was in fact its reinforcement. The dog felt that was what catching a squirrel felt like. But it was reinforcement without fulfillment, so the dog was doomed to toil endlessly around and around, wearing his path deeper and deeper. When we mechanically block a dog this way we are teaching him every day for hour upon hour to have exactly the opposite attitude that we need from him.

It's particularly bad to tie out a puppy. When tethered for the first time, it will scare him, and although he quickly seems to get over his fear, the sensation of vulnerable exposure from all sides is enduring. When people approach he will overload, often with friendliness, and in many cases this will turn into aggression. A dog born with a great disposition toward children can learn to bite just by watching them shout, scream, and dash about in normal play.

Also, they are being set up as an attractive nuisance. If there are people in the neighborhood who like to tease dogs, the puppy is at their mercy.

Since sooner or later a puppy's hunting urge will pull him off his familiar territory, I do believe in restraining the puppy until he's fully trained. I recommend that the puppy have a very sturdy enclosure, preferably a chain-link kennel that is solid on three sides. Stockade fencing could be wired to it on these three sides so that his vision, and his sense of vulnerability, is restricted. The kennel should be built in the quietest place in the yard. Inside should be a comfortable doghouse and a resting bench with a large enough shed-type roof above it so that the dog can lie on the bench outside the house without getting wet in the rain. The ground could either be cement or gravel so that it can be kept clean and periodically disinfected. A minimum size for a kennel is six feet high by six feet wide by twelve feet long for large dogs and somewhat smaller for smaller breeds; of course, bigger is better; too small a kennel and the dog will become nervous. However, a small kennel is still better than a loose dog. If you have a fenced yard, it must be high enough—at least five feet—and secured against digging out. No gap should be left flimsy or makeshift, because sooner or later the dog will find it. Even with a fenced yard, there should still be a kennel deep in the yard's interior, out of sight and locked should you leave the puppy behind. I've known many dogs that were ruined because they ran up to the fence where a stranger could tease them or throw firecrackers at them. It is a sad commentary, but I've found that dogs often bring out the worst in people.

The kennel is a means of prevention so that the puppy can't learn about his hunting drive independent of his owner. The kennel also facilitates the development of self-confidence as the pup will develop a strong sense of place here. It is stressful for a pup always to be underfoot; he's a dog and needs a place where he needn't comply with man's rules and can sleep in peace.

The kennel is not to be a means of mere convenience so you don't have to deal with the dog. In that case, it will have a negative influence on development. It is a holding area so that the dog isn't exposed to negative training.

I know that many people are turned off by the thought of a kennel. They think their dog won't like them if he's put into it, but this association is only possible if they use the kennel as a means of punishment, or if they try to convince the puppy to get into it of his own accord. Don't give a dog a choice. If he's not responsive to some coaxing or a tidbit, just put him in his kennel or crate without fanfare. The normal amount of struggling will quickly extinguish itself if you don't involve yourself. Don't look or talk to the pup; just put him in, period.

By the same measure, if you have to go into the vet's office and the eight-month-old puppy balks, he's too big to be carried and he's not interested in a ball, just go. Don't turn around and address him; you're not imparting valuable advice to him. From his perspective, since you are focusing on him, you are challenging him over his reluctance to go someplace scary. Instead, act forthright; with a displayed confidence in your manner, you will be leading him with an instinct and helping to resolve his conflict. Since you're not feeding the nervousness or giving it room to grow, you are actually reducing stress. Pleading and trying to mollify, on the other hand, magnifies and belabors the point, giving the puppy a big decision to make. Ironically, in this approach the puppy will attribute the negative aspects of kenneling or of going into the vet's clinic *to* his owner. Were one just to put the pup there without fanfare and explanation, the negative association would be minimal.

There are ways to make going to the kennel a pleasant event. I always feed my puppy there; after four or five days he is beating me to the gate and waiting for me to let him in. For many months I am always prepared with a treat to reward this flow. When we play together in the yard I'll frequently get the game to drift in and out of his kennel. Sometimes my wife will hold the puppy and I'll run into the kennel and show him the ball, call him, and he'll be released to run in and we'll play. He isn't allowed to make the connection that the kennel is something bad.

The critical point is not to ask the dog to make a decision to go to his kennel until he is fully trained. Once he is properly channeled, it is not a big burden on the dog to call him and make him get in it. The important thing to realize is that the dog comes to view the kennel as a place of calmness that always produces a happy reunion with his master. As I walk away from my puppy I make no reaction to his crying. This frustration is an inevitable reaction to his group leaving, but quickly this behavior atrophies.

On the positive side, the dog is learning how to contain himself when he is alone, a vital lesson for a dog that is eventually to be left alone in the house. All too often an owner comes to me with a dog that is beside itself when left alone. Unfortunately, they never trained the dog how to handle this abnormal stress when it was young.

It's also helpful to remember that a dog has no sense of time and that a puppy needs a good eighteen to twenty hours of sleep daily. The sooner he gets used to his kennel, the sooner he can get that much needed sleep. A kennel will not be necessary if you are prepared to always attend to him outdoors and crate-train him indoors.

Another way pups learn to tune out their names is when they're called to be confined indoors or hooked up to a lead. When the pup comes indoors spend a few moments to get him excited so he doesn't make the connection that his name has to do with restriction. There must be some instinctive success gained by making contact with you.

Another broad category of negative training that spans all training phases is when commands are used repetitively or casually. Commands must have an explosive impact that totally galvanizes the dog into the desired behavior or the dog will be unreliable. We're not training here merely so the dog looks showy when he works, although there's no reason he shouldn't look great. The point is that if a handler commands 100 percent of the dog's attention in training exercises, in a critical moment more than 50 percent, and therefore control, is assured. But if in training you only get 70–90 percent, when you really need control, you'll fall below the 50 percent mark. And the handler won't be the number one variable. In training, every time you utter a command and that desired 100 percent effect doesn't occur, you are training the dog to be disobedient in a critical moment. This is especially true regarding coming when called.

I think it is well understood by now that one should never call his dog to be punished, but the point bears repetition once again.

Also, there is the more subtle aspect of using the dog's name casually, and repetitively, as in "Scruffy no," or "Scruffy *heel*," and this is damaging as well. I'm not talking here of sweet-talking your dog or of using his name affectionately. That is irrelevant to training; that's just having fun with your puppy. What I mean is using the pup's name when you want his attention, but not for a truly concrete reason as far as his instincts are concerned. You may want him to step outside of your garden while you weed, or perhaps he's grabbed something and you want it back. When the name is used and an attempt is made to control the dog before he is fully trained, one is only training the dog that the name is an irrelevant or a negative command. The dog is learning that his name means a struggle with his owner. There are other ways to deal with the above types of problems, and we shouldn't mix the dog's name in with these issues.

To repeat, control over a dog at a distance, especially if he's in full bore after something, is the hardest thing to achieve and is the major aim of this book. If you make vital mistakes in any of the critical links, the project will be undone. The points I've mentioned are not minor. We must be disciplined as dog owners when we set out to train a dog. It doesn't mean we have to do any more work; in fact, doing things right is efficient and is the minimum effort needed. It means we have to totally manage our influence on the dog.

It would be helpful to develop a household vernacular for the dog so he can slowly learn the household routines that are independent of our training exercises. For example, when I want my dog to lie down and stay put in the house, I say, "Lie down and stay there" rather than a more emphatic, *"Down-Stay"* reserved for when the UPS man arrives.

15

Turning Mountains into Molehills

IN THIS SECTION we'll discuss how to "neutralize" or lower the dog's drive level, which has the effect of making a big problem into a little one. Reducing the size of a problem is the first step to solving it and is halfway to the completed solution.

Since dogs can't see the big picture in a situation, what to us looks like a small issue can seem to a dog, especially a puppy, to be an insurmountable obstacle. In general, a problem for a dog is either a switching of moods or the issue of giving up drive, so its size is relative to the amount of drive a dog is in (how aroused or excited he is). For instance, if a dog is running at full tilt after a bicycle and the owner calls him, it is impossible for the dog to learn to come back to his name in one fell swoop. The dog is being expected to give up chasing something that has totally captured his attention, then turn around and trot dutifully back to his master. That's not going to happen because there isn't a natural instinct available that can switch a mood in this manner. The problem is far too big.

One way to neutralize is to burn off a puppy's drive by tiring him. If I'm going to introduce my puppy to strangers, rather than expose him straightaway, I'll spend a few minutes playing ball with him so that he's emotionally spent when he first meets them. After the on-lead introductions, I'll cut him loose as soon as I see he's calm.

A second way is to distract the pup to a ball or piece of food. You've slightly changed the subject so the dog can better handle the negative in the situation. For example, if you are introducing the dog to a stranger, give the stranger a ball or tidbit so that the focus is off the encounter with this "alien" human. The ball or food activates a very clear and natural instinct, and the negative is reduced from contact with a stranger to access to the food. Since meeting the stranger gains the puppy the food, the stranger is admitted into the group. As a result, the social negative is known as well.

Many times you can do the first and second step all in one moment: My puppy is in the yard and he starts over to the neighbor's when he sees their cat. I've seen this coming, so I've positioned myself in his peripheral vision. I let him get one or two steps into gear and then I whoop and run away, distracting his focus from the cat onto me with my quick motion and noise. He has to burn off drive by chasing me, and when he catches up, I'll throw a stick a few times and then let him drift away to notice the cat again. Then, before he commits to leaving our yard, I'll gently whisper his name and backpedal a little. He comes quickly, we play, and his attraction to the cat has for the time being been neutralized.

I haven't taught him to come to his name because his hunting urge hasn't yet developed to its adult proportions, but I am nonetheless laying a good foundation by giving him a little problem to solve. "Give me your drive, puppy, when I do something really attractive [hoot and run away], and you haven't all the way decided to leave me yet" is the problem the puppy is solving. As he matures, I'll make the problem progressively more difficult.

Another example concerns the city puppy in particular. He has to be walked on a lead through busy streets. When one walks a dog his drive is aroused by the new and interesting things to see and smell, and this pushes him to find a prey focus. This can mean either foraging through litter or straining to meet other dogs or introducing himself to pigeons. Once the puppy has been properly accustomed to the lead, the owner should start to neutralize this drive that's going in the wrong direction. The owner needs to move faster, and in a variety of new directions, so the pup can burn up energy while staying in his group mood. Then every so often the owner can bounce a ball and the puppy can spring on it, then carry it along in his jaws until he loses this focus. Then snatch the ball, switch directions a couple more times, and repeat. Gradually, the pup will be able to sustain his interest in his owner or his focus on the ball while he's carrying it, and they'll be able to walk together calmly for longer distances.

Neutralizing becomes the manner in which problems are first approached. Be creative and use any native instincts to make the problem smaller. This straightens out the road and gets the puppy off the emotional roller coaster in the confrontational approach to domestication.

16

"Let's Play Ball!"

WHEN A PUPPY IS TRAINED correctly with a ball it can be used as a tool to solve problems and to relieve stress. The ball has the power to draw out of the dog a *"pure drive behavior."* This means that the dog is unaware of anything negative in his surroundings; he can only see what is positive because he is fully absorbed by his prey instinct. He feels free and relaxed. He feels he is on the same wavelength as whomever he is with, that he is fully connected to the group. He will work as hard as he possibly can to sustain such a positive experience, and he is very receptive to training and learning when he's in this mood. The puppy views this fuzzy yellow tennis ball as a little furry animal. The ball goes hoppity-hop as it "runs"; it has a meager "hide" to be ripped off; it even comes with rubbery "tendons" to be gnawed on. What puppy could hope for more?

When a dog is "pure" in his drive to the ball, it is as if he were mesmerized by it. He will chase the ball tirelessly. He won't give up looking for it if it rolls under a bush, and he will be wearing a face with a clear expression of positive expectations. He is learning at such a high level that he can anticipate every action of the owner and is stimulated by any turn of events that may occur. The dog is holding nothing back, which is why he keeps on going past the fatigue point. Nothing in life can be more interesting or consuming for him. A lot of this has to do with genetics. Some dogs are born with this drive right off the bat, but many dogs are not predisposed to act this way. Yet all dogs have prey instinct, so they all can be helped to develop a positive and stronger attitude to the ball work no matter what their genetic endowment.

There are two ways that I play ball with my dog. One is strictly for fun and for the dog's exercise. In playing for fun, no demands should be placed on the ball, stick, or whatever is thrown. The other way is serious dog training, and that we will go into here at length.

The most important behavior to cultivate, because it reflects inner self-confidence, isn't the drive to return the ball to the handler. That will come in its own time, when the harmonic pathway is strong enough. The behavior that we want to look for first is the puppy carrying the ball firmly in his mouth in a calm and nondefensive manner.

Once the dog has fetched the ball, the handler, while praising, should be constantly moving away from the pup, which will magnetically draw him in closer. After a few moments, tease the dog with another ball. Quickly, the dog will want in on this new action.

By pretending that we don't want the first ball, and by arousing him to the second one, the pup will drop it as he moves closer to his handler. When he drops the first ball, throw the second one and while he's chasing it, pick up the one he dropped and once again move away from him. This routine can go on until he's exhausted and emotionally content. If he gets bored with the ball, snatch it, tease him, and then hide it. It is more effective to leave him a little hungry than overly stuffed.

While I'm not training him in this procedure to be obedient, I am doing something very worthwhile for our long-term goals. The dog is learning to come to me to get to his prey. I'm not issuing any commands or making any demands that diminish the dog's drive to do this. Most important, we're both having fun.

This brings us to the second more serious type of ball playing. We need the ball to be a training tool that can capture and sustain all of the dog's drive. That grants us access to the inner temperament, which tells the dog how to act and governs how he learns. Few dogs are developed this way. As puppies they chase the ball with all of their heart, and then they grow out of it. They're given the chance to chase real prey: cats, squirrels, kids on bikes, etc., and that teaches them what hunting feels like naturally. Meanwhile, in housebreaking the pup discovers that his owner is unpredictable when the pup is high in drive. When the dog is an adult, the ball will come to have a limited value, and then only when nothing better is going on.

How the pup reacts to his handler relative to his prey instinct will tell us a lot about how much control we can expect to have when the dog grows up and is free. A small prey object is not big enough to be shared by the group, so when more than one member is focused on it, there is high tension. In response to the tension, the pup or dog may want to circle the handler or pin the ball down and rip it or shake it furiously or nervously shift his grip a little too much or, finally, seek to withdraw to enjoy the ball by himself. By moving away and showing a new object of interest, the pup can learn that his handler, the path of most resistance, always brings the highest rate of return to his prey instinct.

What should the finished standard of performance look like? We throw the ball and the dog chases it with all his strength. He grabs the ball without hesitation and runs directly back to his owner and releases it to his hand smoothly. No matter what else is nearby—squirrels, other dogs, or neighbors—the dog doesn't vary his performance.

The first step in this training is to convince the dog or puppy that the ball is indeed a prey animal. With the young puppy, don't throw the ball too far; not only is his mind limited but we don't want to stress his growing body. Just swish it from side to side in the grass, then give it a little roll. Should a puppy or dog lack interest, what will build it is frustration. Throw the ball and run ahead and snag the ball and throw it again, or kick it as if the ball is trying to get away. You can also bounce it off a wall or drag it along tied to a rope while you run ahead of the puppy. A game of "keep away," with another person and the puppy in the middle, is a great motivator. The important rule is not to make the game too difficult. As the dog's drive to the ball increases, note that you are actually building up the dog's resistance to stress.

Many adult dogs will show little interest in the ball, because they will be looking at it through a pack instinct, misinterpreting it as another trick that the owner has in store for them. This kind of dog tunes it all out, preferring to wait for the real prey to come along on one of his neighborhood jaunts. The first step is to take away this dog's freedom. He must be confined in his kennel. The only time he gets out is to eliminate and chase the ball while on a fifty-foot lead. Eventually, the ball starts to look good as the prey instinct kicks on. Never lose patience with such a dog; it will only confirm his initial misgivings about the ball. Mistakes have been made in this dog's development, and it will take some time and sensitivity to correct them. The first objective is to get drive flowing, and then continue below as with the puppy.

Once the puppy has the ball in his mouth, he has captured his prey, and our training task here is to deactivate the naturally occurring instinct to guard it. Dogs selectively bred as bird hunters are called natural retrievers, since they are eager to reunite ball with owner, but the drive to retrieve a small prey is abnormal from the point of view of the fighting instinct. To ensure that the drive to guard doesn't creep into the formula, as I mentioned, moving away is the first step. Meanwhile, I'm saying in a low but ardent tone, "OOoooh what a goooodd dooggie, helllooo puupppy dooog!!" Anything equally silly will be OK. We want the dog to think he is the king, the lord of the forest. From his jaws dangles the carcass of the dreaded "Tennis-Saurus-Rex."

The next step is more difficult because we need the dog to come into our space even though he still has the prey. At this point it's good to ignore the dog and to lower your body height. To draw him over the critical distance, I may have a little tidbit to make him less sensitive to this threshold. The big thing is not to make a play for his ball. Reward him just for being near; then you can stand up and back away and get down again. Finally, when the dog is fully relaxed, give him some food and take the ball from his mouth as he lets it go to eat. The optimal behavior we would like to see is the dog pressing in and making body contact with his owner, all the while maintaining a full and calm grip on the ball. This confident attitude is more important than the handler getting the ball away from the dog, as it means the dog is sure about his drive when he is near his owner. Take the time to build such a solid base; when the harmonic pathway is complete the dog will have a drive to bring the ball to you.

When the dog tires you will see the guarding instinct, or a sensitivity to the critical distance, come back up to the surface. Also, the dog may lose interest in the ball in order to make contact with his handler. At any rate, note this limit and try to extend it as the puppy matures.

The work above is enough for a puppy until he gets to the age of about ten months. Then he can complete the training as it is outlined below. There is absolutely no advantage in getting the pup to the finish line in a hurry. They aren't learning any better by going faster. The more patient one is, the more firm the foundation will be throughout the entire adulthood of the dog. At about ten months ball training will continue, and it will correlate nicely with everything else the puppy is learning in other areas of his training. Our emphasis here is on keeping puppy's interest in the ball "pure," an undiluted expression of his prey instinct.

The next step is to get the pup to bring the ball back to us and then have him jump up to our level with the ball in his mouth. This is another big step for him, and he may become nervous about it, as with this reflex we're training him how to deal with his fighting instinct. That instinct is commonly ignored, especially if the puppy is friendly, but it mustn't be left to seek its own level.

I throw the ball and as usual I back up, but not very fast. I will pat my chest and invite the pup to come up and make contact with me. When he has planted his front feet on my chest, I tousle his jowls and praise him, without taking the ball. I'll disengage again, as I want him to learn that making contact with me doesn't mean he loses the ball. Then I run away, and I want to see him chase me hard. I'll repeat this for as long as I think he has stamina.

The next step is to train the dog to let go of the ball on command. A good crisp word such as *Out* is effective. This training will be done in two steps. First the dog will learn what *Out* means when the handler has possession of the ball. That makes it easier for the second step, when the dog learns that *Out* means to release the ball when he possesses it.

The dog should have a lead on when you let him go to chase the ball. He returns and makes contact. Get one hand on the lead while you offer him food with the other, and take the ball in the normal way without any command. Dangle the ball close to his mouth, as if you aren't paying attention to it. It's hoped that the dog will grab at it. Give him a shock on the lead before he gets to it and say *Out* in a firm tone. Next, you can place the ball on the ground and once again enforce the *Out* command. Then pick up the ball and help the dog sit. With the dog sitting and registering a look of calm acceptance, release him with a hup signal, back up, and have the dog jump up and make contact. The reward for this sequence is another heave of the ball. Do this routine as long as necessary.

Next, train the dog to let go of the ball when he has it in his mouth. You throw the ball and he returns and makes contact. By making the dog plug into us at our height while gripping the ball—an issue covered more thoroughly in the training chapter on heeling—we have caused the dog to make half of the decision to let go of the ball. He has given up his critical distance by coming near, and then he has decided to come up to our level, which is the same as entering our "sphere of influence." Letting go of the ball is a smooth step for him in order to conclude the encounter. After he makes contact for a moment, put your hand on the ball and tighten up the tension on his collar. When the dog lets go of the ball, say *Out*. Have the dog sit, and once again reward the dog with contacting and a throw of the ball. To conclude these sessions, have the dog make contact and let him disengage and carry the ball to the house or to his kennel. Then take the ball away as you give him a treat.

After a few sessions, when the dog is making contact with the ball in his mouth gently place your hand on the ball with the leash loosely held, but only by several inches. Should the dog try to withdraw, or to regrip the ball, make a sharp shock on the lead and when he releases the ball, command *Out*.

The mistake people tend to make in *Out* training would be to make the command and then shock it if the dog doesn't obey. That is dog training from the human point of view, but that will only train the dog that the handler is the problem. The real problem is that the dog is nervous and full of resistance toward this notion of sharing the ball with his handler. Were the dog full of a pure drive behavior, then he would seek to give the ball up so that it could be thrown again. By shocking nervousness, the dog, when prepared properly, is left feeling calm.

When he feels calm he will let go as the focus is shifted to his handler as we have already prescripted in the harmonic pathway we've been developing. Now the handler throws the ball, which channels all of the dog's drive into a pure expression. This reinforces the dog's attraction to the handler, and any shocks that are made after the dog has learned this lesson will actually serve to heighten his attraction to his handler.

The critical point to pulling off this effect is not to become angry but to be a good actor and act silly and happy even though you are going to shock the dog. This will disassociate you in the dog's mind from the shock and then the prey instinct will convert the shock into a stimulation when you throw the ball. The dog is only able to remember the shock in terms of feeling nervous. By throwing the ball, the owner becomes the positive gateway again, and that value can't be tied together with the previous feeling of nervousness.

Now we want to train the dog to return with the ball, to sit in front of us, and then to give the ball to our hand. Once again, train the dog to sit in front first, with the handler holding the ball. Someone else can hold the dog; the handler teases the dog with the ball and then runs away a short distance, turns, and calls the dog. As the dog comes near, use the ball as a magnet to draw the dog in. When you raise it over the dog's head, the dog will automatically sit when prompted by the ball and the verbal command.

When the dog is strong in this behavior, throw the ball and have a second one in your pocket or hidden in your armpit. As the dog is returning, flash the second one for a brief moment. You may also have to be slowly backing up. As he closes in, command "Sit." Have the dog make contact, and then disengage and have him sit with the ball still in his mouth. Then put your hand on the ball and command "Out." Contacting and another throw is the reward. End the exercise by having the dog carry the ball about the yard.

As the dog gets smoother in the contact, sit, and out, start to engage him in tug-of-war so that his focus on the ball stays clear.

All this training should take place initially in a quiet place. Then, when the dog is confident, in the final phases he can be exposed to distractions, and training aids such as tab leads (a short lead, six to eight inches long, that can dangle from the dog's collar without tripping him) and the second ball or food can be phased out. However, don't do the whole routine when you are putting him to such a test. Simply repeat the first steps that you did when he was a young puppy. This is giving him a small problem to solve, maximizing his chances for success. In general, it's always good to go back to the beginning and review and strengthen the dog's drive for this work.

Many parents may be nervous about this whole notion of prey instinct. We are not creating the prey instinct: it is already there. We are channeling it into an appropriate activity. This way it is not as likely to go where it doesn't belong, such as after a child's hand. Otherwise, you are leaving it up to the dog to decide what he wants to do with his prey instinct.

Many people may also think that by leaving lots of toys around for their puppy, they are building his drive, but in fact, they are lessening it. If the dog always has access, it won't hold any special value.

17

Channeling the Hunting Drive into Group Instincts

IN SUCCESSFUL TRAINING, the dog must view his owner as "the keeper of the gate." The owner must have the magical ability to open up the door to the hunt, thereby making him group leader. When the owner is the catalyst and leader of the hunt the puppy can be trained that being in harmony with his owner is the pathway to success. This yields a dog that is always responsive to his name and feels no compulsive need to leave his yard.

If we consider how successful bird hunters train their dogs to hunt we can see that they have almost perfectly solved the problem for our purposes. A properly trained bird dog feels that he needs the hunter in order to get the bird.

The worst way to train a bird dog would be to let him off lead in a field and try to get him to work through the standard prescribed methods of obedience training. Any control that the handler tried to have over the dog would be perceived as a barrier to the prey rather than as a gateway to the prey. The dog would learn to tune out his handler and chase birds on his own.

In gun training, by planting the birds, thereby knowing where they are, we can manage how the dog is going to get to them. My father used to be able to rock a quail to sleep and then tuck it under a bush. The dog would be brought into the wind on a long lead; of course, he felt he had found the bird on his own. Since he was on a lead, he could be made to hold his point and then wait for the bird to be woken up and flushed into the air. The dog learns that this "obedience" brings the hunter near and gets the bird to fly. After that, in a step-by-step manner, the dog learns that not only does he need his handler to come up, but he needs the gun to be fired, and finally, he needs the release signal to be given so that he can fetch the quarry. Since everything is controlled, the dog comes to view as positive guideposts all of these requirements working *toward* his objective. From his point of view, even though he has to inhibit his drive at certain moments, his drive is nevertheless flowing in a straight line, because he can always sense imminent success.

Being high in drive for the bird, he's not aware of the lead. Eventually, even when off lead he feels that only by working near his handler can he find birds. He works happily within these limits because he's never been allowed to experience any other way of hunting.

As discussed in the ball-training section, we can use the ball to mimic the prey and thereby duplicate the hunt for our dog. When the dog finds he can hunt with his owner we see that he orbits us as we walk along in a park or in the woods. It is also possible to create the same mood on a busy sidewalk if the ball drive is high enough. Puppies will do this quite naturally, since their prey and group instincts are virtually one and the same when they're young, and we can take full advantage of that.

A powerful way to become a group leader is to bring the puppy to a strange field or wooded area. Go someplace where you won't run into people or dogs. Should you see someone else ahead, change direction to attract the puppy, and then collect and put him back on the lead before going closer. Then, if desired, you can have the puppy meet the stranger or the other dog and still be in a position to manage the experience.

When the puppy is very young he may not venture from your side at all; it may take his hunting drive many more months to express itself in a strange area. This early phase of immaturity gives us a golden opportunity to develop a close bond with the puppy, as well as a good excuse to get into the woods for a walk. If you live in a city, when in the park, keep the puppy on a long lead so he isn't in any danger. If there are a lot of distractions, move at a brisk pace to sustain the puppy's interest. You must contrive events so the dog learns that he only gets to make contact with people you talk to or with his doggy pals by your action. (*He needs you to open the door to let him outside. The handler controls the threshold point between moods.*) It could be something as subtle as just catching his attention and leading him to the people or dog, or by actually getting him to touch you physically. Be sure the dog is moving to the handler to close the gap, not the other way around. This way he is choosing to plug into the handler instead of being chased by him.

As the puppy's hunting drive strengthens, his orbiting pattern around the handler will grow larger in these outings. Sit down on a log, let the pup wander ahead a short way, then hoot and holler and run away a short distance so the pup will come looking for you. Don't hide so well that the pup gets scared, and if he looks anxious, call him right away. As his orbit and wanderings start to lengthen, his attraction to the owner will start to lessen in the yard or on familiar ground. This is because as the hunting drive emerges it needs novel and fresh stimuli and a higher rate of stimulation to sustain the mood. As he grows and becomes familiar with the yard, the pup's interest will naturally be drawn to the horizon away from the homestead. An important thing to note here is that the dog is not deciding to leave his owner or his yard yet: He is simply following his prey instinct. He will only be deciding to run away or leave his owner once he has been *negatively* trained—in other words, chased—so please read the Avoiding Negative Training chapter carefully. Before he gets the chance to be negatively trained we want to effect this channeling process, as well as taking precautions against roaming.

There is a gray period where the dog's hunting drive will get him into trouble before he can be reliably trained. At this point (around six to seven months), he must always be on lead in his yard or in his kennel if he is to be outside unattended. In quiet woods, however, he can continue to romp about off lead.

When I'm in the woods and I know that we're far from anybody I start to let the puppy range ahead. When he goes beyond the turn in a trail I let out a loud whoop and duck behind a tree. If he looks unduly worried, I step out right away and call him, and have a good play when he gets to me. Throwing sticks for him is a great way to reinforce his desire to find me, as well as fulfilling the training model. You still have to be aware of the puppy's limits and not frighten him; it's easy to overdo things. We want the dog to fully enjoy these outings with his leader.

At some point, however, start stretching out the amount of time you make the puppy work to find you. Normally, when a dog is hunting he learns that these chasing, seeking, and air-scenting behaviors are for finding prey, and his temperament becomes finely tuned through such endeavors. A dog experiences a lot of pleasure with these reflexes, and our objective is for the dog to apply them when searching for his owner. The beauty of this is that he is getting all of the pleasure of hunting, but he is working to find his group rather than his prey. What we are doing is developing the puppy, along the lines of a Search and Rescue dog, to be more interested in the scent of people than of prey when hunting. We are not, however, going to broaden the field beyond the scent of family members. As long as the dog is gaining in self-confidence about finding his missing owner, the work can be made progressively more difficult.

Another good variation on this theme is to go into the woods or the park with other family members. Someone holds the puppy and one of the others walks or runs away to excite the puppy, but not to the point where he becomes nervous. Find a bush or go around a bend in the trail and then call the puppy and he can be let go. When he comes to them they should play, throw a stick, or give him a small piece of meat. Then someone could hold the puppy and another family member about fifty feet away can call, or run and hide, if necessary, and the puppy can look for him. The whole sequence can be like a Ping-Pong game, with the puppy running from one person to the next. As the dog has been trained to enjoy the contact with his family members, going to the park or into the woods will mean the fun of coming when called instead of looking for new hunting buddies or chasing prey animals. The critical point here is that the puppy is learning (*from the inside out, a character trait*) to tune out natural things that normally cause a dog to roam. Our control training later on will be founded on this good attitude.

On the other hand, if one exposes the dog's prey instinct to the real thing in a process of negative training, the dog will be bored with his owner when he feels like hunting. His prey instinct perfectly fits the natural bop and bump of a bunny, whereas he has to learn about the owner's rhythms and how to relate to his owner via the stick. It's the difference between a tailored fit versus one off the rack.

After doing this for a while, as you start to return to your car or emerge from the city park, you will notice that the dog is getting more and more excited to get home. His hunting passion has been taken care of and satisfied, so he's excited to return to the den. I'm always careful at this point, because I don't really have control. The dog may start to race ahead, so I determine on my walks at what distance the puppy starts to recognize that we are returning to familiar grounds. Right before we hit that point, I run away a short distance, give him a tidbit and a rib rubbing, and hook my lead on. Since I stimulated him (the food, stick, or playing aroused his drive) when he made contact with me, he had no idea that he got hooked up to a lead and that he was now confined. We head on out to the car and he's happily pulling ahead, none the wiser.

Taking the puppy for car rides is also a good way to put yourself in harmony with his hunting instincts. The first step here is acclimation; don't go far, at first, as he may get carsick.

It's interesting how many problem behaviors melt in the car. Dogs may be aggressive to each other at home, but in the car they sit calmly side by side. Many dogs are destructive at home and yet remain calm when left alone in the car. A dog that runs from his owner will generally hop right in when the owner patrols the neighborhood to find him. The car represents a perfect harmonic balance that dogs crave since they are connected to the group, and yet feel the stimulation of the adventure.

Another powerful exercise that builds on the above relationship is to take your puppy for car rides and stop at different quiet fields. Let the puppy out and tease him with a ball, then give it a good throw. Repeat the action once or twice, but don't tire out the dog's interest, because we want to end up with the puppy carrying the ball up to and eventually into the car. Go to several different locations around your town. You are now totally fulfilling all of the natural hunting and social instincts in a balance that you can fully manage; you have control over the prey, the ball, and access to the hunt, the car. The dog learns that his highest rate of flow comes from being bonded to his owner along a harmonic pathway. At the end of our training program as outlined in this book, you could take your dog anywhere off lead no matter what distractions were present. When channeled, there is no reason for the dog to *need* to run away from you and every reason for him to remain glued to your movements.

Training a dog that he only gets to hunt with his owner is vital. One morning I let my young German shepherd out into our backyard. He was playful, so I picked up a stick and let it fly into the woods. He charged into the bushes and five deer jumped out, with my dog instantly in full pursuit. I commanded him to lie down and he dropped. I picked up another stick and made him wait a moment, then called him. He ran to me and made contact, and I threw it again into the same area. This time I called him by name instead of commanding him to drop, and he ran right back to me. All of the prey instinct that he felt for those deer I was able to cut short with the *Down* command, but then I wanted to reclaim my dog from that shock. I used the stick to reattract that same energy, the prey instinct, and train the dog that the hunt only comes through me. That was our first encounter with deer, and now he can stand in our yard and, without being in conflict, watch the deer cross the stream below even while in a rapt, attentive state. The gate is not open.

18

Manners: Dealing with the Critical Issues

IN THIS CHAPTER we're going to take a close look at the issue of manners, which is an area of training distinct from the obedience exercises. Usually manners are thought of in terms of an individual learning to respect others. When we think about respect in terms of dogs, the discussion tends to revolve around submission and dominance—the dog must learn his place—and this distorts the way the group dynamic gets each member to subscribe willingly to his position in life.

In canine society, when the inferior learns that he can get what he wants by exerting pressure *from his place* within the group, he has learned manners. The way a submissive dog contorts his body emphasizes his "preyful aspect." At the same time, he goes forward and puts pressure on the superior, extends his forepaw, licks the superior's lips, and crowds the superior's space. The inferior fiddles around with his end of the mood and the superior *has* to adjust at his end in order to stay in the same mood, to stay connected to the pack. The subordinate one discovers he has leverage.

When we set out to train our pup to be mannerly our influence should cause the dog to learn that by being subordinate, he experiences his highest degree of instinctual gratification. Being in his place has to work for him; his instincts need to be gratified so that he will seek out his place and be calm there. By *subordinate* I don't mean submissive; I want the dog to be of a clear mind. He is going to learn that when he acts in an appropriate way, he gets positive results. When he acts in an inappropriate way, *he* makes *himself* uncomfortable. The contrast between these two paths makes it easy for the dog to learn how to behave and to become bonded to his master as his pathway to success. He also gains in self-confidence because he can sense how the world works; he ends up getting what he needs and desires.

I also have noticed that when a puppy is raised on the harmonic principles, very little training is necessary in regard to manners. He grows up to be calm, and a simple word of discouragement suffices to establish acceptable limits on his behavior. Don't overreact to your pup's natural exuberance and zest; spend most of your creative energy on channeling his drive instead of finding ways to thwart his puppy propensity for devilment.

NO: THE MAGIC WORD

When the puppy is old enough, he can learn what *No* means. *No* means the puppy should stop what he's doing or is about to do, not because we're going to be upset with him, but because the distraction is "hot." It will also come to mean there is a shock out there that the owner can see coming, but the puppy can't. If the puppy listens to this word, he can control whether he runs into this shock. The shock has to be made commensurate with the age of the puppy. For a six-month-old dog that is jumping up, the shock would be given in the form of a gradual tightening of the lead while it is held overhead. His front feet are momentarily suspended, which is somewhat uncomfortable. On the other hand, a ten-month-old puppy might get a lightning-quick jerk on a choke collar. Personally, I like to wait until my puppy is grown before I train him to the word *No.* However, most of my clients' dogs—and I'll assume the same for the reader—have been so overly stimulated in their young lives that they may need to learn manners sooner.

Our objective isn't to use the word *No* to discourage the pup from doing something so that he doesn't have to be corrected. First he must be exposed to a shock so he can learn to control the shock by being attentive to the command. The word *No* isn't a threat—it's a warning of danger. Set the dog up; he must experience the shock before he can learn that *No* is the key to avoiding it. No amount of explaining can convince his prey instinct that smelly garbage isn't to be torn apart. Trying to talk things through merely trains him that the owner is the problem. However, once he is blaming the instinct that carried him into danger for his misfortune, he's ready to learn that the word *No* is a precursor to the shock. By being attentive to his owner, he learns he's going to be praised rather than experiencing discomfort. Once he's attentive to his owner, his drive can be redirected elsewhere on to a harmonic pathway and the situation is resolved.

SOCIALIZING

Most dogs would prefer to live in a stable social group. While young, a dog needs exposure to new people and other dogs while his group nature is at its most expansive. But prudent socializing doesn't mean taking the puppy everywhere and simply plunking him down around people and letting him figure things out for himself. If he is sensitive, that will only make him unsure, and if he's outgoing, he'll be learning to be a nuisance and his emotions will end up getting bruised. Always keep the puppy on a flat collar and on a lead so he not only feels secure in his connection to his owner, but can also be managed.

When we think of socializing the puppy we first should think in terms of developing his social skills. Dr. Ian Dunbar, a California-based veterinarian and behaviorist, makes a very valuable contribution in this discussion. His research has shown that if a puppy plays with a wide variety of other puppies, he will invariably grow up to be free of social problems. The more different types of puppies he gets to play with, the more developed his social outlook will be, but take care not to overmatch your puppy with one that is too aggressive.

By knocking heads with his playmates a puppy is becoming less body sensitive. In play, pups learn give and take; a tug on a tail or a nip on the shoulders isn't a big deal. This makes them grow to be infinitely less sensitive to the sudden and unexpected things that children might do. It would be helpful, therefore, to form a play group. The play sessions relax the dog's nerves and develop his social instincts, and he also needs his owner to get him to the play yard.

In daily life, always have a lead handy. Since a big problem area is where guests arrive at the front door, keep a lead hanging nearby. When introducing the puppy to a stranger have the pup go forward and at his own pace; don't have the stranger come toward the pup. Should the puppy be skittish, the stranger should totally ignore him. The ideal attitude that we want to promote is for the puppy to be pulling toward the person. This means that his *nerves* are on the *positive* setting. The puppy is stimulated by this change in the social order, and change is good. If the dog were left off a lead before having been trained, he would end up jumping on people; we don't want to encourage the growth of a nuisance behavior out of a positive attitude.

Instead, to deflect the puppy onto a harmonic pathway, have ready a piece of food or a toy to get his attention; right away the puppy and the stranger have something in common. This reward can be given to the stranger, who will show it to the pup and tell him to sit as the owner is holding the puppy back. The puppy can see the stranger has possession of this food or ball, which creates a new social order and an easy rite of passage for the pup.

The pup should be showered with lots of praise and hearty petting by his owner so that all his drive is being summoned forth and discharged calmly. I encourage my pup to make some degree of contact with me—preferably jumping up—before I let him get a good rubbing from the stranger so he learns that I am his access to this increase of attention. But if the pup is heavily distracted, one can settle for a lesser degree of attentiveness; even if it's just a nudge or a look, because the dog is still getting the connection. Since there is no friction or resistance in the interaction, there is nothing held back deep in the dog's character that could form aggression or hyperfriendliness later in life. The dog is learning by contrast. By jumping up on his handler he is not learning to jump, or to jump up on strangers. He is learning what to do with all of his drive energy, to channel it into the social instinct that his handler arouses. Only when a dog is trained to use up all of the drive energy can the dog learn to be calm and attentive to his owner when people visit. The dog will be left with no drive with which to become nervous. All of his drive found an expression with instinctive reflexes, with outward action that leaves the puppy feeling contented. The dog will have less *need* to jump on the owner or the stranger when he's trained than will a dog that is disciplined and confronted over such matters. His social instinct is in balance.

After the puppy makes contact with his owner, he can go forward to the stranger. This person should bend over and push down on the puppy's frame so that the puppy gets a full contacting at ground level. Were the stranger to just scratch the dog's forehead and praise him verbally, the puppy would have to jump up for more attention. The stranger would be putting more energy into the system—the dog's emotions—than he is absorbing by actual physical contact. While the stranger is pushing down, his verbal tone should be soothing rather than exciting, and he might firmly massage the puppy's neck and shoulder muscles.

A puppy five or six months or older that is really active about jumping up on people can be allowed to correct himself. After the stranger has given him a hearty contacting on the ground, he disengages and stands up. He calmly says *No* and stands perfectly still. The handler allows the puppy to spring up, but not to make any contact. The lead is kept taut above his head, suspending the puppy off his front feet for a brief moment until he becomes uncomfortable. Collect the puppy back into a sit; the handler and the stranger can both calmly and firmly pet and massage the dog again.

Then it would be good to put the puppy away or even better, take him outdoors for a good ball-playing session. It would be very helpful if these little encounters were staged on a regular basis with the help of friends or neighbors, so that the emphasis is on the dog rather than on the company.

Puppies are so friendly around strangers that little thought is given to what the animal is going through in these meetings. If the puppy is having a bad experience, it is usually masked by friendliness or avoidance, which to most owners bears no connection to an aggressive impulse developed later on. But though it may look harmless, the behavior is tainted with nervousness that in certain temperaments will develop into dangerous aggression.

DOMESTICATION

Another big problem area with puppies is raiding the garbage pail or pilfering snacks left on the coffee table. Until the puppy is eight months old he shouldn't be exposed to such temptations; puppy-proof the house when he is around. Later, we will train him to leave these things alone in a controlled way. Prior to this training, should your puppy get into something despite your best efforts, don't make a fuss about it. Distract him with something else and then take away the object in question. Chasing him around with the "prey" in his mouth is going to cause future disobedience.

At the appropriate age—later is always better than sooner—put the juiciest garbage you can find out in the kitchen. Then bring your dog indoors on a long lead attached to a choke collar. Let the dog wander away from you so that he finds the garbage on his own when you're not near, preferably when you're around a corner. The instant he smells the garbage, give a very strong jolt on the collar and run away as the dog comes to find you. When the puppy comes to you, play and fuss over him and give him food. We want the puppy to associate the shock with the garbage. This lesson should be repeated after a few days, and then perhaps once a month until he no longer shows interest.

With a particularly problematic dog, one day when he is hungry, have him in the kitchen on his long lead with another family member sitting down or acting neutral and uninterested, holding the long lead. Drop a piece of food on the floor "by accident" as you're preparing dinner. As the dog goes for it the other person should jerk on the lead. Play with the dog if he comes up to the lead handler and then ignore him. The cook can let another piece fall in two or three minutes and this time say No very calmly. If the dog goes for the food, the other person should again jerk on the lead. Repeat the exercise several times. When the dog is trained to leave alone big pieces of food on the floor, it's much easier to train him in the same way to ignore food on the counter. Also, after every shock, reward him with a treat in his dog bowl.

The same thinking can be applied to the problem of a dog getting up on furniture. We want the dog to blame himself and not the owner for any discomfort he may run into over this, forming a permanent and nonstressful lesson. Should you find your dog on the bed after he's been trained, the best way to deal with it is to calmly hook up the long lead and leave the room. After a minute, make a strong jerk so that you are as neutral a variable in the dog's learning as you can be. If a dog has a strong drive to get onto furniture, he should always wear the lead when he's indoors until he's satisfied with his own bed on the ground.

Someone can put the dog on a long lead and someone else can play with the dog, then run over and flop on the bed or couch, with the other person making the jerk. After the shock is made, the word No can be issued to warn the dog in the next session.

Where dogs rest and sleep is a very strong reflection on where they think their place is. It's a huge mistake to let a dog sleep in your bed, because it will put him in a lot of conflict. He will start to feel that his place is at the top, and he will become very sensitive about issues of ranking. This will make him very defensive when the world doesn't conform to his delusions of grandeur. He will be doomed to live a life of unnecessary conflict and stress.

A dog learns through his instincts, brought into mind by what is going on around him. The dog is not freely or creatively thinking; he is only in tune with the natural pattern that is before his senses. Therefore, we can say that the environment is actually controlling the dog. In this area of manners it is a waste of time to show the dog that you get upset when he does certain things. That only stresses the puppy and damages his self-confidence.

It's more effective if he learns that the garbage, or the bed, or his nervousness caused the shock. The word *No* isn't a threat that the owner will harm him; it is instead a warning that he will harm himself by going near something that is "hot." It's as if he's approaching a cliff and you're advising him of the impending danger. The handler isn't the problem; the danger is. This is a much easier problem for him to solve, and it produces reliable results whether we are nearby or not.

To ensure that this can be pulled off, it's necessary for the puppy to wear the long lead a lot so he doesn't connect wearing it with the shock. You must wait until he's through the chewing phase, but that's OK, because the dog has to be old enough for the shock of the jerk on the lead anyway. This is the kindest way to train a dog; he will come to share the same value toward the sofa, strangers, or other dogs as you do. Then he's not always in conflict between his owner and his prey instinct. In conjunction with all the other positive development that's being done, the dog learns where all of his instincts belong, and his drive can find full expression in ways that bring his family enjoyment.

BITING

A big concern for puppy owners is what to do when their puppy grabs them or someone else with his jaws. Is this the beginning of a wayward and unreliable dog? Certainly not; if the puppy didn't have a healthy temperament, he wouldn't be attracted enough to use his jaws—he'd be sensitive and hold back. It is the reticent dog that is more likely to grow up to bite than the hellion we're talking about here.

I've raised a number of puppies in my life, particularly German shepherds, and I've never taught them not to bite. They've simply outgrown the phase in their own due time, just as human babies outgrow their oral phase. I let them grab my hands and bite as much as they want, while I stay perfectly still. It isn't long before their teeth can exact an excruciating crunch, especially if I overly excite the prey instinct by lying at ground level, and when that happens I yelp in pain. The puppy is more shocked than I am, and his flow of pleasure stops. After the shock wears off, should he persist, I stop interacting with him. Now if we're around strangers and the pup gets excited, I can expect him to want to jump up and perhaps grab a coat sleeve or nibble on a finger. Therefore, I keep the pup on a lead until his drive subsides, or until I've deflected his drive into ball playing or sitting for a treat.

The worst thing to do when your puppy grabs you is to confront him, yell *No*, or hit him. This is only going to make him defensive over his prey drive, put him on a discordant pathway, and maximize his need to bite back as he grows older. His drive will well up, and its overload will produce the very behavior you're trying to inhibit. When I consult with owners who have a puppy that is biting too hard, it's because they fought him over this urge, thereby pressurizing his drive, reducing his cooperative nature, and guaranteeing the manifestation of their greatest fears.

19

Kids and Puppies

DOGS THAT ARE GREAT with kids view all children as belonging to their group. The sight of a child immediately inspires a happy mood. We shouldn't only admire this dog's social flexibility but his stability as well. No matter what the child does, it merely confirms for the dog the child's firm standing in the group. Since most puppies start off friendly and tolerant to children when young, people tend to leave it at that and don't do much to keep them on the right track. However, as the puppy grows, he may develop a problem that ranges from rough play to actual aggression. Or, he may be good with his own family's children but not tolerant of their friends. We have to take measures that ensure that the dog's perception of his group always includes children.

There are two ways to develop a dog's social instinct, which has a lot to do with the way a puppy learns to perceive children.

One way is the dominant-submissive model, which dwells on the rank that everyone holds, thereby emphasizing the pack instinct. Once in this mode, any change in the order is unsettling. When in a pack instinct the dog can only feel completely comfortable around the same members. Since his owner was dominant toward him, he instinctively is primed to respond to a challenge that children may unwittingly stimulate by being on the dog's eye level. Stress is like a hot potato, and once put into play, it is passed gingerly from superior to inferior. Unfortunately, because children are small, they are perceived as acting "out of place" and therefore inferior, giving the dog instinctive permission to discipline them for their transgressions. Needless to say, such a dog is a dangerous liability.

The other way to develop the social structure is to use the prey instinct to develop the harmonic pathways so that every social change heightens the flow of pleasure. The puppy matures to always feel excited by children, and this will never convert to aggression because he recognizes *himself* in the children. They are all on the same wavelength. The child puts the dog into high drive, and the burden can be easily placed on the dog to maintain the pleasurable connection through some simple rules of conduct. Once these are learned, if the dog plays too hard, he feels he is hurting himself. If a child accidentally steps on his tail, he feels it was his fault.

The first step to getting puppies on the harmonic pathway in this regard is to educate the children first and to protect the puppy from kids who are too young or too reckless, so they don't undermine the owner's good work.

Many children are allowed and even encouraged to smother their puppy with hugs and kisses, but this is not the foundation for friendship. A puppy's fighting instinct is being awakened by the child's head being pushed into his, or his own head being restrained, and he will grow irritated. The child is imposing his mood on the puppy, and this generates resistance. Forced contact only brings on the feeling of chaos, because the structure of the group isn't being defined.

Children should be taught right away to perceive the pup's point of view so that they will learn to respect dogs, as well as all animals. A lot of what may pass for cute behavior is actually abuse of the dog, and it will sour the potential for a strong relationship. Parents shouldn't permit children to pick up the puppy. Besides the chance for physical injury, the dog doesn't like it; he has four legs and prefers to use them to get around on his own. Grabbing and carrying him will produce apprehension at the child's approach. Instead, when the puppy is small, the child can sit down and the puppy can be placed in his lap for some calm petting. If handled roughly, the puppy's pack instinct might always mask his nervousness toward his owner's children, but he could still become defensive toward strange children.

A large part of compassion is learning that there are other points of view besides our own. Every dog encountered needn't be fussed over. For example, I tell my children never to approach a strange dog, because they might scare him. He might like them as much as our dogs do if he knew them, but it would be kinder in the meantime to simply leave the dog alone.

The big issue between young children and puppies is biting and rough play. The natural way a child acts stimulates the puppy's prey instinct: Their voices are high pitched and they move suddenly. The puppy thinks he has found his soulmate. He acts toward the child as he would toward another puppy. The only problem here is that the child's threshold for play is so much lower than another puppy's would be. That the puppy has the desire to bite the child doesn't mean the puppy doesn't like the child, or that he's manifesting the potential for later aggression. It simply means he likes him *too* much. Once again the puppy's potential for a problem is also his potential for a healthy disposition. It's very tragic that many puppies' attraction toward children is so grossly misinterpreted. This energy is a positive force that is easy to mold and shape into a harmonic pathway if the dog and the children become immersed in the same mood. The wrong approach is to scold the pup and smack him on the nose when he's attracted to a child. He'll take it when young, but should his temperament have a defensive element to it, the seeds for later aggression are being sown.

In general, there are many nice kids who are simply too aggressive with puppies. Their prey instinct gets as aroused as the puppy's, and they think that play means "Wrestlemania." When a child is aggressive it becomes a real turn on for the puppy, and it starts to hyperpower his prey instinct. The resulting nervousness leaves the puppy unable to control himself.

Also, you should never tie or confine a dog where he can see children play. This will frustrate him and hyperstimulate his prey instinct to their innocent sounds and movements. The horror stories all too frequently found in the news concerning a dog mauling a child are usually due to a history of the dog's being tied where children can be seen but contact can't be made. In some of these cases the prey instinct is so heightened that the dog may lie in wait for the chance to pounce as the child approaches him. The child doesn't sense danger as the dog isn't growling and seems to be acting passively, so the child comes within range.

Another way to create problems is to let the puppy out unattended with the neighborhood kids. The risk is that someone will find it amusing to tease the dog. The pup gets worked up and rushes the gang of kids, then he pulls back short of the bite, performing with a lot of intensity and barking. The children get the thrill of being chased without the real feeling that they're in danger. They can see that the puppy (usually six to ten months old) is in control of what they feel is his better sense. But it will only be a matter of time before the puppy matures and his frustration overcomes his inhibitions. He wants to bite in that moment; it's just that his prey instinct is limited by his nerves. It is imperative that parents always supervise neighborhood children when with the puppy until his character is formed. To turn the puppy loose with children is to entrust his development to the whims of those who just don't know or won't do better. We don't think of taking the same risks with our infant children, and the issue is exactly the same with the puppy.

The following techniques are the proper ways to deal with the standard problem areas. *One must take nothing for granted, plan for the worst, and fully manage the puppy's time with children.*

One of the easiest things to do is always keep the puppy on a lead when kids are around and when the puppy is high in drive (for example, when the children come home from school or when the pup awakes from a nap). It is counterproductive to fight the pup over his exuberance toward children, serving to reinforce a negative impression. Besides, it only takes a few minutes to get them all off on the right foot. Always have a toy or tidbit ready to give to the child, who will ask the dog to sit. The owner can nudge the dog along if necessary. After a round of rewards, the pup should be taken outdoors, where the child can throw a ball, exerting control over the puppy in this sport as well. By changing the subject via the ball or food, the dog is quickly able to be let off lead, free to run about burning off drive, all the while learning to relate calmly to kids. Discourage your children from making overly passionate scenes when they are reunited with their dog. Quite frankly, I feel these episodes are overcompensatory, or self-indulgent, on the part of the child, and at any rate accomplish nothing more than making the dog nervous. Constructive action is a more healthy expression of love, and it focuses the pup's drive into calm attraction.

When I raise a puppy I like to take him for long walks with the children as a means of neutralizing his prey attraction to them. When we first come out of the house the dog is full of fire, so he's kept on a lead. His drive usually fades by the time we get to the woods, so once there I turn him loose. Now there are lots of pleasant distractions like grass, mud, leaves, and butterflies to occupy his attention. He'll hop on and off logs and eagerly accept our children's fondling and caressing without feeling the need to mount or grab them. He has bigger fish to fry, and soon he has a calm attraction to the children as fellow hunting buddies, interested in their explorations more than he is in them. These walks have a wonderful bonding effect; the stimulation of the voyage into the unknown heightens his connection to the children. After the walk the puppy can come indoors and hang around the children until he starts to become aroused again. I have a kennel outdoors that he can go into, or I might put him back in his crate in the kitchen. Since he gets the daily exercise he needs, he is always due for a nap.

It would be a big mistake to let the children play indoors with the puppy, other than when you want to distract a young puppy from chewing up the indoors. All heavy play action should be outdoors. The thresholds outside are *expansive,* so there is less chance of the dog becoming defensive. A dog is very sensitive to the releasing effect that these wide open spaces offer, and we want to condition him that this is the normal place for play. There is a lot of room to run and discharge drive, and that has a calming effect. There also is enough room to throw a ball or stick so that the prey instinct can be broken out and defined as separate from the child. When children play indoors with the puppy the dog's nerves will be more burdened than relaxed, as an indoor environment has *compressed* thresholds. When a dog is full of drive and held in tight quarters or tied he has no clear focus and there is no natural conclusion for his excitement. This distorts drive so that intermixed with a puppy's mouthing and gripping, one will start to see barking and a curled lip. Eventually, this may turn into nipping, but it has its beginning with the above conditioning, and then comes the inevitable confrontation between the child and ultimately the parent.

Sadly, some puppies are afraid of children. This generally has to do with being overdependent on their owners, especially if they aren't raised with children. But it can also have a genetic basis if the prey instinct is brittle, not easily deflected into the group instincts. These kinds of dogs are destined to become centered on their owners if not handled just right. They come to interpret all social beings as a block between themselves and their owners. Such a dog lacks a happy and free prey instinct, and using a ball to get him to play may not get us very far. Exposing him to children when he is very hungry and the child can offer food as the owner controls the dog can, over a long spell, effect a bond. From this bond, he may even start to feel attracted to a squeaky toy or a ball bounced near or away from him. Go slowly, and try to find a child composed enough to help you. As their play progresses, the child could start to give the dog commands, to stabilize social structure.

If you and your dog live without children, it's still easy to develop a puppy's social skills. Whenever you encounter an unfamiliar child who asks to pet your pup, give the child a tidbit and coach him on how to get the dog to sit. When you see the dog become stable about sitting, expectant of the next treat, give the child the green light to start petting.

One of the best ways to strengthen a pup's social character is through play with other pups. The hearty biting that goes on in a group of dogs strengthens the harmonic pathways so that, by contrast, the pup is more readily able to learn to play in a softer style with kids. Puppies that get the chance to play with a lot of other puppies develop a very good attitude toward children almost on their own.

A frequent problem is a puppy mounting children. The pup is stimulated, but there's no prey object to absorb his drive. Rather than scolding him, pull him off and distract him into ball playing. With a dog five months or older, put a lead on his collar and pull up gradually until he becomes uncomfortable, but don't issue any command so he doesn't attribute his discomfort to his owner. You want him to learn that he himself is causing his own discomfort. Then throw a ball to dissipate his drive. Yelling or disciplining over the issue of mounting is only training the puppy to be defensive about children. It isn't training him how to behave around children.

Children playing outdoors really fire up a puppy's prey instinct. With all those coats and sleeves flying, the dog thinks he's in a herd of stampeding gerbils. Put the puppy on a long lead (when he's about five or six months old—before that the situation should be avoided if there is a problem) that is attached to a flat collar. Coach the children ahead of time on what their job is to be. You want them to run and shout as usual, and everyone will have a ball or a piece of food held out of sight of the puppy. The role of the handler with the lead is to be totally neutral (no commands are given to the dog), so as to have no value in the puppy's memory of the situation.

The handler lets the puppy plow into the group. Right before the pup makes contact, he slowly checks his forward progress. Then have a child stop in front of the dog and tell the pup to sit as he produces the reward. A ball is somewhat preferable to food because with it you have more clearly broken out the prey instinct apart from the child. The puppy can find total fulfillment with the ball, but even more, he is learning that the child's *being* controls the prey when the child stops and says "sit." This defines the social place of the child without teaching the puppy any defensiveness to the child. All the children in the play group should get a chance to do this with the puppy. After the puppy has chased the ball, you want all the children to praise him, and you want to encourage the puppy to run through the group carrying the ball in his mouth.

Next, take the ball away. Then let the puppy plow into the group of children again, but give the puppy slack in the lead and let him run alongside a child so the pup learns patience. If the pup jumps to nip, he gets a quick jerk on the lead. When he shows just a moment of self-restraint have the child produce the ball. It's not that important that the puppy sit; he just registers that the child is imposing a condition on him to get to his prey. The puppy is learning by contrast; when he goes to grab the child he gets a shock, yet a moment of restraint yields the prey. When the pup has learned this lesson let him run with the lead dragging behind. Every so often one of the kids should have the dog sit; then someone throws the ball. With this technique the children can go about their play and the dog can learn to play alongside them, immersed in his own game. As he gets older, just being aroused and in harmony with the kids is reward enough.

Some children are too young to know when to throw a ball. In that case I hold the puppy on a lead and ask the children to run to a tree or bush and get back to me before the puppy does. Thinking they are in a race, they tend to run in a controlled direction. I let them get a head start and then feed the puppy out on his long lead. When the puppy tries to make a grab he gets a jolt, and then I lob the ball into the fray. The puppy doesn't see where the ball came from, so he thinks it has something to do with the child. After several repetitions when he's calm, you can proceed as above.

In all these issues of puppy development, imagine the worst thing that can happen and then work to safeguard against it. That's how wills are drafted and insurance policies are formulated. Look around at your situation and see where a big disaster might come from, despite all your hard work. Two such examples are given below, one concerning the issue of feeding and the other the possibility that a neighborhood child might surprise and frighten your dog.

It's not unusual for dogs to become defensive over their food or possessions, and a lot of children are bitten when they innocently come close. For a young puppy, food is clearly his prey, and to maximize his calmness about feeding, he should be left to eat in a quiet place where he isn't going to be disturbed. Children should be instructed to leave him alone whenever he's eating. Only through peace when at a vulnerable limit does a puppy learn security.

It is wrong to take food away from the puppy, thinking you are training him to accept your control over this issue. You are making the puppy unsure about his chances of finishing his meal.

Still, the puppy has to learn how to deal with people coming near him when he's eating. Instead of leaving this to random occurrences, train him to perceive such instances as a further stimulation of his pleasure rather than a threat. I take a small portion of the pup's rations, put it in his bowl, and set it down in the kitchen. Then I have one of my children take a small handful of his meal, walk up to him, and lay it in the bowl next to his muzzle as he eats. This is repeated until he gets his complete dinner. Once a week I repeat the procedure. In short order he is eager for someone to approach him while he's eating, because it means more, not less.

Another potential for defensiveness, especially with the guarding types of breeds, is when a neighborhood child walks into your house unannounced. I always make sure to have a filled cookie jar available, which all our kids' friends know about. Whenever they visit, I want them to call my dogs and give them a biscuit. At times the dogs may be sleeping inside, and if a child comes by, I'll have him go to within ten feet and call the dog, waking him up. Then they head for the cookie jar together. In this way, I'm building in a safety mechanism so that if I'm careless, or a child is careless, no one has to be sorry. Should a child startle the dog, there is a clear pattern established for the dog so he can suppress a defensive instinct.

To reiterate, by using the prey instinct to develop the puppy, he and the children can fit into the same mood without friction; they are all aligned on the same wavelength. The puppy clearly learns where his prey instinct belongs and that his place is secure in the group. Furthermore, the puppy quickly learns that he gets the highest degree of satisfaction by staying in his place within the group. Our puppies need to see where they stand with their little companions at all times.

20

Housetraining the Puppy

A PUPPY CAN'T BE EXPECTED to be reliably housetrained until he is one year old. Before that, he should always be considered "in training." However, during this first year there is absolutely no reason why he should ever eliminate or be destructive indoors. Anytime there is an accident, it's due to a handling error by the owner.

Training a dog to keep a large indoor area clean for long periods, even when the dog needs to eliminate, has a lot of little steps to it.

The first step is to create a preference in the puppy to want to eliminate outdoors. Most puppies would actually prefer to eliminate *indoors* if they're given a chance. Outside there are many things for the active puppy to do, and for the sensitive puppy, the outdoors can at first be too scary for him to relax and be able to eliminate. Additionally, the commotion inherent in getting a puppy outside can take his mind off relieving himself. Then the owner spends twenty minutes outside with the pup, nothing happens, and the owner thinks it was a false alarm. He brings the puppy back inside and bingo, behind the couch he goes. After a few repetitions of this sort, the puppy starts to feel that the objective is to romp outdoors and eliminate indoors.

The first rule is never to give a young puppy any freedom indoors so that he becomes patterned to the ritual of elimination that only the outdoors can evoke. The wide-open spaces and the fresh air, the strong scents of grass and dirt, the scenting and circling behaviors, must be the only releasers that put the dog in the mood to eliminate. Another important factor is that a dog be exercised on a regular schedule. The puppy learns *where* to go and the owner learns *when* the puppy has to go. Then it's easy to get the puppy to the right place at the right time.

Nature has equipped the puppy with an ability to learn to be clean, but only in a wild setting that is very different from a household. There is no instinct in the dog's mind that allows him to grasp the concepts that the indoors, which is vast from the pup's point of view, is a den and that his elimination habits have to come under the control of his master.

In nature, the puppies would live in a cramped den hollowed out of a woodchuck hole or a crevice in a cave. When they're very young the mother consumes all waste material so the den is never dirty. Also, a dog in the wild never has to learn to be alone except when he's occupied with his prey instinct. This means that a wild canid never has to learn to control his bladder or bowels when he's anxious by being separated from the pack. And as wolves or feral dogs mature, they always have access to the outdoors.

As pups grow older, they start to feel a need to increase their distance from the pack in order to eliminate. This has to do with the emergence of the fighting instinct and sexual development. As the prey instinct exerts its influence, the dog is compelled to mark territory, not to claim it but to push out the "known" realm around his den. This drive can motivate our growing puppy to wait for a long time to get outdoors and express himself in this way.

A dog owner paralyzed by guilt is the single greatest source of misdirected training. Whenever owners feels guilty about a house-training procedure they should spend either money or time to deal with the problem instead of giving the puppy freedom. They're not doing the puppy any service by lacking in decisive control of his learning process.

The first instinct we have to work with is the den instinct. This is a desire to keep a small, compressed area clean, which makes the dog want to move away a short distance in order to eliminate. To stimulate the den instinct a young puppy must be in a small crate when he's indoors. If the crate is too large, he may go to one end to sleep and to the other end to eliminate. I prefer the plastic airline crates and not the open wire ones; however, summertime heat has to be taken into consideration. I buy a size that will accommodate the grown dog, and then fill it up with cinder blocks to give the puppy only the room he needs to sleep, stretch, if necessary, turn around, and lie down again. As he grows, the cinder blocks can come out.

The plastic crates give the puppy a greater sense of security when he's sleeping; the wire ones leave him feeling too exposed.

Don't think in terms of giving the puppy a sense of freedom. That would be logical for a person, because we have an intellect to amuse. If the dog feels free but then is blocked, he will become frustrated. He is to be confined, and he has to get used to it. The den instinct and the need for a calm resting place will quickly inspire him to like it. When the puppy is in the crate totally ignore him. Don't talk to him to try to calm him or scold him for crying; that will only create or reinforce nervousness.

This crate is an essential training tool and is the most humane way to go about housetraining. Many people feel at first glance that it is cruel to put a puppy into a crate, and that the puppy won't like them because of it. But who is crueler: the owner who puts a puppy in a crate and then returns to a happy reunion, or the one who leaves the puppy free and comes home to attack him for being dirty or destructive? A puppy has no sense of time. When a crate is used he finds himself in a den, which is the easiest way for him to cope with being alone. He quickly falls asleep. The next major change in his mood is the owner's return, and they then enjoy a happy outing together. The crate is less of a trauma for the dog, and it takes the "break" out of housebreaking.

The crate allows the puppy to teach himself that calmness produces the return of the owner. When he's left behind by his handler there is nothing in the crate that can reinforce the puppy's nervousness, and anxiety will quickly extinguish itself. If a puppy is allowed to have the run of a room or the house, he can gnaw and tug at the door or moldings, and whatever activity he pursues does, indeed, end up producing the return of the owner. Whatever corrections are made upon the owner's return will have no connection in his mind with the mess he made.

During the teething phase some chew toys can be left in his crate, but as he grows beyond that phase, nothing needs to be left in. His life revolves around his handler, and he can easily learn to wait for his return for a rousing play session outdoors.

Sometimes a puppy can't be expected to keep even his small den clean if the owner has to go away for more than a few hours. In this case a compromise has to be reached. Depending on the weather and security, an outdoor kennel with a snug house in a quiet part of the yard is the ideal solution. Another option is a kennel set up in the garage or basement with woodchips on the floor. Indoors, one may have to give a utility room up to the cause. The main thing, though, is for the puppy to have the opportunity to leave a nesting area in order to get to an eliminating area.

In the eliminating area there should be woodchips or peat moss so there's an "alfresco" quality to his site selection. (Unless the pup eats it; in that case, use a mat of paper, with shredded paper on top.) The nesting area should be raised a few inches to highlight the distinction between it and the soiling area. The woodchip area can be progressively made smaller so that the puppy makes more of an effort to use it. His sense of discrimination is being developed.

Having the puppy on a regular feeding and watering schedule has the dog ready to eliminate when you are able to exercise him. Do some research on natural dog foods; these are very important in giving the puppy a firm stool and a healthy digestive tract so he can control his bowel movements. These natural diets give the puppy a maximum of nutrition without an excess of filler or toxicity so puppy doesn't have to relieve himself too often. Being consistent and faithful to the routine puts the puppy's insides on a rhythm that greatly aids our housetraining.

The next thing the puppy has to learn is that he needs his handler in order to "go to the bathroom." This is easy for him to learn; he has no freedom indoors and needs the owner to be let outdoors.

This directly sets up the next lesson: The puppy learns to indicate to his owner when he has to relieve himself. At first the puppy will start to whine or circle inside his crate when his elimination reflex is frustrated by the crate. If you're attentive, the puppy will learn you are always aware of his internal need, just as he learned that his owner is aware of his hunger drive.

When the puppy is old enough this drive to indicate and then to find the owner can be strengthened. Let the puppy make a fuss for longer periods when he is in the crate to let you know he has to eliminate. This could be done at age ten months and first thing in the morning. Then have a family member let the puppy out of the crate as you call him to another part of the house. Have the puppy come to you and make physical contact, then get him out the door right away. When he's doing very well with this, don't open the door right away until he makes a fuss to show he needs you to open the door. Teaching the dog to speak on command would be helpful for this phase, but don't overdo barking on command until the dog can be trained to be quiet. Again, this is at around ten to twelve months and is done in conjunction with the *Down* command.

Any time a puppy is excited or stressed he will need to eliminate. Whenever he's given some freedom in the house and has been excited, even if it is only to be awakened from a nap, let him outdoors right away. No matter how small the change is from our point of view—if he's let out of his crate, given a biscuit, petted or talked to, a friend visits, etc.—he should be taken outdoors.

When he is about seven or eight months old a dog can be trained to control himself despite being excited. The owner could pet the dog and play with him and then watch him like a hawk. Should he look as if he's going off to look for a spot indoors to eliminate, put him into his crate for five minutes and wait for him to indicate his need by whining or circling, then take him outdoors. On the other hand, if after you play with him he goes to the door and indicates his need, by all means let him out right away.

At age ten months and on a weekend when you're at home, start to train him to be clean when he's alone and outside of his crate. I have a three-foot tie chain that is secured in the foyer of my house. I tie the puppy there in midday so there's a chance he may have to go, but his need isn't as pressing as it would be first thing in the morning. I can watch him through a window without his seeing or hearing me. I go around the house doing small chores and check on him every five minutes. If the puppy is anxious, I keep a constant watch. When the puppy gets up and starts to circle I crack the door and try to get him to bark to indicate he has to go. I get whatever I can out of him by way of the bark and let him out to relieve himself and then have fun.

A dog living in a condo or apartment won't have this opportunity, so you just have to go on a schedule of gradual increases of time left alone outside of the crate. Tie up the dog, leave for five minutes, then return and take him outdoors. Increase each repetition by several minutes.

One of the best ways to help the puppy to be clean outside the crate is to make use of the night, when he doesn't have to eliminate for a long stretch. I like to have my dog sleep in our bedroom, so at around eight months, I tie him to the bedpost on a light chain lead for several weeks. Then, when he's about ten or eleven months old and knows how to lie down and stay, I give him the run of the bedroom overnight with the door closed. If he gets restless during the night or gets up too early in the morning, I make him lie down and be patient.

When he's good with this phase I start to give him the run of the kitchen during the day, with a baby gate in place to confine him to that room. I go outside and wait for ten minutes, then come in and go out again. I want him to get excited, then learn to calm down again on his own. Each time I leave I come back in after five or ten minutes, and I do this for thirty or forty-five minutes, totally ignoring him while inside. Finally, when the puppy looks really good in his calmness, I take short trips away from the house, slowly building him up to six or eight hours.

When I first leave him for a long time he will only have eaten lightly the day before. I want to give him the smallest possible problem to solve.

It's very important to go slowly enough so that the puppy never has an accident in the house. When the puppy does make a mistake it doesn't do any good to correct him after the fact. Go back to the step before for at least another month. It is also critical to monitor your puppy closely for parasites; these internal pests make house-training impossible.

A word about paper training: This trains a dog to eliminate indoors and is not the proper foundation. With a tiny breed or for an apartment dweller, there may not be an alternative and so you should construct an indoor area that will allow the dog to distinguish between the house as his den and a discrete area for eliminating.

What should one do if the puppy does make a mistake in the house? There is no point in correcting the dog; that will only make him defensive. It's almost as meaningless to correct the dog as he's relieving himself; simply interrupt the dog and get him outside as quickly as possible. The point is that the dog was already *moved* to eliminate, and it's this emotional process that we want to influence in its first phases. It doesn't do any good to react to a dog's behavior; we want to influence the process that produces behavior.

There sometimes is a place for shocking the drive to eliminate if the puppy proves resistant to house training, but this is only when crate training has been carried out for a full year, and longer if the crate wasn't used from the start. One morning let him out of the crate and keep him confined in a room where you can watch for twenty minutes but he can't see you. When you see the dog start to circle in preparation for finding his spot, lob a "throw chain" directly at him. Don't say *No* or any command or behavior that will cause him to attribute the chain to you. Open the door, run away outside, and, when he follows you, play heartily with him. A throw chain is a two-foot length of brass chandelier chain that is very light and noisy. Leave it lying where it falls until the dog is not around; we want him to think it's a thunderbolt from Zeus.

21

Selecting a Breed and a Puppy

THE IDEAL DOG IS CALM indoors, yet full of life outdoors. These are very minimal goals that are easy to attain, but there's also a genetic factor to consider. Many dogs are simply born nervous, and this is a fact many breeders and the American Kennel Club aren't addressing. There's a growing movement to use temperament testing to evaluate breeding stock, but that isn't a full answer, as the standards are too low. Unless the breeders fully train the breeding stock in their original working trade they can never truly know what their dogs are made of. One flaw in a single area and the whole formula of a breed is out of balance. Instinct is designed to keep organisms alert to danger, and such sensitivity in reality means less of a resistance to that which is negative. The entire thrust of domestication and breeding programs has been to lessen this survival impulse in our dogs, making their moods more flexible and resilient. A breed of dog is nothing more than a manifestation of one or more of the harmonic pathways. Any breeding program that doesn't closely follow the original working standard developed when the breed was created will allow naturally occurring nervousness to come to the forefront of the offspring's character. To breed correctly in the modern era, one must always work against this ever-present natural force by using the prey instinct to balance character.

The modern breeds were created with a lot of painstaking work and represent a very delicate balance between owning a dog that is an effective working partner and companion and owning one that is a complete disaster and liability. In general, the optimal dog is medium-sized with strong nerves and a sound constitution. When the physical or mental characteristics of a dog are stretched or condensed severely in any direction (giant or toy breeds; superactive or lethargic breeds), rigorous standards have to be imposed to maintain the animal's mental balance and physical health. It's easy to produce lemons and very hard to attain reliability.

Every breed was created with an emphasis on a certain component of the prey instinct. For instance, bird dogs have an insatiable attraction to small prey. The point where their drive becomes aroused is very low; these dogs like to run all day. Dogs with a "higher prey threshold," such as rottweilers, learn to tune out birds; their prey instinct quickly tires chasing something they can't catch. That low flash point that a bird dog has could easily convert to nervousness if the breeding isn't tested for "gunsureness." The ability of a dog to work under the boom of a 12-gauge shotgun is important to the stability of the animal's nervous system. And in field work there's a real burden placed on the dog's drive; the dog must wait for the hunter to flush and shoot the bird before it can go and pursue. Then the dog must return it without harming the carcass. This is a very delicate piece of genetic engineering and a few generations removed from such a working formula and one is most likely to get only the genes for hyperstimulation with a resulting low point at which the dog becomes irritated.

Many nervous puppies are being bred today, and that low irritability threshold is producing an increased defensiveness. These puppies may be overly friendly not because they like people but because they are unsure but tend to channel drive into the group mood. The sporting breeds are beginning to produce higher numbers in the biting statistics, because every harmonic pathway has its breaking point.

If I were going to buy a puppy, the last place I would look, except perhaps for the toy breeds, would be to the show ring. The show ring doesn't evaluate how the dog's nerves fare when he is apart from his handler and has to deal with stress or resistance to his drive. In shows, the traits that are promoted can have nothing to do with health, agility, or physical soundness. Dog breeding has become a whim of fashion. It reminds me of what happened to the American car industry in the sixties. The cars were designed strictly for the consumer's emotional consumption. We had big fins and big engines but they didn't handle well or go very far on a tank of gas. The same thing is happening to the American dog. The consumer thinks a German shepherd is a German shepherd, like a Chevy is a Chevy. If the dog has American Kennel Club papers, that makes the animal certified, as if it had garnered a favorable rating from *Consumer Reports*. It's time the consumer became educated and insisted on function as well as form.

Where I would look for a puppy would be from the breeders who use their dogs for their original purpose. I would watch these dogs at their native work and then decide if I could handle or appreciate such a dog's enthusiasm and style. If I decided I wanted a dog just to fill an emotional gap, I'd get a toy breed and not a dog that was bred to work. If I wanted a golden retriever, I would make sure he was steady to a gun shot and could sustain a focus on a pheasant. I'd like to see a collie with an instinct to herd farm stock or a Newfoundland that was agile enough to swim and eager to keep working.

There are certain rough guidelines to the temperaments of each breed, although there are individual exceptions. The physical traits are the easiest to pin down. Find out the grooming requirements and any special needs the breed may tend to have. Veterinarians should be consulted about the medical tendencies in the breeds.

In general, the smaller the prey the breed was designed to chase, the more active the breed's nervous process and the more outgoing the breed tends to be, as they are less able to process resistance into aggression. At the other end of the spectrum are the ancient guarding breeds such as the mastiffs, which have a nervous process with a high threshold and are less outgoing. In the middle of these two extremes one finds the herding type of breeds. In an apartment setting, a very small dog is very convenient; however, the larger breeds are less active, so either can be handled successfully. The medium breeds need the most exercise, but with a conscientious owner there's no rule that says one breed will work and another breed won't.

It's very important to see the puppy's parents. All puppies look cute and generally are outgoing. As they mature their defensiveness and sensitivities become more evident. Evaluate the mother off lead and somewhat apart from the breeder to see if she has the temperament you're looking for. Perhaps the father will be available, but often he's a stud from a distant location. The mother is more important for evaluation, anyway, because she has contributed 50 percent of the genes and 100 percent of the primal conditioning of the litter.

The ideal way to pick a puppy would be to see previous litters that are now one or two years old. A repeat breeding would be a big advantage. You're not picking the puppy, you're picking the genes, and that necessitates looking at the parents or the other off-spring. Take the time to research several generations of the breeder's stock.

Many people misunderstand the role of genetics when they select a breed. They may want a dog that will be protective of the house but go out and find a puppy of indeterminate breeding or a puppy of the sporting breeds. In a way, a dog's genetic makeup is like a TV set. It comes from the factory equipped to receive certain channels having certain hard wiring that can't be changed. One can fiddle with the fine tuning all one wants but you're not going to get cable television if the TV isn't wired to it. Too much fiddling is just going to scramble the picture. There-fore, it's wrong to try to get a dog to do a task he wasn't designed to do. Pay close attention to the parents and previous breedings because that's what you're going to get.

A lot of puppies are purchased through pet shops, and that's a big mistake. I'm not all that concerned with the health problems, as many of those are treatable. The real problem is with the genetics and with the early experiences of the puppies. They need a calm environment not a glass bowl to live in. Socializing should be a de-liberate and studied process instead of via a sales pitch. I'm sure most of the people who work in these shops treat the pups as well as they can, but the concept of a puppy as a commodity is never workable. The gene pool the customer is selecting for is totally un-known and there's no chance it's from acceptable stock. I would much rather go to a dog pound and select an adult dog; what I see is indeed what I get. While it's true that at the pound you're inheriting someone else's problem, most dogs are redeemable with an enlight-ened training program and there's something especially gratifying to saving such a dog.

When you adopt a waif from a shelter you must train the new behaviors the same way you create new behaviors with a puppy. The work is harder because the new behaviors have to compete with the old ones, which will always have priority in the dog's memory bank.

The best way to pick a puppy or a discarded shelter dog is to trust your emotions. The one most outgoing and independent is the one I would choose, but I know that not everyone wants such a dog. More sensitive dogs are harder to train but they are the easiest to inhibit and don't show as much drive, which is easier for many. The emphasis with such a dog has to be on building and maintaining his self-confidence so that his sensitivity doesn't make him apprehensive in new situations.

In my experience I've found that people have the most problem controlling dogs with a lot of drive. A dog can't have enough activity drive for my taste, but those who don't want to deal with that need a breed with a high nervous threshold and yet one that is still socially flexible. An Irish wolfhound or Newfoundland is an example of these kinds of dogs. Bear in mind that no matter what breed or temperament you select, *all dogs need training*.

Most serious problem behaviors originate with dogs that are defensive about their drive. Closely examine the breed at a dog show and see if you're prepared to deal with the sensitivities and limitations of those breeds you're considering. Find out how the breed reacts to stress and follow the advice of the experienced handlers when it comes to selecting a breed. Seeing is believing, so rely more on your own evaluations and the advice of handlers and experienced people than on the reading found in the breed books. Those are usually written in such a glowing style that there is little hard information to help in your selection process.

Finally, be honest with yourself about your patience factor; get the most outgoing breed if you have a short fuse and get the less spirited breed if you don't have much time.

I'm often asked if someone should get two puppies to start out with so they keep each other company. That would be a big mistake. Select one puppy, develop him, train him, and then when he's two years old, if you want another puppy, go ahead and find him. If one owns two puppies, or a puppy and an older dog, one must do a lot of individualized work with each so that each develops a complete character. Two dogs is four times the work!

22

Taking the Dog for a Walk

THERE ARE TWO WAYS to walk a dog on a leash. One way is a casual style, with the dog being allowed enough freedom so he can eliminate and investigate interesting smells. This style, the subject of this chapter, permits dog and owner to enjoy a walk together. Even though the dog is going to be given a great deal of latitude about what he can do, there are certain rules that have to be followed.

First of all, the direction and rate of travel is up to the handler. Second, while the dog is going to be encouraged to smell about and amuse himself, he's not going to be allowed to pull on the lead excitedly or invest his attention in an inappropriate direction, like scavenging garbage at curbside. Whenever the dog grows too excited, he'll be commanded, *Easy*, or another similar command.

The other style of walking on lead is very precise and we use the command, *Heel*. This will be the subject of the next two chapters. Heeling means the dog is immediately by his owner's side with his attention fully riveted on his owner. This kind of work is demanding for a dog but is quite necessary to control a dog under difficult circumstances. Additionally, training a dog to be both enthusiastic and precise has a profound effect on positively forming his character and on developing the right attitude for work. Training a dog to heel can be likened to training soldiers to march precisely in parade formation, and given its demands, I like to start this training when the dog is about ten months of age.

However, dogs need to be walked on lead—especially those dogs who live in the city—well before they're old enough to learn how to heel precisely. We need to train our dogs to walk in a more relaxed manner while still under control. This style of walking can be compared to soldiers marching over long distances. Soldiers are allowed to shift their gear around and needn't walk in perfect formation, but they have to remember they're still soldiers and can't go off on a side adventure. The unit's overall objective must remain in the mind of each individual. A good age for this kind of training is about six months.

Before we can even consider training the dog in either of these two styles of walking with his owner, and especially if we're dealing with an older problem dog, we have to see exactly what the nature of the problem is from the dog's perspective.

FROM THE DOG'S VIEWPOINT

Whenever a dog *moves ahead,* particularly outdoors or into an open area with lots of new and interesting things, he is put into a hunting mood. His drive is strongly aroused and he begins to look either for prey or for a new social order (making contact with other dogs or people) that carries with it the increased potential for finding prey.

When a dog is hunting he will, depending on his temperament, either orient with his eyes to the horizon, or lower his nose to the ground as he moves along. Aroused, the dog will move at a trot in order to keep sensory data flowing to his brain at a rate commensurate with the heightened state of experience that dogs are in while hunting.

The function of a hunting group is to look for something positive that can absorb all the drive generated by its motion and activity. An animal to chase would be the ideal target and that motivates the group to cover ground quickly. The group wants to get to the horizon unless it can find something particularly absorbing right at hand.

If my dog were actually in a group of other dogs, all of them would be able to move in unison at a comfortable trotting pace. All the dogs can smell and are tuned into the same interesting stimuli. They are all on the same wavelength so they can move in concert without any degree of tension or conflict. Their nervous systems are relaxed, their bodies are aligned, and the body language of each group member is reinforcing the others. They are stimulated by whatever little twists arise in their adventure.

In the hunting mood, the need to be connected to a place or to each other becomes displaced by the relaxing aspect that flow has on the nervous system. A singular focus suffices to bond the group, leaving each member free to concentrate on hunting.

The potential for a dog and his owner to be at odds over how to go for a walk is inherent. The owner wants to go from point A to point B and at a pace that's humanly possible. However, the dog feels that since he is with his group, and they are moving into new territory or novel surroundings, they are on a hunt together. Since he's restrained by a lead, he is compelled to pull, and the tension on the lead reinforces for him that the group is indeed moving together. The tight lead becomes the substitute for being in the midst of fellow group members all in sync with his inner lust for the hunt. With repetition, pulling on the lead on these outings with his owner comes to represent for the dog what hunting should feel like.

There isn't any instinctive reason why the dog would feel the need to pay attention to his owner. The only way he would feel attracted to his owner is if the owner demonstrated through his body language that he was hot on the trail of a promising scent. Otherwise, the dog will rely on his own senses and keep moving along, with his peripheral vision tracking the progress of his comrades.

Meanwhile, the dog owner, who isn't trotting and who has a different idea of what the outing's objective is, finds life on the other end of the lead precarious to his health. I've had many clients come to me after their dog pulled them over and they had broken an ankle, a wrist, or a leg. One elderly client even suffered a heart attack as he tried to walk his strapping young German shepherd.

The time quickly arrives for a rambunctious dog to learn how to walk properly. Unfortunately, the scenario often finds the owner stopping, yanking back on the lead, and yelling, *No!!* or *Heel!!*

Many things are going on in the dog's mind at this point. The owner is asking the dog to switch from a hunting to a pack mood, and also to proceed at a lower drive level (not to be excited and pull so hard). Yet the dog cannot see anything in the owner's stimulation that would attract his drive. In fact, he sees quite the opposite. He perceives his owner as trying to take away his drive, to make him stop hunting. This has the effect of stimulating the dog to avoid his owner, getting even deeper into his hunting mood. And as the dog tries to resume trotting, the handler yanks the dog backward. The dog feels the lead growing tight, upsetting his balance.

Before we begin we need to understand a simple point about dog behavior. A dog works to preserve his emotional balance the same way he will work to preserve his physical balance. When the dog feels the lead pulling him back, he reacts just as we humans would if we felt someone trying to pull us over. To maintain our balance, we would resist that force as hard as we had to. The harder the owner pulls back on the lead, the harder the dog will strain forward in order to maintain his emotional balance. And the more unattractive the owner is making himself to his dog by becoming confrontational, the more the dog will seek to find an instinct with which he can avoid his owner: garbage at curbside, the form of a person, animal, or bush on the horizon. The dog learns that by pulling forward against the resistance of the lead, he is able to keep drive flowing into his hunting mood.

A common postscript to such a scenario is that the dog owner becomes thoroughly frustrated and finally gets the dog's attention by blowing up. Depending on the dog's genetics and upbringing, the owner has aroused the dog's fighting or defensive instinct. This in turn sets off a new series of negative learning patterns: an attitude problem solely produced by a struggle between dog and owner about how to go for a walk.

When dogs encounter these leash problems for the first time relative to their urge to hunt, they may bite the lead, either in play or with a little snarl or a curl of the lip. This should indicate to the handler that the dog isn't able to include his handler in his hunting mood, rather than that the dog is being defiant. Of course, it's human nature to conclude that the dog is being rebellious or stubborn and to challenge him over his behavior. As this goes on, the dog's urge to resist over the long term is being reinforced even as the owner may be winning the struggle in that moment.

As the dog matures, and if his drive to hunt is strong enough, whatever happens to him—shouts, threats, corrections, smacks on the rump—will come to represent for him what hunting with his pack is supposed to feel like. Eventually, the dog will become hardened and oblivious to all his owner's screaming and jerks on the lead. In fact, some dogs are stimulated to pull harder on the lead by these very corrective measures. Such dogs learn that resistance within the pack is an acceptable price to pay, as long as hunting continues.

At some point, with some kind of organized training, the handler may work out a compromise with his dog about how to walk nicely on a lead; this may work most of the time, but it never works when the dog is high in drive—when he sees another dog, a cat, a squirrel, or a particularly absorbing smell.

With dogs that have a weaker hunt drive, the corrections may inhibit the pulling on the lead; however, the central objective of channeling the dog's drive into the handler won't be accomplished either. The dog will develop a self-confidence problem, and he'll learn that being with his handler when there are normally positive and exciting stimuli present is a stressful experience. His defensive instinct will constantly be aroused to keep the urge to hunt in check.

All these neurotic conditions are the result of the dog learning that his drive couldn't flow in harmony with his group. He therefore needs to get away from his pack in order to become in balance. Thus, we find the worst result of such a bad foundation in training: Whenever the dog is off lead and starts to get aroused with drive he must dash to freedom, where he can pursue a natural style of hunting. Not only has the resistance between dog and owner been intensified by the training, but the dog has actually been influenced to run away from his owner by the very effort to train the dog to walk on the lead.

What are we asking a dog to do when we command him to heel or to walk nicely? Since heeling or walking calmly means to be attentive to a lesser or higher degree to his handler, and to be aroused by the prospects of a hunt, we need to use the principles of group life to channel the dog's drive into the appropriate reflexes. In the system of training covered in the next two chapters, we will see that the dog can willingly learn to channel this strong drive into his handler, and that it can easily flow under the control of the handler, when the dog learns that by "plugging in" to his handler he gets to make contact with stimuli (food, ball, stick, handler) that leaves his hunting urge satisfied.

This chapter, which examines how to walk a dog, is a training program that will quickly teach the dog to walk calmly on the lead with enough range so that he can pursue canine matters. The next chapter will discuss a precise method to produce an exact form of heeling obediently under any conditions.

PHASE ONE: *"BE WITH ME"* MAKING CONTACT

When the handler moves out and wants the dog to walk along with him, he's saying to the dog, *"Be with me;* move with the group." Before a dog can be put into a group mood so that he wants to be with his handler, the dog should exhibit the desire to touch his handler. He should have the drive to make physical contact so that he is emotionally "plugged into" his handler. The physical reflex we want to activate in the dog is the same reflex that puppies use when they jump up to touch people with their front paws.

We can see the same parallel when we consider how children talk to adults. A young child is too instinctive to understand abstract mannerisms of social intercourse such as social distance. When they keep their distance it's because they feel uncomfortable about being too close. Similarly, when they're attracted to someone, they can't feel connected solely through language and eye contact. For a child to want to talk to someone means he has to be in the mood to want to *be with* that person. Children are compelled to make direct physical contact. In short order they close any gap that existed between them and others and are touching the person they're talking to. They're either leaning on the person's arm as they chat or they actually slide into the person's lap. For children to feel they have guaranteed access to a person's attention, they need to be touching him.

The same holds true for a dog. If we're inviting a dog to be with us, given the instinctive definition of what heeling means to him, he can't understand that he should walk with us without trying to touch us. The mood to be with us invokes a distinct physical reflex, one which we will associate with a command. I use the command *Hup*. The object here is to get the dog to jump up and touch me on my chest when commanded. Then, as a measure of the dog's commitment, I encourage him to sustain the contact for several moments by wrestling with him and backing up. This reflex will be strongly developed in our training program so that all the drive aroused by the instinct to hunt that is normally conducted by a tracking or airscenting instinct can be redirected into and accommodated by a group instinct: the reflex to touch with the two front paws.

From basic to advanced training, we will be using this reflex of contacting as a solution to virtually every training problem the dog has to solve. The answer in any situation is always for the dog to want to be with his handler.

If the handler doesn't feel up to such a physical and active style of contacting with his dog, he can develop an alternative style. He can, instead, bend down, pressing into the dog as he engages him in play, then backpedal so he is working to sustain the contact. As soon as possible, this drive can be directed into ball chasing or food treats to deflect the dog's attention from the jumping-up reflex. In terms of his handler, the dog learns he is only praised at ground level.

In the compromise described above, the dog is getting as much drive flow as in the more physical style, although the level of the dog's commitment to his handler may run lower and the handler has to be sure that the dog sustains the contacting. Once again, food is an excellent way to reinforce the connection between dog and handler. From here on in this book, one can substitute one's own style of contacting whenever contacting is called for in the text.

Each time I train a dog, I start with food, using fasting if necessary to develop the level of intensity behind their drive to make contact. I then try to graduate to the ball for the final phases of training.

When I command *Hup,* I move away from the dog, pat my chest, and talk to the dog in an ascending tone: "Come on, puppy dog, hellooo, goood booy," and so on. It's almost the same way one would talk to a baby. This tone of "Motherese" activates a group instinct in the dog.

The first few sessions are strictly to encourage the dog's drive to be with his handler. The dog is always to be on lead. As I verbally encourage the dog, I backpedal away from him, then pat my leg or chest so the dog will be attracted to follow me.

After the firm sound of the command *Hup,* my tone remains encouraging. A common handler error is to become frustrated if the dog is hesitant about making contact. His tone becomes stern and commanding, which repels rather than attracts the dog.

When the dog jumps up and makes contact, I massage under his chin, tug at his jowls, and rub his ribs. This is a good point at which to pause and evaluate the dog's disposition. Is he calm or tense? Is he in drive or is he inhibited? If he's excited, is he overstimulated, nervous, or anxious? Is he looking off to the distance?

Touch your dog. Does he flinch or is his body supple, excited, and stimulated by the touch? The more relaxed the dog's skin and body are, the more his drive is flowing into the group mood. This is important because it means the dog isn't holding anything in reserve (at least in that moment). The dog is getting as much gratification as if he were hunting.

The next step is to disengage without a command, back up a short distance, and repeat. When training outdoors, start out in an open area away from bushes and trees or you will be presenting distractions to the dog ahead of our schedule.

This simple act of inviting the dog to make contact with his owner can pose a serious dilemma to older dogs and those dogs who have been trained along avoidance principles (correct and reward). These dogs have learned that their pack instinct carries with it an intense amount of social resistance. They have to break through this pressure in order to want to make contact with their handler, especially up high at the handlers' level and in the presence of natural stimuli. This defensive instinct dampens the normal flow of drive, and while such a dog may be attracted to his handler, it won't have enough drive to get over the hump to enter his handler's "sphere of influence."

To encourage the dog and get his juices flowing, I'll use inducements and special handling according to his temperament. These stimuli have an attractive power to the dog's natural instincts and, like priming a pump, can start the flow of drive to get it up to a higher peak. These inducements and special treatments for the different temperaments are described below.

Sensitive Dogs

It's easiest to start contacting by getting down to their level, so I start the process by walking to a bench, sitting down, and inviting the dog to make contact with me. I'll even lie down on the lawn and encourage the dog to smell, nuzzle, or even scratch at me. If the dog can be encouraged to play that would be ideal.

When I see that the dog is starting to be attracted, I'll get up and run a short distance, fall down, and try to get the dog to play again.

With sensitive dogs I start with a flat collar. It's good to use food or a ball as an inducement for the dog to touch his handler in one way or another. Because of their sensitive nature, however, these dogs may not show any interest in the reward for several sessions.

It's especially helpful to fast a sensitive dog so drive is aroused from inside the organism. Sensitive dogs are easily inhibited, and if not truly hungry, they can easily misinterpret the food being offered to them as pressure being exerted upon them. If they misconstrue the food as pressure, it will have the adverse effect of making them want to increase their distance rather than to make contact with their handler. It is also important to proceed very slowly when fasting a dog, for the hungrier he gets, the more intense his fear of disconnectedness.

It also may be best to start the sensitive dog on contacting indoors rather than outside.

As the dog starts to make contact on the ground and gets more and more excited about it, in many short sessions over several days progress the dog so that he's making contact with the handler, who is standing upright.

Arouse the dog into a play session on the ground, run away a short distance, and then command *Hup*, pat your chest, and praise the dog with a rising inflection. When he comes up to your level, renew the playing. Stop the session before the dog loses interest, leaving him full of drive instead of reminding him of the social resistance he generally associates contacting with.

Nervous Dogs

These dogs express a lot of drive because their nervous threshold is so low. They can't sustain a focus, especially outdoors. They're usually very easy to attract and willingly jump up to make contact; however, they jump away even faster.

They may also exhibit a lot of social frustration while they're contacting by nipping at your hand or shirt sleeve, or by not aiming squarely for your chest. I try to ignore this nervousness as much as possible because it will recede as the dog's drive starts to flow clearly. Also, in these early stages, try to displace the nipping (a nervous prey instinct) into the ball (a pure prey instinct).

Running and chasing after the ball is good for the nervous dog because it burns up a lot of energy. Food can then be used to build the dog's focus so that he calmly learns to sustain contact with his handler.

Nervous dogs should be started on a choke collar. By the final stage of this chapter they can be put on a pinch collar. (With all dogs in all the stages of training until the very end, whenever you work them at any distance from you they should be on a long lead.)

Dogs with Strong Hunting Drive

This kind of dog makes an uninhibited kind of contacting. He readily jumps up and splatters your chest with his front feet. He likes to grip the handler's arm and usually not too hard. It's a purely social "harmonic" gesture; however, it can be tinged with nervousness if the dog has a learning block through previous training.

In these early stages, it's best if any nervousness can be ignored. If it's too severe, even after distracting him with food, choke up on the dog's lead and collar when he's contacting and thinking about grabbing your arm so that the dog makes *himself* uncomfortable. Then praise him heartily on the ground to keep his good feeling of making contact with his handler. Remember, the dog must learn that his nervous behaviors cause his problem, not his group instinct (attraction to, and desire to be with, his handler).

The common mistake that's made with such a dog is to confront him over his gripping of the arm, telling him *No*. The problem is being misdiagnosed. It's not that the dog is trying to dominate the handler, or even that he's aggressive. It's simply that he has more drive than the group instinct has been developed to channel, so he feels compelled to use his mouth to deal with his frustration. What he needs is a prey instinct to absorb all his surplus drive. Produce the ball when he's making contact and throw it to burn off the dog's emotional energy.

Also, this dog can be engaged in contacting, and if the handler were to backpedal away from the dog faster, rather than slower, the dog's drive would be burned off by the running activity. Then the ball can be thrown after the dog closes the gap and makes contact. Such a training session will leave the dog feeling very calm about his group instinct and emotionally spent as well.

Dogs with strong drive have the problem of being solidly focused in the hunting mood and are easily distracted by prior learning. However, the advantage to such dogs is that within several sessions, if not right away, they can be worked on the pinch collar and can breeze right through all the training steps in these chapters on heeling.

With any dog, the first step in using the pinch collar is to acclimate the dog to it without any training involved. Let the dog pull you around on the lead. In fact, before I ever shock a dog on a lead, and throughout the course of the training program, I always encourage the dog to pull me. This ensures that the dog will never lose drive, even after receiving a shock. After the dog is acclimated to the pinch collar, show him a morsel of food held at chest height, back up, and when he's comfortable with your pulling on it, command *Hup*, and then encourage him with an ascending tone of voice.

At first, he may jump right up and gobble down the food. But soon this contacting ends up being more work than the food is worth, and the dog will disengage and look for a stimulus more worthy of his hunting prowess. Exactly at this point, while the dog is looking away, a shock is made on the collar, the handler quickly backpedals as if he, too, wants to escape from the shock, and profusely praises the dog as the dog turns around and catches up with the handler.

Don't wait for the dog to get to you before you praise him. The outpouring of praise should start right after the shock, so that you not only disassociate yourself from the shock, but you simultaneously attract the dog's drive by your movement away from the dog. The handler can also pat his chest as he is backing away from the dog.

If the dog's drive is strong enough, the dog's drive will quickly channel back into the group mood. The important thing is to praise your dog so heartily that the group mood brings the dog intense pleasure. In this way the dog won't be able to attribute the shock to his handler; he will only remember that the hunting mood focused away from his group wasn't successful.

After the shock, if you see that the dog wants to make contact but doesn't have enough drive to complete the jumping-up reflex, kneel down and give him the same profuse praise at his level on the ground. As long as he's stopped hunting you're halfway to redirecting his energy into his group mood, so spend the time praising and trying to arouse in him the desire to play. Once again, the group instinct needs to be widened so that it can handle more drive.

In three to four sessions of five minutes each, the dog should be making contact and sustaining it until he's released with the OK signal.

Learning Block

Many dogs, no matter what their temperament, have learning blocks in place because of previous training. They may have always been confronted over their misbehavior or perhaps they were kneed for trying to jump up to make contact with people when they were young. These dogs have learned that making contact with their owner or another person is a negative if not dangerous experience. Despite their varying temperaments, no matter how positive the handler may act, the dogs will interpret it as just another negative thing that people unpredictably do. Take such a dog out into an open area and just make him sit and wait. Let him look around at whatever is going on, but enforce that he must stay in the sit position.

Stand patiently next to him, keep the lead a little tight, and watch the dog for signs of frustration at not being able to respond to the attractive stimuli that abound outdoors. This nervous energy is the resistance between the handler and the dog and when the dog gets fidgety the handler has an opportunity to channel it into the group instinct of contacting.

Don't get too confrontational about the sit exercise. I prefer to manipulate the dog physically into the sit position and keep my hands poised so that I can keep the dog in that position. If we dominate the dog too strongly, his drive will subside and we won't have it at the surface of the dog's temperament, available for training.

As the dog grows restless, tousle him on his right jowl, whoop and holler, and race backward a short distance. Stop, kneel down, and try to engage the dog in play. If the dog gets excited, produce a ball or some food and encourage the dog to press against you in order to get to his reward. Let him have the food or the ball for a few moments. Normally, after the dog's little burst of drive activity, resistance will set back in and the dog quickly loses interest either in his handler, the food, or the ball. At that point, collect him back into a sit and make him wait again.

Repeat this process over several days until the dog will leave the ground and jump up for his reward as you are standing instead of kneeling. Then you must continue to develop this dog so that he will sustain the contact and play heartily during the session.

If a dog is particularly sensitive, nervous, and burdened with a learning block, I'll train the dog to sit/stay before I do the training to walk on lead. If you feel that's the case with your dog, refer to the Training the Sit/Stay chapter and do that phase of training now.

Don't Overdo Contacting

It's very easy to overdo the contacting. It shouldn't be used as a way of relating to the dog; it's only a training tool to ensure that the dog is committing his drive to his handler. As we go along in the training program we are going to shape the contacting reflex into heeling behaviors and into the sit position.

PHASE TWO: THE COLLECTIVE PURPOSE

Now that the dog is responsive to the *Hup* command, the next step is to show him that by making contact with his handler, he gets to a desired objective. This further reinforces for the dog that contacting is the conduit for high drive flow.

During this phase the dog will need to be shocked because initially, he will be in conflict about being with his handler and getting to the distraction. Of course drive must first be strong enough to convert the shock into stimulation.

Before being shocked, the dog must first learn that the handler is on his wavelength. When he's distracted, keep the dog on a tight lead and praise him exuberantly, both physically and verbally. We want him to soak up his handler's infectious excitement. We want the dog to end up feeling completely uninhibited and in sync with his handler even though at the moment, his focus is the distraction. Once the dog is sure about being high in drive and near his handler, we're ready to think about the shock. Let's discuss how to handle the lead in this delicate matter.

The shock should be made as far from the dog's sight as possible, preferably when he is absorbed in the distraction. (In other words, when he's in a hunting mood.) The point of shocking the dog is not to teach him that he is a bad dog or that his handler is displeased, but quite the opposite: to train him to feel more attracted to his handler *especially* in the face of a distraction. And most important, that his group instinct produces more success than a hunting instinct.

A common handler error is to brandish the lead in front of the dog's face, causing the dog to see a quick motion of the handler as he feels the jerk on the collar. It becomes difficult for the dog to feel attracted to his handler in the face of that negative stimulus.

Hold the lead at hip level and make the corrective snap behind you with a whiplike action in your arm. At the same time, dramatically increase the verbal praise and genuine affection that is oozing out of every pore of your being. As you become more adroit at giving the shock as you praise and attract, you should try to wiggle a ball or a tidbit of food as an added inducement.

When you shock the dog you have to be a good actor, pretending that you have absolutely no idea how your dog was shocked. You end up looking good to your dog because your enthusiasm is contagious and you become the answer to his problem.

Another common handling mistake when trying to shock the dog is that it's human nature to try to communicate with another being about a conflict rather than to take physical action. People tend to stop what they're doing (which was training the dog how to move together), to lower their head toward the dog, and to express either frustration or anger in their tone of voice. This only puts the dog deeper into conflict because the handler isn't doing anything to attract the dog's drive. On the contrary, the handler is repelling the dog's drive, and that makes the distraction look even more attractive than before. We're trying to train the dog to move smoothly with the handler, as opposed to a hectic stop-and-go activity, so always keep moving away from the dog, especially if he bogs down.

If the handler fails to attract the dog with enthusiastic and sincere praise, and fails to firmly shock the dog's hunting instinct, then social resistance will be increased and the dog will become even more confused.

However, when the shock is crisply delivered in conjunction with a happy, infectious attitude in the handler, the drive is diverted from the hunting instinct and will smoothly course back into the group instinct. Although it may at first seem paradoxical, only in this sequence of events can the handler and the dog be on the same wavelength.

It's also necessary, although from our human point of view, illogical, to make the shock without any preparatory command. We aren't going to give the dog the chance to comply as a means of avoiding correction. He must experience the shock because it is vital information. It is a pulse of dynamic energy that he will emotionally convert into a mood of attraction toward his handler. After all, we all agree that a dog must be corrected, but it's the timing of the correction that is critical. We cannot assume that the dog will understand why he is being corrected. None of our training objectives makes any sense to him. He just wants to follow his prey instinct. The concept of fair play is exclusively human. In this sequence, the dog learns that the shock is an incentive to be with the handler thereby neutralizing his need to get to the distraction. This premise is the most humane way to train the dog to accommodate to the ways of life in the human world. If you still feel indecisive about this issue, please review the section of disassociation in the Training Tools and Equipment chapter. The worst mistake a handler can make is to be indecisive. It's better to do something wrong than to do something halfway.

After the shock, if your act is convincing enough, the shock will be converted to a stimulus, and you will see your dog *happily* making contact with you with his tail high and his body energized.

A dog that will not make contact means one of two things: Either the dog is not attracted enough in your beginning work, or the shock is not hard enough. If you feel unsure of how to evaluate this problem, be conservative and build up the dog's attraction to you for four or five more sessions. Also, in regard to a puppy, you often must wait until he is ten months of age.

Now we need to select a target (distraction) that will be the focal point of the group's activity. Choose something that the dog is enthusiastic about. For some dogs it may be food held by someone or set up on something like a bucket stood on end. For other dogs it could be a chance to hop into a car. Or it could mean getting to another family member who could give the dog a ball throw or a good rib rubbing.

What I use most often is a doorway. I collect the dog into a sit at the door and pause for several moments as I praise him and reward him with food.

Holding him at sit with my left hand, I open the door with my right, and while praising him, I release the lead. He will, of course, bolt through the door, but as he heads in that direction, I move away from the door and give him a crisp shock. I intensify my praise and encourage him to make contact. Next, I run in and out of the door several times, with lots of rewards, praise, and stroking.

After the dog is calm, I let him smell around outdoors for a few moments, bring him back indoors without any command, close the door, and repeat three or four more times. In the next day's session, I'll have him sitting before the door and command *Hup*, but as he goes to jump I'll spin counterclockwise and collect him back into a sit. I'll praise him for a second and quickly open the door. The next time I might do the spin and then stretch it out for a few feet so that he's moving by my side as an additional precursor to getting through the door.

If the dog loves to ride in the car, I'll take him to the parking lot and let him hop into the car on his own and pet him up when he's inside it. Then, I'll take him out of the car, about ten feet away, command *Hup* as I back away from the car, and as soon as he makes contact, I'll break away from the dog and race him to the car. It's important to demonstrate in your body language that you're trying to get to the objective, too, so that the dog doesn't have the sense that he's leaving you to get to his goal. We want the dog to feel that the target is mutually shared by the group and its attainment is a collective activity. When he's made the connection that I'm his access to the car I can progressively get him to glide near me as I make a couple of swift turns before letting him in the car.

This training is a lot of fun for the dog and not very hard work because he only has to make one second of contacting to get to something that's very pleasurable for him. He's also learning that his handler is the "on switch" for his pleasure circuitry and so there isn't any need to resist the handler's influence.

Continue this work until you see the dog becoming attentive to you, waiting for the *Hup* command so that the two of you can get to the place of high drive flow. You should also "feel" in the leash a certain looseness; the dog isn't in conflict and isn't straining on the leash anymore. He's starting to look to his handler for access to something he wants.

Now that the dog has learned these two skills we can put them together so that the dog can heel in a casual manner down a city street and through traffic. This is a *middle way* of walking on a lead for a dog, whereby the lead will be kept moderately tight as a signal for a casual style of walking. This won't equip the dog to deal with intense distractions, but it's sufficient to train a dog how to walk nicely on an evening constitutional in the manner we discussed earlier.

To train the dog about this middle way it's important to remember that your objective is not to get to a particular place, but to achieve a certain mood in your dog. Once the dog is in the appropriate mood, you can think about getting somewhere.

The first step is to pause at the threshold to the outdoors and command the dog to make contact. When the dog makes contact he gets to go out, either through the doorway for country dogs, or out of the lobby to the street for city dogs. Give the dog a few moments to sniff around and relieve himself.

Then command *Hup*, and when the dog makes contact, disengage and break away at a fast pace, being careful to keep the lead loose. Now start to slow down, which means you're not generating as much attraction to the dog's drive as you are when you're going fast. Since you're going slower, the dog will begin to drift into his hunting mood. He'll forge ahead, and the slack in the lead will be taken up.

Abruptly, let the lead go slack by extending your lead hand forward, reverse your direction, and shock the dog. When the dog turns around to see what's going on, the handler should be backpedaling and moving away from the dog in the opposite direction from the original course. Be sure the shock precedes the dog's notice of your change of direction.

As the dog catches up, praise him. Then break away once again in the opposite direction. Again, give the dog an opportunity to forge, and repeat the shock sequence.

You will quickly discover that the dog is now paying very close attention to you; the lead is loose and the only way he can monitor your direction is to look at you. At this point reward the dog by telegraphing with body language that you are about to change direction. The dog will snap up this clue, so praise him mightily for being attentive. When he is especially attentive to you, you can even give the command *Heel,* then change direction, making an exaggerated commotion, and praise the dog.

Now that this pattern is well established in the dog's mind, he can learn the middle way of walking with his owner. In this mode the dog doesn't have to pay strict attention to his handler and can engross himself to a degree in smelling and exploring those things that only dogs take delight in. In this style of walking the dog can pull ahead somewhat. Whenever the dog starts to pull too hard the lead goes slack, the handler changes direction, and the dog is shocked.

The first step is to channel the dog into the handler with a rapid series of changes in direction as described above. When the dog is very attentive, move ahead with the dog at a slower pace. As he relaxes, slowly tighten up on the lead and say *Easy* to the dog. As you walk along, slowly play the lead out so that the dog has the full six-foot length with which he can explore.

The command *Easy* is going to represent a mood where the dog can drift into his hunting mode, but where the tight lead won't be a stimulus to pull harder. Rather, it will be a reminder of his group instinct and of being attracted to the handler. Because of this delicate balance the handler will need only a very slight shock to enforce the *Easy* command should the dog start to pull.

The handler has reached a new dimension in his training. After creating the fifty–fifty balance in this middle way of walking a dog, he can shock the dog for violating this emotional balance without doing any motivational work. The dog will work to restore the fifty–fifty balance in order to continue with the outing.

Soon, a strong tone by the owner, *Easy,* without any shock, will be sufficient to inhibit the dog's nervousness, that tendency to break out of the existing mood. By continuing to walk along smoothly the dog learns that the middle way is the path of least resistance and highest rate of drive flow.

To an observer, it would appear that the handler was doing traditional praise-and-punish dog training when the reality couldn't be more different.

This middle way is a very positive experience for the dog, because he's also learning that he gets to hunt *with* his handler. He's learning that he can still be a dog, he can be in medium drive, and that outings with his handler are lots of fun without any measure of social resistance.

If you run into another dog, or something that is too distracting for the level of control that you have over your dog at this point, repeat the change of direction sequence. At this level of the dog's training the handler must always be the answer for the dog by going very fast and attracting the dog. But with young dogs, try to avoid such difficult situations as much as possible.

Finally, you can end up at a park or a field and throw a ball or stick for your dog, and the prey instinct, which is the ultimate objective of any hunt, finds its fulfillment.

23

Training the Dog to Heel

STANDARD

THE DOG WILL WALK on his handler's left side and will look up at his handler's face at all times. He will work to keep his shoulder next to his handler's hips no matter what pace or direction the handler takes. When the handler stops, the dog will automatically sit without any command.

CONCEPT

The foundation of off-lead control starts with heeling, which refers to the dog walking very precisely, as if in a marching drill for a parade. He is very attentive to his handler and does not pull on the lead. As the initial step in training, heeling is crucial, for it is here that the dog first begins to funnel all of his drive into his handler. When the dog's drive is channeled in this way, we find that he works very hard to be with his handler, and that the obedience work is actually stimulating for the dog. Drive training increases and strengthens his spirit.

In a practical sense, we need a dog to heel precisely so that we have strict control over him in difficult circumstances. What we're actually doing in gaining such control is training the dog's temperament to switch his emotions, or drive, quickly from one mood to another.

It's in the nature of a dog to find this mood-switching very difficult to do. The dog's drive seeks to follow an instinct to its natural conclusion, and when this process is interfered with, dogs are designed by nature to experience resistance toward that which is dis-rupting their concentration. This resistance is the basis of emotional memories and equips the individual with the survival reflexes he'll need to be successful in the natural world.

Training a dog to heel substantially reduces resistance between the dog and his handler, and heeling can be used to relieve tension whenever it occurs in the dog's life—especially in those critical mo-ments when there are strangers at the door or when the dog is intro-duced to strangers.

Not only are we going to train the dog to switch moods quickly, but also, since the dog's drive is channeled into his handler, the dog learns that a group mood (focus on the leader) rather than the hunt-ing mood (focus on something outside the group) is the path of high-est flow.

DEVELOPING THE DRIVE TO MAKE CONTACT

In this phase we're training the dog to maintain a 100 percent focus on his handler as they move together. In the previous chapter, the dog learned through experience to be on the handler's left side, but without the degree of intense focus we are now going to require. Now we're going to be demanding his undivided attention. We will concentrate in the early stages on eliciting and developing the in-stincts that we need before we put them together into a finished exercise with the dog on our left. Putting all of the components together with the dog on the handler's left side will only happen at the very end of the training program. It's a mistake to start the dog out on the left side, because he is most likely to learn this is a posi-tion of danger.

What's new here is that the dog has to maintain a steady concen-tration on his handler as he covers ground. He's not allowed to look at something else or to drop his head down to the ground to find a scent. Whenever the head starts to drift away from its focus on the handler the dog should be shocked, with the handler snapping the lead from behind his right hip. Immediately after he's shocked the handler must pick up his pace, and then praise the dog. The shock trains the dog that a hunting instinct is unsuccessful whereas a group instinct produces high drive flow.

PHASE THREE: CHANGES ARE GOOD

In this phase, we're going to train the dog that all changes that occur in the exercise are good. No matter which switches of direction or variations of speed the handler may make, these are positive events. Even a jerk on the lead is a positive stimulation of the group mood.

In this work the handler has to generate a lot of enthusiasm and dynamic body language, because we want the dog to be crazy to make contact with us.

Start to play with the dog and abruptly break away, as if you're trying to get away from him. Fall down and wrestle with him if he's not too rough, or just let him catch up and play with you. Then get up and run off again. When the dog looks to be at his peak of enthusiasm, start to face the dog by backpedaling, and fake going either left or right, like a basketball or football player would "throw moves" at a defender. After your most convincing effort, *try* to get away from the dog. When he catches you reward him with more play. This is a lot of fun and a good workout for both the handler and the dog. But it's serious, too, because we're training the dog that rapid shifts in the speed and the direction of his handler aren't dangerous events; they don't get him into trouble with his handler over which way the group should be going. Rather, they are stimulations, and they cause the dog's drive to flow even higher.

Normally, around the house or in traditional dog training, the dog learns quite the opposite. When the handler moves abruptly and quickly, the dog gets corrected and finds himself in trouble. The dog associates a sudden move from his handler with the correction, and he has to internalize his drive in the form of stress. The only way it can come out is through avoidance instincts. For the rest of the dog's life, a jerk on the lead reconfirms his wariness about this kind of work.

A ball can be an ideal focal point and reward, but if the dog doesn't have much drive for a ball, use food, and make sure the dog is very hungry. If the dog has a lot of drive (likes to jump and mouth while contacting), sometimes he won't require any more inducement than your body language. However, the ball and the food are especially helpful training aids for channeling the dog's drive back into the sit position when the handler disengages from the dog, as we discussed earlier.

I start by roughhousing with the dog and working him up to an excited state, and then I start to move away and encourage the dog to keep up with me. I break away from the dog in an abrupt and helter-skelter manner, and run away as fast as I can. When the dog catches up to me I play with him even harder and reward him with food. As he is chasing me, I fake going either left and right, or running away, and at the same time I make progressively harder and harder shocks on the collar as the dog is facing me. If he looks at my hand rather than at my upper body or eyes, or if he shows any degree of concern, the shock is too strong and I work at getting the dog more interested in the food. But as long as the shock is having no inhibiting effect, its intensity can be slowly escalated. The dog is learning to be unaffected by the progressively stronger jerks; nevertheless, I'm making the jerk behind my hip and not directly in front of his face.

When I see that the dog is at his peak, I let him catch me. I command *Hup* and engage the dog in contacting, making sure to massage under his chin with my left hand as he feeds.

I disengage and collect the dog into the sit position, calmly continuing to praise him. You should keep the lead somewhat tight and guide him by holding the food over his head so that the dog doesn't get up from the sitting position. Then you can repeat the series several more times.

If the dog has strong ball drive, there is another exercise that one can do to help in this phase. Tie the dog to a post or a tree on a two-foot lead. Stand a short distance away from the dog and tease him with a ball, and then roll it to him. Steal the ball and repeat. The next several times, roll it past a little bit out of his reach so that he'll give himself a little jerk on the collar. Keep building up the dog's tolerance to the point where he will lunge for the ball even when he's on a pinch collar.

The session can be concluded by massaging underneath the dog's chin, putting on his long lead, releasing him from the post, and giving the ball a good throw.

In short order the jerks will be converted from being a shock to being a stimulation.

When done properly, the shocks add energy to the dog's "system"; they reinforce his group mood and insulate him from his hunting mood.

If the dog winces with each correction or becomes inhibited, his drive is not high enough, and you have to work on becoming more attractive to the dog.

Some dogs of strong drive may become inhibited by anything the handler does because they have a profound learning block due to previous training or handling. To get them into high drive, the handler may have to put them into a state of deep conflict. These dogs can do best when they're distracted by something they really lust after, perhaps other dogs or cats to chase. Spend a week just strolling around your yard with this dog, sitting down and giving him treats when he comes near, and then take him off to work in a distracting environment. It may be advisable to have a professional who is familiar with these techniques assist with the training, because when the dog's drive is released, it will first come out as aggression. The owner may be shocked that such an ugly mood is inside his dog, but it has been brewing there for some time. The training exercise, although it produces the aggressive response, is the first healthy expression the dog has enjoyed in some time. Don't correct the dog! He most desperately needs praise in this moment so that his drive can assume a more direct and pure expression. Becoming aggressive is the first step in the recovery process.

PHASE FOUR: INCREASING STAMINA

After the dog is proficient in sustaining contact over short distances and is excited by the shock, the next step is to increase the dog's drive with lots of changes in direction, to make contact over longer distances. This can be done by strongly blocking the hunting mood. The technique is to shock the dog for breaking off the contacting when he's lost interest before the handler has released him with an *OK* signal.

Command *Hup* and reward the dog as usual, but taper off your praise as you continue to backpedal. Allow the dog to break off the contact as he loses interest in the handler, and when his front feet hit the ground, make a shock on the lead and collar, run away as fast as you can, at the same time telling the dog how good he is. The dog should quickly make up the lost ground and renew the contacting. Praise the dog profusely for this positive response.

As the dog makes contact, continue to walk backward with tiny waddle steps so that the dog is working to sustain the contacting.

The important thing the dog is learning here is to stay committed to the group mood and to cover ground to remain with his handler.

In the next three or four sessions, work on increasing the dog's stamina in maintaining his focus as he covers ground to make contact with his handler. Remember that this is very difficult work for the dog because his nervous process is still telling him to look for a hunting stimulus. Try to increase his stamina in small increments, a few extra yards at each session.

The dog's drive to maintain contact should be developed to the point where he will work with full focus on his handler while they're moving together for about fifty feet. After this distance is achieved, the handler should engage the dog in contacting and a brief play session.

The critical point with this technique is to keep the lead loose. As the jerk on the lead is made, the handler should verbally praise the dog, then quickly backpedal. The handler becomes a lightning rod for the dog's drive energy because of his praise and because he's moving away from the dog.

By this point, all but the most sensitive dogs can be worked on a pinch collar.

PHASE FIVE: THE SAFETY POSITION

At this point we have an opportune moment to teach the dog that there is a safety position he should work to attain whenever he is shocked. This will be an added signal we can develop so that later we can attract the dog to our left side when we finish the heeling training. We've been planning for this since the dog was being encouraged to make contact, but now I want the handler to take the time to develop this one particular training tool.

While the dog is making contact with you, make a point of massaging under his chin with your left hand as you feed him with your right. At the same time, in a low voice, praise the dog with your most soothing tone.

Gently disengage from the dog by shifting all of his weight onto your left hand as you step back six inches or so away from the dog. All the while as you lower the dog to the ground, sustain the contact with the dog with your left hand. Then, when the dog is near the ground, command *Sit* as you guide him with the food.

To help the dog make the transition from an excited state of focus on his handler, you can tighten up on the lead with your right hand

and give the dog a little jerk toward your belt. This way, the dog will end up sitting snugly in front of you as his front feet make contact with the ground.

As the dog goes to sit, step back in close to the dog with the rest of your body and make the exact same kind of soothing and massaging praise underneath the dog's chin. A piece of food would be appropriate here as well.

Then, the handler commands *Hup*, breaks away by backpedaling at a quick pace, and engages the dog again with contacting. Put the left hand under the chin again, disengage, and have the dog sit as before.

The point of this exercise is to train the dog that the left hand is a place of safety. Later we can train him that the left side of the handler is the place of safety by luring him to our side with the open palm of our left hand. When he nestles his snout in our clasp, our right hand can reward him with food.

This is a necessary precaution because it's likely that the dog will be under some stress, and this teaches him how to deal with it. If later in the training program you see your dog trying to avoid your left side, either by diving between your legs or trailing behind you as you come into a turn, it's because not enough time was spent in this area.

PHASE SIX: BEGINNING THE AUTOMATIC SIT

Now the dog can be encouraged, and then trained, to disengage from the contacting and sit automatically when the handler stops attracting the dog's group instinct.

Sitting is a natural position for a dog when he's attracted to something but not quite triggered to take action toward it. This reflex to sit automatically is already on file in the dog's inner computer; it doesn't have to be created. The handler should first work on putting the dog into the proper mood of being attracted so that the reflex to sit is at the surface of the dog's temperament. The worst thing to do is to command *Sit* from out of the blue. The dog learns that a change associated with that sound is bad; he fills with resistance and can only work sluggishly. Before you give the dog the command, he must first be trained, and to be trained he must first be attracted to his handler.

This mood of attraction fits in perfectly with our system. The dog has already learned that sit is a position of focus on his handler, and, since the handler isn't moving, to wait patiently for the next stimulation from the handler.

The first step is to get the dog excited, backpedal, and command *Hup*. As the dog makes contact and is being rewarded up at the handler's level, produce some food with your hand and position it over the dog's head and slightly away from your body mass. With your other hand tighten up on the lead.

As the dog starts to show an inclination to sit, the *Sit* command can be issued with a sharp tone and rising inflection. When the dog is sitting give him the food.

This can be repeated many times in one session. If the dog works better for a ball, that can be tried, but food is the best way because the session isn't interrupted by the chasing sequences. Moreover, some dogs are overly stimulated by the ball, and this new mood of attraction is not yet able to channel such high drive.

As you progress, the dog is learning by the contrast in his handler's body language. One moment the handler is going very fast and the dog is driving to make contact. The next moment, the handler becomes still and the dog is encouraged to sit. The more the handler dramatizes the difference between these two moods, the quicker the dog will learn to anticipate the sit position as the handler stops.

After several sessions, the mere tightening of the lead should be all the help the dog needs to disengage and collect himself into a sit without a command. This cue trains the dog to sit automatically without the incentive of the food visibly at hand. Then the food can be produced and given to the dog. Also, the dog should be massaged under the chin as a further reward.

Once the dog has mastered sitting immediately for the food, it's time to train the dog that a shock is a stimulation to sit.

Engage the dog in contacting on the *Hup* command, then abruptly stop and simultaneously shock the dog with a hard tug on the leash. Then give the dog the command *Sit* as he gathers himself into that position. Make the jerk as soon as you stop so that the dog associates the stopping with the shock. The command *Sit* is being used to help the dog deal with the shock and to associate it with the mood to sit that the shock helped engender.

The point of the shock is not to correct the dog, but to neutralize the dog's nervousness, which in this case is a hyperstimulation toward the handler, as the dog didn't notice that the handler stopped.

Continue this session until the dog breaks off the contacting as soon as you stop and no shocks on the collar are needed.

When the dog has mastered this phase it's time to add a new twist. This step trains the dog that the sit position is a substitute for contacting.

Get your dog really fired up, backpedal, but don't command *Hup*. As the dog closes the gap and starts to leave the ground out of his own enthusiasm to make contact with you, abruptly stop and command *Sit* before the dog makes actual contact.

Make a shock on the lead as you stop, and then use your left hand to absorb his contacting and to guide the dog into the sit position. Massage under the dog's chin as he's sitting. As the dog becomes calm about sitting, give him a piece of food.

Then, the dog is commanded *Hup* as an additional reward, which completes the learning cycle that *Sit* is a substitute for making contact with the handler.

Since this is a new behavior for the dog I only use it as a substitute for contacting on an intermittent basis. As the dog gets more advanced with his training, the ratio of sits to contacts can get higher and higher. Eventually, from the dog's point of view, the sit will come to have the same connectedness value to his handler as does the actual contacting.

PHASE SEVEN: CONFLICT TRAINING

In this step we train the dog that by making contact with his handler he gets to make contact with a distraction. (With the problem dog we are going to use the distraction as a device to put the dog in conflict, which raises his drive. Then the dog can learn to channel this drive back into his handler.)

Using another dog that is friendly with yours is best, but if none is available you can use a person offering a food treat, a ball, or a favorite toy.

If you own two dogs, one could be tied out as the distraction, and he can carry on while you train the other one. Later you can switch the dogs around.

If you find yourself on a city street and dogs are all around (but of course not participating in your training program), carry a ball or food to use as a reward for your dog making contact on command.

If your dog is aggressive to other dogs, just work your dog

around other dogs. If his fighting instinct is very high he may not be interested in either a ball or food even if he's fasted. In that case the contacting is reward enough for this kind of temperament. This kind of dog will be covered in more depth in the section on aggression in the Training the Down/Stay chapter, but it can be noted here that in some cases it's best to postpone the conflict work until the dog has perfected the down training. Usually, these kinds of dogs have a lot of problems with the down exercise, and solving them is a good springboard to solving their aggressive problem.

The critical point in this training phase is that the dog must make and sustain contact with his handler until released by the OK signal. As the dog is making contact with his handler, the handler goes through all of the phases that led up to this one. He fakes going left and right, he runs away, he shocks the collar as the dog is stimulated to chase him, he engages the dog in contacting, and then collects him into a sit. In the course of running through these steps the dog ends up sitting in front of his handler next to the distracting dog.

Then the dog is commanded *Hup*, and finally he's released with an OK signal to play with his friend. The dog learns that an intense focus on his handler yields the highest drive flow (the play session with the other dog).

When the dog attempts to make contact with the distracting dog on his own initiative (hunting mood), he experiences a shock.

This step is different from the collective purpose phase because of the intensity of the distraction and the degree of focus the dog must sustain while he's making contact with his handler.

This phase is effective even if your dog isn't going to get to play with these other dogs. The imperative point is that the dog must make contact and that the handler compels the dog to focus on himself. Thus, all the draw the dog feels for the distraction becomes channeled into his handler; no instinct came to fulfillment when he was focused on the distraction. The faster the handler works his dog, the more this effect will be true.

If your dog has a strong attraction to a ball, then after sustaining his contact toward his handler under these trying circumstances, he can be given a good ball throw on the long lead as a reward.

When a dog is made to do something that requires a lot of exertion he ends up emotionally spent and calm about being focused on his handler rather than on the distraction. There is no margin for error with this exercise. If the dog isn't 100 percent committed to his handler, the dog is still in conflict and will never be reliable off lead. But if the dog ends up perfectly focused on his handler, he'll never miss, by comparison, the stimulation of the distraction.

PHASE EIGHT: HEELING ON THE LEFT

During these building steps, you may have sensed that your dog is primed to pop right into position on the left side of the handler. Now the time is right to put all of the smaller steps together to get very close to the finished behavior we're striving for.

In general, whenever you give the dog a new twist to learn, repeat the first lesson he learned by commanding *Hup* and engaging the dog in contacting. Being with the handler is always the answer, either as a reward after an improvement or to convert a correction into a stimulation of the group mood. So even though the dog is advanced to being on the handler's left side, never hesitate to use contacting as a reward for surmounting a new learning obstacle.

Command the dog *Hup*, make contact, disengage, and then as you are backpedaling, slowly turn to your right, continuing to move along a straight line in the same direction in which you started backpedaling away.

As you turn to your right, use your left hand to guide the dog into position alongside your left thigh by alternately touching underneath the dog's chin and patting your thigh as you move along. As you do this, give him a lot of verbal encouragement.

If he's moving along smoothly with you, pat him on his ribs on his left side, being careful to maintain a smooth pace as you do so. Then, as you're walking, flick your left hand against the right side of his chin to keep his focus on you in cadence with your gait. Find the speed at which your dog feels most comfortable. Too fast and he may get overly stimulated; too slow and he may lose drive.

If there is no resistance in the dog's system, you can sense a certain bounce to his gait. It's helpful if the handler tries to "catch it" and match it with his own stride. If you are able to get in sync with your dog in this way, your verbal praise to celebrate the event will become a very powerful motivation to your dog.

Once the dog is in position on the left side, the handler can flick the dog's right cheek with his left hand, and then instead of patting his left thigh the handler can pat his own chest to raise the dog's focus toward his face. I also will tease a dog I'm training with a tidbit as we're heeling, and then, cupping my right hand around it, hold the food tight to my chest, wiggling my hand somewhat. Instinctively, the dog's gaze will be drawn to my eyes to see when he's going to get his treat. It's important to work toward this clear focus because it means that the dog is solidly in his group mood.

In the beginning just go straight ahead with your dog on your left side for very short distances of ten to twenty feet. Then reward the dog with contacting. Keep careful note of your dog's stamina threshold. He may be able to go for ten, thirty, or fifty feet before he starts to break down (reverts to a hunting instinct); before that point, get the dog's attention, switch directions, and engage the dog in contacting. I'll reach down and bump the dog's rear end with my hand in a playful manner, hoot, and then reverse direction, teasing him with a tidbit by waving my hand at his nose level.

If the dog is stimulated by changes in the handler's direction, then constantly turning to the right can be used as an additional stimulation to get the dog to maintain his focus on his handler. As you make this rounded-off right turn, the handler can give the command *Heel* in a soft tone. Also, be sure to use the left hand to guide the dog along through the turn. Now, should the dog forge ahead, position the food or ball over his head and make left turns.

In the first few sessions the handler's emphasis should be on motivating the dog to want to be on the handler's left side, instead of correcting the dog for mistakes. Therefore, we want to do something to attract the dog to his handler and maneuver our body in such a way relative to his that the dog just happens to be on the left side by being attracted to us.

After we see that a strong behavior has been created in the dog's mind to be on the handler's left side, the dog can be shocked for losing that calm focus in later training sessions.

The command *Heel* can be introduced in a firm and commanding tone as we see that this heeling behavior on the left side is becoming strong.

Use of the ball and food is critical in increasing a dog's stamina. Heel with the dog for a short distance; before you sense the dog is going to lose his focus on you, reward him with a ball throw or the food. Then engage him again in contacting, disengage and encourage the dog to get into the heeling position, and work on his stamina again.

Up until this phase of training the dog has been trying to go straight at the handler because he wants to make contact and the handler has been facing the dog and backpedaling. The dog may still try to get in front of the handler now that he finds himself on your left side. If that's the case, just go faster and tone down your praise to help him get over this hump. Don't be concerned if the dog is not yet precise; it's enough just to motivate him.

When you're working the dog on your left side the leash should have an inch of slack in it and it should be held in the right hand at hip level. The dog's head should be near your left thigh and cocked up toward your head.

A common handler error is to keep the lead tight, either by choking up on it or by raising the lead hand above hip level. This is human nature because most handlers want their dogs to avoid making mistakes, thinking this shows improvement. But bear in mind that the dog doesn't learn anything by being steered into position; *he has to choose* how to position his body so that he's on the handler's left side. Since being focused in the group mood is the key to success, we have to give the dog ample opportunity to learn that a hunting instinct is unsuccessful.

The loose lead stimulates the dog to be attentive to his handler because he can only know where his handler is by maintaining eye contact. To repeat, the tight lead has the effect of stimulating the dog to resist the handler, which dampens the attraction.

From a practical point of view, we need the lead to be loose so that this training works when we take the lead off. By loose, I mean one inch of slack. As soon as the dog drops his head down from the focus on his handler position, or looks off to the side, the handler makes a lightning-quick shock with the lead and immediately speeds up and praises the dog. After a shock, the dog must always be stimulated, as the dog is doing something that requires action. Should the dog not become energized by the shock, then spend more time on building his stamina by teasing him with the food or ball each time he loses focus.

After several sessions of the dog doing very well, don't be surprised if the dog starts to drop his nose down or tries to go ahead toward the horizon again. After traveling a short distance it's normal for the attraction to wear out and for a hunting instinct to come bubbling to the surface again. When that happens, shock the dog and backpedal in the *opposite* direction. The correction shocks him out of the hunting mood and stimulates him back into a group instinct.

Make the shock before making any *Heel* command and before the dog notices your change of direction, because the dog's mind has already drifted into the hunting mood and that's the issue that needs to be dealt with. If you call the dog's attention to you before the shock, the shock is attributed to the handler and the attraction is dampened. By default, the hunting mood grows.

After the shock, go only a short distance backward and then engage the dog in a contacting session and reward him for choosing to be in his group mood. Be sure to go backward in a line that is 180 degrees opposed to the direction that the dog's hunting mood wanted to take him. This has the effect of neutralizing the drive completely in that direction because drive is "spatially sensitive." This way the dog more effectively learns that the group instinct to make contact is the answer since it's going in the opposite direction of the hunting mood.

Continue this training to increase your dog's stamina to work precisely on your left, to remain focused on his handler, and to be patient for his reward. Also note that after a shock the dog's focus on you becomes especially intense. So reward him generously with food so that he gains confidence in this sensitive mood.

Since heeling properly is so unnatural for a dog, the handler should always review these phases. The emphasis should be on building the dog's spirit higher and higher and being sure it stays channeled in the behaviors we've been shaping. While it may seem like a lot of steps, a good session of heeling that reviews everything needn't last more than two or three minutes.

The next chapter will deal with some other specialized aspects to training the dog to heel as well as some typical problem behaviors that may be encountered.

24

Heel: Problem Solving and Polishing

PROBLEM SOLVING

IF A DOG HAS A *learning block*, you will find that he wants to avoid being on the left side of the handler and doesn't get into drive. He's either stuck in trying avoidance behaviors or grudgingly submissive obedience responses, or he'll grit his teeth, endure, and try to maintain his old hunting mood.

This type of dog starts to lag behind and you'll find the lead is always tight. He's burdened with resistance, his whole body bound up with dread of a correction, and as he grows more nervous he moves more and more slowly.

The worst thing to do is to engage this dog in a struggle and to increase your pressure. That's exactly how the dog is misinterpreting your attempts to motivate him, and we don't want to confirm his negative expectations.

With this kind of dog you have to go very slowly from the backpedaling position, to the position where the dog is on the left side. The dog has had a bad experience learning how to become subordinate to his handler and that takes patience to work through.

Engage the dog in contacting and start to backpedal, then walk sideways so that you're half facing him and the dog can always see his opportunity to make contact with you.

As you see the dog enthusiastically work to keep up with you, slowly turn your body to the right, in no particular hurry to get the dog into the correct heel position. The problem for this dog is that when he can't directly see his opportunity to make contact his drive shuts off and he tries to avoid the handler. He has associated being on the handler's left side with that negative drive flow condition. It will take time to nurse him into the left side, with both the dog and the handler facing forward. Your work is to gradually bend the dog's drive (the relaxed nerves make the dog's drive supple and it can be bent). When the nerves are brittle and you give the dog's drive a corner to go around, it can only break as he perceives any change as a dead end.

One must be very sensitive with such a dog, when he's at the point where he's ready to break down into avoidance behaviors again. Before that happens, I'll revert from the heeling position back to the sideways gait and engage the dog in contacting as a reward for drive flow. Or, if his drive seems strong enough, I'll try to encourage him back to my left side.

This kind of dog needs frequent stops and play sessions to build up his stamina. The dog can also benefit by being fasted and using a food morsel as a magnetic draw to your left side. As he reaches forward to grab the food, pick up your pace little by little and try to get him to break into a run. Also, to build up this dog's spirit, he should be encouraged to pull you around on a lead, thereby lessening his inhibition.

Another technique that's effective, especially with sensitive dogs that are easy to arouse in their group mood, is to collect the dog into a sit and massage him under his chin with your left hand as you hold the lead with your right hand. As your dog is enjoying this massaging, move your left hand away from his chin and pat your left thigh with it. As you see the dog becoming aroused, gently command *Heel*, make a quick spin in a half circle, and collect the dog back into a sit. The quick turning after the stimulation of the praise is an attraction to the dog's drive to stay focused in the group mood and to move his body accordingly. This exercise is easier work for a sensitive dog than the heeling in an open area.

The dog is learning to be with his handler on the left side, but he's learning it relative to the changes of direction before having to do it in a straightaway pattern.

When you stop, help the dog into a sit if necessary, massage his chin again, and repeat. If the dog gains in enthusiasm, you can straighten out the turn and prolong it into a few straightaway steps so that the dog starts to learn the straight-ahead portion of the heeling exercise. End the session with a contacting and play session.

FORGING

Dogs with a strong hunting drive will tend to forge. The problem is that the dog isn't focused in a group instinct; he's not attracted to his handler. The first step in dealing with this problem is an inductive training technique that shows him how to make left turns. (See page 229 and the section About-Turns to the Left.)

In this case, a shock should be made, followed by a command to make contact, and then a ball can be thrown so that the dog learns that his hunting drive can come to fruition, but only by being attracted to his handler. Once the dog learns this connection he grows calm and is in a position to learn what heeling is all about.

NERVOUS DOGS

Nervous dogs tend to get stressed, and then they press in very hard on the handler's left leg and may even attempt to dive between his legs. They are burdened by their drive going in an unnatural direction and they need to be relaxed like the sensitive dogs.

Also, the dog is confused about what his handler wants. In the past the owner may have pressured the dog and he has learned to deflect the pressure by acting submissive, usually by lying down. This is what the dog now tries to show his handler.

Any positive inducement to calm the dog is helpful, but the problem can be best addressed in the automatic sit training that will be discussed later in this chapter. The handler should go back and review the contacting and disengaging into the sit position as preparation for that.

Some nervous dogs are hyperstimulated and anxious about the group instinct especially when the group gets rolling. These dogs are trying to show active submission to their owners and often will try to get directly in front of them. Some spectacular upendings can result with the dog so underfoot.

With such a dog, I once again try to relax him and build up his self-confidence about being in his group mood and dealing with the commotion of moving together with his handler. I'll use the mood swings of going very fast to going very slow as a means of focusing the dog's drive with a steady stream of food to reassure him that every change isn't a discordant reminder of the old pack mood. Another antidote for the problem of active submission will be discussed later in the program when we train the dog to lie down. Training the dog to lie down very fast out of the heeling exercise will inhibit the dog's nervousness when he is in the group mood.

OVERENTHUSIASTIC DOGS

Another problem area, particularly for outgoing dogs, is when the handler makes the dog heel at a fast pace and the dog gets over-excited, jumps up, and *tries to grip the handler*. This dog needs to get a shock on the lead at the moment he leaves the ground. At the same time, the handler must continue to heel straight ahead. The dog is simply showing us too much of a good thing and only needs a little tempering rather than correcting.

A common handler error, while logical, is to stop and tell the dog *NO*, and then repeat the *Heel* command. However, this is only training the dog that heeling involves a struggle, that it's a stop-and-go affair. A dog can't connect the stop with the go.

With such a boisterous dog, the solution (after having redoubled your efforts in using food or the ball to deflect the urge to bite) is to go as fast as you can, and to shock the dog as hard as you can. The dog has to learn what to do with all his drive (running at full tilt beside his handler) rather than being confronted over being high in drive.

After the shock, the pace can gradually slow and the dog can be calmly praised for heeling in a calm manner. As you see the dog becoming simultaneously contained yet still attracted to the handler, slow down to a very slow walk with even more intense praise. It's imperative that the dog work very precisely; don't let the dog's enthusiasm break out of this contained mood.

As you go slowly, you may find the dog gets rather antsy, and this fidgeting should be inhibited by a series of staccato-type shocks on the collar as you continue to praise him for the slow walking style. Be sure to shock the dog for becoming nervous; don't wait for the dog to make an overt mistake by jumping up or pulling hard ahead. Only a focused, calm attitude toward the handler is acceptable.

After the dog has been shocked several times, reward him with food and engage him in a rough contacting session, break away into a rapid heeling pace, and then throw a ball for him to outlet some of his drive and to complete the learning that the prey instinct doesn't belong targeted on the handler's body.

AUTOMATIC SIT

The automatic sit is a good barometer of where the dog's head is at. When a dog is high in drive, when his nerves are relaxed, and when he's fully focused in his group instinct, he will sit automatically and quickly when the handler stops. It's an involuntary response. And, if the dog will sit quickly, he will sit straight at the handler's side as well.

Where the dog aligns himself is a very good indication of how he defines his relationship with his handler, especially relative to high drive. A straight sit parallel to the handler, which is the preferred position, isn't a trivial matter from the dog's point of view. When we train a dog to heel, we are training him to be subordinate to his master, *to be by his handler's side*. The dog's temperament feels what the instinctive issues are in this work and what's at stake here.

If the dog doesn't sit properly, it could mean he is nervous about his handler, is overly stimulated toward his handler, or is burdened with a lot of resistance. Unsureness resulting from a pack instinct (submission or dominance) can make the dog want to get in front of the handler. A flight instinct can make the dog want to kick his rear end out wide away from the handler when sitting.

In training the dog to execute this exercise flawlessly we are polishing his character to fit smoothly and calmly into his master's.

We were also encouraging this reflex in the dog when we were disengaging from him in the contacting sessions. We helped him assume the sit position with the left hand and by subtly tightening the lead held in the right hand.

So, go very fast in your heeling pattern, stop, abruptly jump backward one step, and engage the dog in contacting. Then, command *Heel* and go forward again. Stop, and make contact as before.

The next time, start to slow down and switch the lead to your left hand. Let the lead grow tight as you stop, which gives the dog a subtle cue of the impending change. It also puts the handler into position to arrest the dog's forward motion so that the dog remains beside his handler.

Command *Sit* as you stop with a rising inflection. Sit is a position of action for a dog so the tone, while crisp, shouldn't be harsh but attractive.

As you command *Sit* you can reach across with your right hand, holding it back and over the dog's head, which will cause the dog to look up at the food cupped within it. This action, coupled with your change of speed (stopping), encourages the dog to sit quick and straight as you stop.

For several sessions you can continue to assist the dog as described above. But soon it's time to assess the dog's attitude. If he is fully focused and committed to being with his handler, he is soon anticipating the impending stop and sitting without any help or command whatsoever.

If you find this is not the case, the dog will have to be shocked for either being nervous or distracted by his hunting mood.

Start to heel with the dog, allowing his mind to drift away, and when you sense he's not paying attention, make a very strong shock on the collar, jump backward, and engage the dog in a spirited contacting session.

Disengage and heel away. Test the dog again as you heel to see if his mind drifts off again. As soon as it does, shock the dog again and repeat the contacting.

The third time, heel with the dog very fast, making sure the dog is highly attracted to you, jump backward, and engage the dog in contacting. Disengage, heel away very fast, and then stop abruptly; the dog will sit automatically and correctly.

Praise the dog intensely for this proper response. If he appears to be a little nervous or unsure, or confused, then not enough motivational work was done with food and his sense of touch, as discussed in the Training Tools and Equipment chapter.

GOING VERY SLOWLY

This exercise really solidifies in the dog's mind what heeling is all about. It's very hard work for a dog to walk slowly and yet be high in drive and intently attentive toward his handler. For that reason the exercise should be spaced in between periods of very fast heeling. The handler commands *Heel* and moves out at a very brisk pace but with little praise, then he repeats the command *Heel* and goes very slowly, but with intense physical and verbal praise. When the dog shows that he's happily attracted to his handler, command *Heel* and move out at an even faster clip. The dog will learn to blend the slow pace with the overall drive flow of the preceding and following session of fast heeling. If the dog starts to put his nose to the ground, repeat the first lesson, *Hup,* and make contact. Then repeat the above exercise.

ABOUT-TURNS TO THE RIGHT

The only turns we really have to train for are the about-turns, where the handler completely reverses his direction. When the dog is correctly focused on his handler simple left or right turns require only minimal work as the foundation was already laid in our early training.

Training the dog to heel should be done in wide-open spaces so that you can really stretch the dog out and give his group instinct a good exercise by long, straight heeling legs.

As you come to the edge of your training area, you'll encounter a new problem: turning the dog around. Should the handler always turn to the left, the dog will develop a lagging tendency. That's because he has to inhibit his drive somewhat since he's on your inside and has to go slower than the handler to stay even. Therefore, do many turns to the right; then the dog has to go faster than the handler, which requires more drive. This is the proper spirit to cultivate in the dog.

Since the dog has to go faster than his handler, the dog will tend to spin off out of orbit and degrade into a hunting mood. So after the turn, pick up your speed as a reward.

As you're going through the turn, monitor your dog's head position very closely and shock him for any deviation from the heads-up and focused position.

Many handlers tend to choke up on the lead and try to steer the dog through the turn. That has exactly the opposite effect and actually trains the dog to go wide and not to pay close attention to his handler.

As you come out of the turn heading in the opposite direction, feed the dog or throw the ball.

ABOUT-TURNS TO THE LEFT

Turning to the left is really just an extension of the automatic sit and you may find your dog trying to sit as you make this turn.

The first step is to be sure the dog is especially aroused in the group mood and paying close attention to you. When the dog is excited about being with his handler we are going to give him some instinctive reasons for making the left turn. Finally, we will package all this learning into the *Heel* command.

Before you start with this training, do some heeling on a straight stretch and quickly jump backward and engage the dog in some contacting several times. After this the dog will be paying very close attention to you. When he's focused this way, start to slow down and lean over the dog as you turn to your left, drawing his attention to a morsel of food that you are cupping over his head. To get the dog to check his forward progress, press the food against his muzzle so that he must stop to eat. Open your hand to oblige him as you make the turn. These stimulations, when combined, allow you to complete the left turn with the dog high in drive, focused on his handler, yet almost backpedaling to accommodate his handler.

As an additional reward, go very fast on the straightaway after the turn and praise the dog enthusiastically. You can also engage the dog in contacting and a ball throw as a way to end the training session.

Many handlers are taught to use their left knee to ram the dog in his head or shoulder area so that he gets out of their way as they turn to their left. This does train the dog to get out of the way, but unfortunately, it also trains him to avoid his handler. At any rate, this approach, besides being ineffective, isn't at all necessary.

Any problems you encounter with this exercise are because the dog isn't high enough in his group drive. If the dog were aroused and focused in a group instinct, he would notice the handler giving some subtle body language that would stimulate him to try to sit. The dog should always be watching his handler's body language for any hint of a change. He is almost always on the verge of sitting automatically, except that his handler is constantly in motion, save for occasional stops.

Once the dog is aroused and focused in this behavior, the *Heel* command can be given before the turn is made. As this behavior grows stronger in the dog's mind, when he is shocked for not being attentive he will become even more attracted to his handler.

Training the dog to heel very slowly on a straight leg also helps in training the dog to make about-turns to the left. For example, you could heel very slowly, command *Heel*, make the left turn, and then run as you straighten out and give the dog lots of praise.

In another technique the dog can be caught napping. I'll race very fast ahead with the dog and then out of the blue do a left turn. The dog is caught hopelessly out of position, but the dog isn't shocked. Instead, he is encouraged with the ball or food to make contact again. That's always the answer: By being more attentive to the handler and stimulated in his group instinct, the dog can learn to be more and more precise.

PHASE NINE: CONFLICT TRAINING

Now that the dog has all the tools he needs to solve problems, it's time to expose him to distractions. It's best to use another dog that's playful with yours, but you could simply take the dog to a busy area. A city park or a grassy area next to a shopping center would be fine.

All one has to do is repeat the steps from the beginning to the end. This can be done in one five-minute session.

First, command the dog to make contact, then proceed to the distraction: the friendly dog, with whom your dog gets to play or some food or a ball if you're working by yourself. Let the dog play with his buddy, then have your helper pull this dog away. Both dogs must be on leads.

Command your dog *Heel* and go very fast away from the group, then make an about-turn and heel slowly toward the group. As you near you will sense your dog starting to slip into conflict. His focus will waver, and he may whine or make play motions toward the other dog. At that point tighten the lead and praise the dog and then explode back into a run away from and back again, ending with a contacting session ten feet away. After the contact, release your dog with an OK signal to resume playing with his friend.

Then wade into the fray, grab your dog by the collar and praise, and command *Heel* in an emphatic tone. Go very fast out of the group, about-turn, and proceed slowly back toward the group, then speed up and go past the group again at a lightning clip, contacting as a reward for the dog being focused as you passed the distraction. Then release the dog to play.

As the dog's drive toward the distraction starts to flow into the handler in order to get to the distraction, the automatic sit can be added to test that the dog is both high in drive and relaxed about being fully focused toward his handler.

From a distance, proceed toward the group at a very fast pace and stop abruptly in front of the dog. When the dog sits automatically, command *Hup*, contact, and release the dog to play.

If the dog fails to sit automatically, heel again very fast toward the distracting dog. At the point where you want to stop and train the dog to sit automatically, reverse your direction without warning and shock the dog. Command *Hup* and make contact. Heel away from the group and return, going very fast, and do exactly the same thing. On the third try, stop without any command, testing for the automatic sit. The dog should comply willingly.

25

Training the Sit/Stay

STANDARD OF PERFORMANCE

WHEN THE DOG IS MADE to sit and told to stay he will hold that position until released. He should be highly focused on his handler to the exclusion of any distractions.

CONCEPT

There are three basic problems for a dog to solve in learning how to stay put: 1) the length of time the dog has to stay; 2) how far the owner goes from the dog; 3) to resist all distractions around him.

FROM THE DOG'S VIEWPOINT

The easiest way to train the dog is to tackle the above problems one at a time. The training can be done simultaneously as long as each problem is addressed in separate lessons. A lesson should last only three to five minutes. When the dog is calm about each problem they can be combined.

Solving these three problems requires the same mood in the dog: the predictability of success within the group mood.

Duration

The first step is to introduce this exercise to the dog in a relaxed fashion. Let the dog relieve himself, then go out away from any distractions. Collect the dog into a sit position without turning it into a struggle. Simply arrange for the dog to be in the heel position, then pull up on the collar and push down on the dog's rear end. Say *Sit* only as he starts to sit. I want to concentrate here on focusing the dog's attention on the stay exercise and not on training to sit, so there's no need to make sit an issue.

When the dog is sitting calmly, produce a piece of food. I prefer to use food over the ball or contacting because the drive involved is a calmer instinct in which to learn.

Show the dog the food in your hand then gently stimulate him by shaking your hand. At the same time, command in a firm but not hostile tone, *Stay*. The left hand should be holding the lead with only one inch of slack so that the dog is working freely but you're still in a position to control the dog.

Be poised to correct the dog for any nervous fidgeting. Don't wait for him to break; we want to affect his emotional process, not his motor responses. Be 100 percent attentive and ready, and when he shows any nervousness by fidgeting or whining, quickly snug up on his choke collar and repeat *Stay*, being careful to keep the dog in the sit position. It's very important here not to start backing up to adjust to your dog. Keep your feet rooted to the original place and make it uncomfortable for the dog to try to get away. Meanwhile, try to keep a steady stream of food flowing so that drive can start to displace nervousness.

Don't let the dog bend down to the ground to clean up any morsels he may have dropped. He has to be trained to eat calmly from your hand. The dog is only to receive success in his group instinct by maintaining a constant focus on his handler's activity with the food.

As you progress with this lesson over the next few days, start to stretch out the length of time in which you deny your dog the reward. Slowly increase how much you shake your hand with the food and how much you move it around, and shift your weight a little bit, so that the dog learns that calmness and attentiveness toward *Stay* produces his success.

The point of using the food is to calmly train the dog that the spoken word of the handler has a positive impact on the simple, natural instinct of eating. Meanwhile, the handler can both hold the lead and massage the dog's back and rump with his left hand so that there is no resistance between them.

The dog is clear on this exercise when he demonstrates patience, no matter how much you move the food or how long you make him wait for it. Working the dog up to the point of waiting for one or two minutes will be sufficient for our purposes.

I conclude the exercise by releasing the dog with a *Hup* command and by jumping back and encouraging the dog to make contact with me. Then, when the dog is focused on me a ball is produced and thrown to him. The lesson ends with play. I'll use a second ball to reattract the dog as I want this to be fun and not obedience training. Nevertheless, if necessary, I'll have the dog on a thirty- or fifty-foot lead.

Distance

Now it's time for the dog to learn that *Stay* means *the handler will be right back*. Logically, that would suggest that the handler has to leave, but moving away from the dog would be an error since it would be putting him into conflict over his group instinct. I'll discuss this further at the end of the chapter, but for now let me say that a dog can only learn calmness if he feels that *Stay* causes the *return* of the handler, not his departure.

Rather than moving away, if we move around the dog in a very tight orbit, maintaining physical, verbal, and lead contact as we go, the dog will learn to ignore the natural attraction that our moving body exerts. As we're circling the dog we'll keep the lead somewhat tight near his right ear and we'll use a hand signal so the dog doesn't feel we're moving away from him.

Earlier, when we trained the dog to heel, the dog learned that the heel position on the left of the handler is a secure and pleasurable place to be. Now we'll use the heel position as the beginning and finish point for our orbit of the dog.

First, we want to arouse the dog's group instinct. We start with a very brisk heeling exercise on a long straight line, preferably in the middle of a spacious field. After going a prolonged distance the handler should stop abruptly. The dog automatically makes a fast and straight sit. This means that the dog is fully focused on his handler and that there is no resistance in his system.

The handler issues a *Stay* command and makes a hand signal. The hand signal is made by extending the left hand toward the dog's face.

Then, switch the lead back to your left hand and repeat the *Stay* command with your right hand. Gently touch him on his forehead and repeat the *Stay* command once again. Touch the dog only for a brief moment, and then withdraw your hand a few inches back into the *Stay* signal. If the dog makes any attempt to nuzzle or lick your hand he should be shocked, depending on how strong his attempt is.

Meanwhile, the left hand maintains a hold on the lead and keeps it a little tight to keep the dog from becoming excited by his handler's motion.

Next, exchange the lead to the left hand and reemphasize the stay command with the right hand. If the dog shows any stimulation or nervousness to this slight motion, he should be shocked.

Our next move will be to take a half step in front of the dog, but it's vital that the dog is calm before we move our entire body as this is a critical moment in his learning.

A dog gets a lot of important social information by studying people's body language, and this is an opportunity to teach him what we want him to feel about his handler's body language. Is it to be instinctively positive—is he going to follow the handler—or is it to be instinctively neutral—is he to stay put? When the dog figures out what instincts the master stimulates by command the handler can also use these commands to teach the dog what the body language of strangers is to mean to him.

When we're training a dog either to heel, stay, or come when called, we are training the dog that his handler's spoken command outweighs the instinctive information he's gathering through his other senses. Then the handler can condition the dog's temperament to what value any body language is to have, be it that of an animal, a child, or a stranger. The handling of the dog in this simple exercise is vital to our long-range objective that the world works for the dog through his owner's mastery of it.

Anytime we change our body language through our motion or height, we have to tell the dog what that is supposed to mean to his instincts. It's wrong to leave it up to the dog, to step out from the dog one inch without first giving the dog a command, which in this lesson is *Stay*. I'm making this a big point because in my experience working with thousands of dog owners, they universally make this mistake: They step away from the dog and then belatedly give the command, either *Heel* or *Stay*. The dog's nervous system processes information at a lightning-quick pace so the dog is being left to himself in that first instant to decide whether he should move out with the handler or stay in place. That's a critical error because we have to train the dog that all vital information comes from the handler's spoken command, the master's version of the group's order.

Stepping away from the dog is a big change for him; up until this point we have been making him highly attracted to our body motion by training him to heel, and now he has to learn to discriminate.

As I touch the dog after making the hand signal, I study the way he reacts. If he makes submissive gestures toward my hand, or if his tail is wagging a lot, that means he's not stable about staying in the sit position. When I move out he's likely to break. Therefore, as I touch him, I will give either a few preemptive jerks on the lead, or tighten the lead up even more, repeating the command as I do.

As you step out, shift the lead from your right hand to your left so the lead can stay fixed at the heel position by the dog's right ear. Be sure to command *Stay* before you adjust your lead or shift your feet.

Think of the lead as being secured to a post that doesn't allow it to budge and pivot. Most people, when trying to go around the dog, tend to drag the lead across the dog's chest or neck and this pressure, plus the handler's momentum, will cause the dog to get up to follow his owner. Keep the lead slightly taut by the dog's right ear as you walk around. It's a very delicate maneuver, so be very studied about every message you are conveying to the dog with your body and tone of voice, and with the lead.

As you circle around the dog it's OK to touch his forehead again if he looks like he's going to get up. Maintain this contact with one finger the entire time you're circling the dog if you have to.

With dogs that are really squirrely, I'll put my palm over their eyes and virtually cradle their head to get back to the heel position before they can see where I've gone. Should a dog get up despite your best efforts, calmly recollect the dog back into a sit position and keep circling him until you successfully complete one orbit without the dog getting up.

A common handling error with a dog that gets up is to start the exercise over again. That's a big mistake because the dog will interpret your "pulsation of effort" as a victory for his nervousness. Convey the impression through your calm and firm handling that only his patience produces his success. At all costs don't become frustrated. After the dog learns that you return, he will quickly gain in calmness.

As you circle the dog you have to be able to do two things at the same time: First, you have to give him the security that staying put is successful; next, you have to repress nervousness. It's not something one can learn by reading; it will have to be mastered by doing.

A clever training suggestion I heard once was to practice the lead techniques and vocal timing on a stuffed dog or chair. This is a great idea because when you get to your dog you won't have to remember what the words and the moves are. It'll be easier to learn the timing that way when you turn to your live student.

A critical moment arrives when you cross behind the dog as you orbit him. He may want to get up for a multitude of reasons. He could be excited, wanting to see where you're going, or he could become unsure with someone on his rear flank, out of view. You may have to contort your body so that you can simultaneously touch his forehead, then his shoulders or rear end, and then quickly touch the right side of his face to suggest your return, in order to have a calming influence on him. Keep the lead snug near his ear and get around him in a quick but smooth way.

This is another important moment for the dog. The simple act of turning his head away from his left shoulder to pick you up again over his right shoulder is the moment he learns to inhibit a natural impulse to respond to instinct in deference to the command *Stay*. He is in fact using his group instinct to discipline, or to inhibit, the motor response to get up. Naturally, he isn't doing this on his own; the handler's skill is contriving for this lesson to be learned. Be patient with yourself, because it's a tricky move. Take the time to master something that seems so simple. There's a lot going on in your dog's mind here and this is an opportunity to really develop a rapport with him. Watching him really learn your commands is exciting and gratifying, especially when you can see nervousness being converted into calm attraction to the handler.

Be careful not to let the dog get up upon your return. The dog must only experience success by being under your calm influence, not by nervously taking things into his own hands. If he should manage to get up, continue your efforts. Don't stop and start over, because the dog will get deeper into conflict and the notion that training is a struggle will have been reinforced by your pause.

When you return to the heel position, calmly pet the dog and slowly escalate your praise so that he gets somewhat excited; however, the dog is not allowed to get up. Don't give him any more praise than he can handle.

In order to maintain control over the dog while you praise him, shift the lead back into your right hand as you pet him with your left hand.

A common handling mistake at the point of return is to leave a gap, even of only a few inches, between the dog and the handler. A dog learns through physical reality, so give the dog full contact upon your reunion. Make sure there isn't any distance between the two of you. End up at the finish facing exactly in the direction you left at the beginning, dog and handler on parallel lines. Press against the dog with your left knee or thigh; with your left hand, massage his left rib cage and shoulder area. This dramatizes the positive sensation of the handler's return. Also, a strong but gentle style of petting/massaging absorbs the dog's drive so that it's easier for him to stay put. If you pet the dog too vigorously on the head, or pound him too hard on the side, or have frustration or aggression in your voice, you will put him into conflict and he will want to get up. This kind of praise is counterproductive because it makes the dog nervous instead of reinforcing the desired state of calmness.

By keeping control in all these moments, which are distinctly different from the dog's point of view, the dog learns that when the owner commands *Stay* and there is movement, it's to have an instinctively neutral value. When the handler returns it's a positive stimulation of his group instinct.

It will only take a few sessions before your dog will be "grooved" to the imminence of your return. You should start to see the dog becoming excited as you slide up next to him. When the dog starts to display this excitement after the third repetition, don't praise him as you normally do when you return to the heel position. Instead, command *Hup* and explode backward. Encourage your dog to make and sustain his contact with you as you continue to move away. When the dog is very enthusiastic, give him a *Heel* command and go once again into a straight and brisk heeling pattern.

Collect the dog into a sit and begin again. All told, three sets of three orbits would be sufficient to comprise a lesson that should only last five minutes.

The next step is to let the lead drop to the ground as you give the *Stay* command. Practice bending over and picking it up, commanding *Stay* with every change of body height. Since you haven't moved and returned, only praise the dog very softly so he doesn't misinterpret this new twist as an invitation to make contact with you and break the *Stay* command.

Next, command *Stay*, drop the lead, and walk around the dog in a circle of one meter. Keep your hand extended with the *Stay* signal and praise quietly when you return to the heel position. We don't want the dog to get too excited, since we have little means of control. As the dog shows calmness in this phase make the orbit bigger and bigger. Over several days you should be able to get it up to twenty yards easily enough. There's little need to go beyond that in terms of the *Sit/Stay* command.

At first, go around the dog only once, but when he's calm about the distance factor, you will find that you can go around the dog several times and in the opposite direction. Read your dog very carefully for the reemergence of any nervousness and determine exactly what tone to use to either calm or inhibit him.

To conclude the lesson, pick up the lead after returning to the heel position and reward with contacting, heeling, and then a good ball session. Be very disciplined in your timing of the command *Hup* before you move backward, just as you commanded *Stay* when you moved out.

Finally, we can combine duration and distance quite easily with the following exercise: Command *Stay* and step in front of your dog, facing him squarely. Have the lead gathered into your midsection. With your left hand, thrust the lead toward the right ear and repeat *Stay*. Walk around the dog back into the heel position. Start to build up the amount of time that you are facing your dog before you complete the orbit.

As the dog seems very calm about staying while facing you, take one step backward to the end of the lead when you're out in front of the dog. Build up the amount of time your dog will calmly wait here. Remember to thrust the lead toward the dog when you repeat the command *Stay* and circle the dog back to the heel position.

Then you can drop the lead, command *Stay*, walk five or ten yards out in front of your dog, wait several moments, and circle the dog, returning to the heel position. You're on your way to a well-trained pet.

Distractions

If the dog proves to be a willing worker, in that he shows calmness and patience, and enthusiastically heels as a reward for staying put, it's time to "harden" the behavior. As always in dog training, whenever you add something new, you do it within the context of the first lesson. This means that as we expose the dog to a variation in this exercise, the handler is either near the dog and/or will be making a small, tight orbit as he moves around the dog.

Start the training session with some contacting and some spirited heeling to arouse and focus the dog's group instinct. Command *Stay*, make a fast, tight orbit of the dog, and simultaneously jiggle the lead in front of him. You're no longer to hold the lead in the post position. Make very intense praise upon each return, and as you see the dog anticipating your return, make the jerks progressively stronger. The timing here is important because you're training the dog that the pressure from the front is a precursor to a joyous re-union. After three repetitions, do contacting, heeling, and then repeat.

What the dog is learning here is to tune out distractions like the snap of the lead by remaining in his group instinct and focusing on his handler. This establishes a strong foundation; the more energy put into the system, the more the energy reinforces and strengthens the group instinct and therefore the ability of the dog to wait for his owner's return. A distraction actually heightens the dog's com-mittment to staying.

The dog is also learning what a shock means. A snap on the lead and collar doesn't mean he's a bad dog; it simply means to stay put, as the handler will be right back. Even though to the logical mind it would seem we are correcting the dog, in the dog's mind, the shock is in fact a positive inducement, a stimulation to wait, and a reliable indicator that the handler will be right back.

This behavior could be hardened even further by having an assis-tant handler exert the pressure on a fifty-foot lead as you run around the dog in a bigger and bigger orbit. This exercise will show you how strong the dog's drive is as it courses through his group instinct. You will know the limit of your control before you ever take the dog off lead.

Now we want to train the dog to be resistant to other distrac-tions. As always, we will use the group instinct as the stimulation to stay and we will work close to the dog from the heel position.

Have a friend bring another dog, who is playful with your dog, toward you, but they should stop a fair distance away. Allow your dog to view them, physically and verbally praise him, and then jump backward, commanding *Hup*; then the dog must make contact. Quickly heel your dog back toward your friend, ending up closer than before. The helper advances again, cutting the distance between you in half, and repeat. On the third try, heel right up to the dog; if your dog makes an automatic sit, he's commanded to make contact with you and then released to play with his friend.

As your dog gets better at this maneuver, instruct your friend to start to play with the other dog, making more and more of a fuss over it. As your helper escalates the distraction, the handler should increase the dog's group instinct as he orbits the dog by more and more attractive body and verbal language, and by stronger snaps on the lead.

This is channeling the drive away from the hunting mood and back into the original group mood. The dog learns that by making contact with his handler, he eventually gets to make contact with a hunting buddy. Be sure not to use dogs that are aggressive with each other; that would give the dog more problems to solve that obscure the original intention of this lesson.

The exact same scenario can be done using people as the distraction.

All of the learning described in this chapter is on a straight line and is "clean" because it always raises the dog's drive flow. From the dog's point of view, even though we're constantly contradicting the natural flow of instincts, it's all part of the same continuum; his drive to his handler grows higher and higher and so it's easy for him to learn patience and calmness. All the outside distractions eventually are brought within the original group mood.

There really is no need to make the *Sit/Stay* command into a bigger lesson. Sit is a position that means ready for action for a dog, and it's wrong to use it if you're going to make the dog stay for a long period. For a dog, sitting is like standing at attention is for a soldier; it's hard work, and that's another reason not to use it much in everyday life. The *Sit/Stay* command is ideal, on the other hand, for making the dog behave when introducing him to company at the door or on the street. *Down/Stay* is much better for exercising control over an extended period under trying conditions. Down is a position of passivity and of low drive. A dog feels more secure when he's lying down; when he's made to sit and left alone he feels vulnerable. If you feel the need to train the dog to sit/stay for long spells, you could train for it the same way we'll train for down/stay later on. Stand/stay could also be approached in the same way.

Let's contrast this system of training the dog to stay with one that's "concept driven," because logic, which is how we survive in human society, is naturally going to compete in the handler's mind for the same space this system needs.

The first logical error we've already discussed: putting the dog in conflict over his group instinct when the handler walks away. A dog is a group animal, and his survival depends on staying in constant contact with his group. In that sense he's a lot like an infant baby. When a parent leaves a baby alone for a quick dash into another room, he constantly uses his voice to reassure the baby that although he's moved away, he's still near and almost on the verge of returning.

If we correct a dog for responding to his group instinct when he goes into conflict, he becomes unsure and defensive in that instinct. The group instinct becomes the source of the dog's problem instead of its solution, in other words, it becomes a pack instinct.

It's logical to think in terms of praise and punishment. If the dog stays, he's praised or rewarded. If the dog moves, he's corrected. With repetition the dog is supposed to learn logically that by staying put his owner is pleased and the dog is rewarded. Conversely, when he moves the owner becomes unhappy and the dog is corrected. It's assumed the dog will make this association to the command *Stay*.

What actually happens is that the dog is put into conflict over the group instinct and he learns to be inhibited, submissive, or defensive in order to cope with the situation. He will be made to sit when he's in that mood. He may even develop a little patience on his own because the handler does indeed return. However, this kind of learning is contingent on constructing a containment vessel of pressure around the dog. Because of this pressure the resulting pack instinct won't be able to handle a lot of excitement; when the dog is exposed to a strong distraction he weakens rather than being strengthened.

The training program is actually making the dog more sensitive to pressure instead of raising the genetic thresholds with which the dog was endowed. A training program should raise a dog's nervous thresholds and that is the main function of the stay exercise, as we will see in the *Down/Stay* command section.

The real value in training the dog to sit and stay is in preparation for the stay, particularly in the down training. In this *Sit/Stay* command exercise we are building and calming the dog's focus on his handler even when he's in conflict. A dog with full drive that is still composed enough to sit calmly is halfway to learning how to lie down on command.

26

Training the Dog to Down

STANDARD

No matter how excited the dog may be, he hits the ground as if shot when he hears the command *Down!* He becomes calm and fully focused on his handler at this point.

CONCEPT

For the dog *Down* means giving up all his drive energy to his handler. It's our primary means of training the dog to go our way instead of nature's way when he's off lead. Before we can train a dog to come in answer to his name, we have to train him to give up a chase, to stop him from leaving the group. Before we can train a dog to be quiet and not bark, we have to train him to be low in drive, to be calm. We can use *Down* to do these things, as well as anytime we need control. Once the dog is trained to down properly, it can be used to take him out of conflict, which helps him to learn calmness around the house and in social situations with strangers. *Down* ends confusion in the dog's mind between what his survival instincts are telling him to do and what his owner is telling him to do. In a moment of chaos you needn't fight your dog; simply command *Down*. In fact, I never scold my dog or discipline him in any way. Whenever he's doing something inappropriate, I make him lie down.

We need to differentiate between training the dog to a lightning-quick *Down* for control purposes and the more casual use of another command, such as *Lie down*, when you only want the dog not to be underfoot or to relax in a noncritical situation. Don't mix these up in your training program.

Verbal tone and inflection are very important. *Down!* should have a harsh tone and a descending inflection to it, in order to activate the reflex in the dog to drop down quickly.

FROM THE DOG'S POINT OF VIEW

For the dog, learning to lie down rapidly is natural in one sense and yet very difficult in another. Dogs quickly and instinctively drop down in the presence of danger, be it the approach of a fearsome predator or of an aggressive, superior member of their pack. However, when a dog is excited and happy about things, it's very hard for him to lie down, as a change of height means a change of mood. He has to go from being exuberantly excited to being subdued, and that's a very difficult transition that, if mismanaged, can easily generate resistance. In this program we will be going step by step so the dog will learn that the *Down* command, while necessitating a change of mood, is going to lead to an ever-higher rate of flow than he was currently in. This increased dividend will make the issue of resistance moot.

Fortunately for our purposes, there is the reflex to lie down in response to the approach of the *prey*, and in the final training steps in this chapter we will use that reflex to teach the dog to go from high to low gear in a flash. When the dog masters this lesson he learns that the command *Down* brings his world into order by activating the dog's group mood. We train the dog that his drive flows through a group instinct and he experiences great success and pleasure. He feels that the world conforms to his instincts and to his advantage.

This increases his attraction and bond to his handler because the handler becomes the superior member within the group mind. The handler demonstrates that he knows where the danger is, and therefore is the key to the dog learning how to successfully convert the danger into a positive sensation. Therefore, the master's commands will come to have tremendous value to the dog.

TRAINING PROGRAM

We're going to train the dog to go down quickly on command through a series of steps that progressively get more difficult. The main mistake that most handlers make is to present the exercise to the dog in terms of a struggle. They approach the dog with a confrontational style either through a lot of eye contact, or verbal pressure, or simply a dramatic style of emphasizing one's presence. This will only generate resistance in a dog, because in order for a dog to lie down calmly and quickly, there must be a clear focus on his group leader. This is why training the dog to heel is the halfway point to training the dog to lie down. We cannot just be arbitrary and tell the dog to lie down from out of the blue. He must first be attracted to his handler.

The dog can easily misinterpret even a progressive approach to this training phase, because trying to get a dog to lie down can fill him with resistance of either the dominant or submissive variety.

STEP ONE: FOOD AND TOUCH AS AN INCENTIVE TO LIE DOWN

When the dog learned to heel, he learned that sitting was a position of calm focus toward his handler. We will start with the dog in this position as it puts him halfway in the mood to lie down.

From the sitting position we will create the reflex to lie down, using hunger and food as a magnetic draw. In a sense, we're carving a circuit in the dog's brain that programs a reflex to lie down.

The main value in using food is that it helps the dog to learn that the down reflex can channel a lot of drive. The dog can then learn to flip-flop from the active polarity (up) to the reactive polarity (down) quickly. When we use food to train the dog to lie down we need to remember our precise objective in this phase of training. We are getting him to respond to the number one variable in the environment—food—and not to his handler. However, at this point we're only interested in creating the circuitry in the dog's mind, and as you go through the training steps you will see the focus gradually shift to the handler.

Start the exercise by getting the dog's attention on the food and having him drive into you as you slowly back up a short distance with him on a lead. When you stop, the dog automatically sits as you hold the food poised toward the middle of your chest.

Command *Stay* and circle the dog. When you come back to the heel position, hold the food in front of the dog with your right hand and use your left hand both to restrain the dog on the lead and to hold his rump down if necessary to keep him sitting.

248/ NATURAL DOG TRAINING

As you entice the dog with the food in your right hand, keep the lead tight and pull back on the dog's neck as your left hand leaves the dog's rump and travels up the lead so that you can squeeze the dog's shoulder blades with a slight downward pressure.

Don't try to squash the dog into the ground with your left hand. It's up to the dog to do the actual physical work of lying down. He can only learn to lie down if he *chooses* to lie down, not if he's crushed into the down position. The handler's role is to arrange for the dog to come to that decision.

Be sure to keep the dog in the sit position and shock him with a jerk on the lead if he tries to get up to grab the food. Meanwhile, you will bait the dog with the food by letting him lick your closed hand to get at the treat clasped within. The subtle pressure on the dog's shoulder blades will at the same time suggest this impulse to him. As his drive for the food mounts, slowly lower your hand to the ground so that he cranes his neck downward. If the dog is stable in his sitting position, he will lie down in order to find a more comfortable position in which he can feed. As soon as he assumes the down position, open your palm so that at the moment of lying down, the flow of pleasure reaches its peak.

In this exercise, it would be helpful to have three hands, because the left hand first has to ensure the sitting behavior and then help the right hand suggest the down behavior. It can be a tricky move, but don't become frustrated.

At this point, the dog may try to get up right away. If you sense this inclination, don't fight the dog; release him with an OK signal and then start him on a new exercise. This way, you're not training the dog to be unfaithful to the *Down* command.

At the point at which you sense the dog is deciding to lie down you can make the *Down* command in a firm but not too strong tone. I don't want the handler to call attention to himself. In these early stages the command is relatively unimportant. The dog simply has to learn that by lying down he gets the food.

When he's down, keep the food coming so that the dog grows comfortable with the down position. It's handy to wear a food pouch that you can quickly turn to for additional treats. Gently massage the dog's topline but remain in a vigilant position so you can influence him to stay down. Talk to the dog in a soothing but not exciting way.

Before the dog gets restless, release him with some contacting and then collect him back into the sitting position. Five minutes of ten to fifteen repetitions is enough for one session.

In this early phase, after the dog starts to get the gist of the exercise, a big learning opportunity presents itself. As the dog commits himself to lying down, he'll simultaneously be stretching his neck forward to get to the food. Exactly at this juncture of the commitment and the overexuberance, increase the squeeze on his shoulder blade with your left hand and abruptly draw your right hand away from the dog's nose as far as you can reach. The dog feels that his overexuberance chased the food away, and for a moment there is no clear releaser for action, so that he ends up being calmly focused on the food that, through force of habit, is about to be his. When you see this calm, poised expression, immediately dose out a food treat and then quickly draw your right hand away again. Repeat this process several times and then eventually leave your hand about six inches from his face. If he stretches his neck a smidgeon toward the food, quickly withdraw it once again to arm's length. Again, this causes him to study the food, and so you can reward this focused expression with another tidbit. The dog is learning to correct himself for feeling nervous about getting up to get the food. By contrast, when he becomes calmly focused on it, in a poised state of drive, by jiminy, that feeling causes the food to be brought magically right into his mouth. Also, this exaggerated body language is a helpful stimulant to get the dog to drop into a down position while he's heeling.

Once the dog learns that the down position produces the food reward, the handler can taper off all the physical assistance he's giving the dog so that the verbal command *Down* starts to stand out in the dog's mind. As part of this process, start holding the food higher off the ground so that the food itself isn't coaxing him into the down position. In the early going, you will have to apply stronger pressure to the shoulders so that the dog can remember to lie down in order to get the food. If the dog gets confused, then use the food to help him as in the beginning.

You should schedule as many sessions as necessary so that the dog lies down smoothly and calmly when he hears *Down* and when he sees the food before him. Continue this phase until you can see that the dog has made an association between the food and the command.

STEP TWO: THE SHOCK AS AN INCENTIVE TO LIE DOWN

The next step is to teach the dog that a shock on the collar via the lead is a stimulation to down. The easiest time to teach the dog this lesson is when he's already down, not when he's up and is most likely to learn a response of resistance to a shock.

Collect the dog into a sit and lead him down with the food draw as you did when you started the training, but then pull it out of reach; don't give food to the dog for lying down. Allow the dog to grow a little frustrated, and when he makes an attempt to get the food either by leaning, lurching, inching forward, or raising up slightly, make a sharp jerk on the lead to inhibit this nervousness and then wiggle the food to elicit a focused look. As soon as the dog is poised in his composure, immediately reward him with his treat. Move the food back and forth, from side to side, shocking and rewarding as necessary. As an overall tone of calmness starts to manifest itself in the dog's demeanor, command *Stay* in a soothing manner.

It's imperative that you use good timing so that the shock nips in the bud the impulse to go forward. Notice that we're giving the dog a little problem to solve. He's being shocked for going forward, not for getting up. It's easier for him to learn to stay in these terms since he is still somewhat committed to the mood of down. Should the dog break down altogether and get up, there's most likely either a timing error in the exercise or the dog isn't yet ready for this step.

Logically, one may think that if the dog doesn't make a mistake he's learning quickly. However, eventually we need the dog to try to get up so that he can learn how to lie down in response to a shock. Therefore, don't look at an error on the dog's part as a training setback; rather, it's an opportunity to teach him how to respond to a shock, so be ready to take advantage of it. After the dog displays a lot of calmness about the shock and his patience for the food, tuck the food away when he's lying down and wait for him to get up. Remain carefully positioned so that the dog doesn't get more than a millimeter into gear before you can shock and touch his shoulder blade in order to reestablish the down position. Reward immediately so that the dog doesn't attribute the shock to you and become sensitive.

Repeat the routine until you see the dog displaying a lot more calmness than he did when he came into the session. The dog has internalized this step when he stops fidgeting in response to the shock only, with no other physical help from you. When he's down, command *Stay* in a soothing tone.

STEP THREE: THE *DOWN* COMMAND AS AN INCENTIVE TO LIE DOWN

Now the dog is ready to learn that the spoken command *Down* is a stimulation to lie down. This lesson will be further reinforced as the dog learns that by listening to the spoken command, he can also control the shock.

Show the dog the food, excite him about it, and then tuck it away. Command the dog *Heel*. Go a short distance, stop, and command *Sit*. Command *Stay* and circle the dog. Don't praise the dog when you return to the heel position. Bend over slightly to position yourself and extend the lead in front of the dog with your right hand, and then with your left hand squeeze the dog's shoulder blades and press down slightly. Note that this exaggerated body language is consistent with the food being drawn outward to arm's length.

Command *Down one* time, then make a series of staccato jerks on the dog's collar. When the dog goes down, command *Stay*. Don't offer verbal praise at this point, because any stimulation will make the dog want to get up. If the dog is calm enough you can bend over slightly, massage the dog, and repeat the *Stay* command. Be very careful that the dog doesn't misinterpret your lowering of height, praise, or touch as an invitation to get up. Your influence must be to calm the dog, not to put him into conflict.

The reward for the dog will be some spirited contacting after he has shown calmness in the down position. During this contacting he can be given the food. Command *Heel* and repeat the exercise.

Over the next five sessions the dog should be going down without resistance. At this point you can concentrate on phasing out your body language so the only stimulus in the dog's mind is the *Down* command.

STEP FOUR: INTERRUPTING MOTION TO LIE DOWN

Now we have to train the dog to lie down from a moving position. Engage the dog in a little contacting and then casually walk a few paces with him to let his drive subside. Before the dog starts to lose interest in the handler, speak; *Make*. . . . This new command will catch the dog's attention and he will turn to look at his handler, which lessens the shock of the *Down* command that follows. As the dog looks at the handler, he sees the exaggerated body language that he learned in step three, and hears the command *Down* . . . and feels the handler's left hand on his shoulder blades.

After the dog has dropped down, wait until he's calm and then command *Hup*, and give the dog lots of praise and contacting. Disengage and repeat the exercise. In one session it may be possible to phase out completely the body language and the *Make* preliminary command. At this point the dog should be dropping somewhat quickly into the down position on the verbal command alone. Also *Make down*, or *Make your place*, is the correct way to tell your dog to lie down in the house or outside when you don't want him to interrupt an outdoor activity such as gardening.

STEP FIVE: DROPPING FAST WHILE HEELING

At this point the dog has learned all the components of the exercise, so we can put all the pieces together. The dog is ready to learn how to drop lightning-quick while moving out in high drive.

Do this work in the wide-open area where you have done much of your training. Since dropping quickly is such a rapid interruption of flow, we don't want to do it out of the *Heel* command so that the dog makes a negative association to being on the left side of the handler. Just invite the dog to make contact, rough him up, and then build your pace up to a fast run, irrespective of the dog's position.

When you're at your peak speed, give a shock on the collar at the same instant that you come to an abrupt halt. Touch the dog's shoulder blades and command *Down*. The faster you run and the quicker you stop, the faster the dog will drop. When the dog is down, command *Stay* in a firm but reassuring tone so that the dog can learn that this down position is indeed the place of safety.

Watch your dog very carefully to gauge how quickly the dog is dropping. If he looks like he's going down as fast as possible, don't make any shock on the collar the next time, just use the *Down* command. This allows the dog to learn that by paying very close attention to his handler he can avoid the shock. With this training step the dog now views his handler as the number one variable in the environment: The handler knows where the danger is. The dog's attraction to his handler grows immeasurably. As a reward for lying down, channel the dog's drive back into fast and precise heeling without any down training. To repeat the down exercise, break off the heeling exercise with a roughhousing session.

As the dog progresses, start making the command softer and softer. This makes the dog work even harder to pay attention and glean from his handler where the danger is and then how to get back into high drive flow.

Think of the handler's job as warning the dog about where the danger is. It's the way a parent would say *Stop* when he discovers his child one foot from a sharp dropoff. That's the purpose of saying *Down* harshly. That tone quickens in the dog's temperament the sensitivity toward danger.

Only when the temperament knows where the negative is in the environment can the handler train the dog how to successfully cope with it. Therefore, our reward will not be praise but contacting after the dog is calm about the response he chose. An army sergeant in combat doesn't have to praise his squad for hitting the dirt when he yells "Sniper." The response to drop rewards itself by mere survival. But we're going to go beyond that. By our rewarding the dog through excited contacting, the dog gains a lot of self-confidence and bonding with his handler. Danger is converted to high drive. Also remember that if you get your dog back into a high drive state he can't grasp how he was shocked; in fact, the shock is transformed into a stimulation of the group instinct.

As I mentioned, we can work the dog to listen to a soft *Down* eventually, and then the harsh tone can be reserved for those off-lead moments where we need total control.

At this early point, however, because this training is so dramatic, there is the risk that your dog will start to lie down as you slow down. After the dog has mastered this lesson, in your next training sessions, you have to neutralize this effect so that the dog retains his enthusiastic heeling and automatic sit. Most handlers fail to praise the dog enough so that he gets high in drive again. However, this problem will never crop up if the dog remains uninhibited about pulling on the leash when given an OK signal.

In addition to using food or a ball to bring up the dog's enthusiasm, increase your physical and verbal praise of the dog as he's heeling, especially in the automatic sit. Do three or four automatic sits for every down. Another aid is to run very fast, slow down, and immediately praise your dog as you keep up the heeling at this slower pace. At this point you could have a contacting session or a ball throw.

In one session, you should find your dog will master this exercise since all his instincts are cooperating with each other. If you find there is a continuing resistance, spend more time on the heeling and contacting, because that's where the real problem is.

On the other hand, there are some dogs who learn how to heel properly once they're taught how to drop quickly. Heeling and down, although they look diametrically opposed to each other, are in fact behaviors that are opposite sides of the same coin. In the next chapter we will look exclusively at potential problem dogs that require special handling.

STEP SIX: COMPLETING THE CIRCUIT

Now we want to use the prey instinct to complete the circuitry to lie down quickly as the shortest and quickest path to high drive flow. We're going to train the dog that by dropping when he hears the *Down* command, he gets to his prey, but of course the dog must like to chase a ball as a prerequisite to this.

Stimulate the dog with a ball and as you do, back up and maintain the dog's interest. When he's at his emotional peak, bounce the ball nearby and let him pounce on it. After the dog has seized it, move along with the dog on a long lead so that he is orbiting you with the ball in his mouth. Kneel down, praise, and pet your dog.

As you're petting him, pick up the lead, and when the dog wants to disengage give the command *Down*. Then tell the dog *Out* as you take the ball.

Release the dog with an OK and work him up to chase the ball again. Throw it and get it back in the same manner as before.

On the third repetition, work the dog up to a high drive state, shock him, and then instantly change your body language by abruptly becoming motionless. Give the dog a shock on his collar and command *Down*. Your hand can wrap around the ball with an index finger extended toward the dog to emphasize that the ball is now inert, not poised to be thrown.

Make a rapid-fire series of shocks on the collar if necessary to enforce the down reflex, and also move in to touch the dog's shoulder blades if necessary. These shocks are training the dog to inhibit any nervousness he may have, since the prey isn't moving in accord with the simple prey instinct. The dog has to learn that the prey follows the rhythm of the group instinct, so don't vacillate with these shocks. Remember that the shock is a learning aid as valid and valuable as praise. This knowledge is one central fact that separates successful from unsuccessful dog trainers.

When the dog is down and calm, display and wiggle the ball a little bit to arouse the dog's drive again. Give him a few moments to recharge, and then command him to make contact and give him a ball throw. Get the ball back as before and give him another throw. On the third try, drop the dog as described above. If the dog's drive is high enough, continue the exercise until the dog will drop without any shocks being made. Then slowly decrease your body language, leaving the verbal command *Down* to stand out as the primary stimulus for the dog.

The more attracted the dog is to the ball, the quicker he will learn this lesson. Take care to give him enough actual chases and carries so that his drive to the ball remains uninhibited.

SUMMATION

While it may seem illogical to use the danger response to calm the dog, from the instinctive point of view it makes natural sense: In this positive training sequence, danger is reduced to a manageable level. Your dog is born feeling that there is an undefined negative energy out there, and he needs to learn how to cope with it.

When a deer unknowingly wanders close to its predator, the predator drops down. The danger for the predator is in being highly aroused when there isn't a releaser to permit biting. Nature doesn't equip the predator with redundant circuitry; the same reflex to down for danger or for submission or for striking a prey animal is in effect for all of these moods.

The training in this chapter is not designed to make the dog submissive. We are training the dog that he can use his down reflex in response to the *Down* command as an incredible way to get the world to conform to *his* advantage. Amazingly, this heightens to an exponential degree his attraction to his handler, since from the dog's point of view, *he* is controlling the situation by lying down. The dog is learning how to align himself in his place within the group so as to get back into high drive flow.

27

Training the Problem Dog to Down

THE DOWN EXERCISE is so essential that there is no room for any error. We can expect that certain dogs are going to be very problematic about having to lie down since they have encountered a lot of resistance in their upbringing, but since they are still trainable they deserve to be the subject of a separate chapter.

All problems in down and down/stay training are due to dogs not having a clear focus on their handler, since they are burdened with social resistance. With these dogs it is always expedient to constantly review contacting, especially with distractions, and to soothe them continually with your touch.

There are three types of dogs that will overreact to down training and will have to be handled carefully: 1) highly excitable types that have a very active nerve process; 2) dogs that are oversubmissive and nervous; 3) dogs that can be called overdominant and aggressively sharp.

THE NERVOUS DOG

This dog gets hyperfriendly or hyperfrightened when he's touched in training. The friendliness is masking an inner panic that is only revealed when the dog has the chance to get away or is forced to do something he views as unnatural. This kind of dog should be worked when he is profoundly hungry. Feed him lightly in the morning of the day before and then train him on the following afternoon. He can eat his ration in the training routine from your hand.

I will walk such a dog on my lawn, then pause and kneel next to him and offer him some food. I'll sit on a bench and get him to make contact on my level and then touch him as he eats. If he seems to be relaxing, I will start to move from resting place to resting place where the handling and touching occurs. The running will burn up some of the dog's nervousness and mitigate his negative feelings about the lesson. When he seems at his calmest I will train him to down with food, as outlined in the previous chapter. Every time he lies down and starts to overreact, I will break away and run to the next resting station so that his nervousness is quickly converted into a purer form of drive expression. Slowly, we're getting this dog to see his group instinct as a means of success instead of a survival instinct.

An important point about nervousness: Every dog has some best-loved activity that is his particular version of drive activity. With fearful dogs the sensation of running is relaxing; frequently these dogs like to engage their owners in games where the owner chases them. Study your dog and determine what activity he seems the most relaxed in, the most fully absorbed by, the most free when doing, and use that as a reward for him when he chooses calmness. Nevertheless, if he likes to run, don't reward his flight instinct by chasing him. Put him on a long lead, focus on him so that he gets charged up and is ready to run, and then run away so that he chases you. In this way stress is converted into a pure form of drive activity.

THE OVERSUBMISSIVE DOG

This dog will be overly stimulated by his handler's presence and his touch will elicit much nervousness. As the handler tries to influence him, the dog will prostrate himself, perhaps on his back, and he will totally misinterpret our objective. Rather than doing a simple down with a focus on the food, the dog will keep his focus on the handler. In other words, the dog is defensive rather than clear in his drive; he is driven by nervousness to show submission to his handler.

Making this dog hungry is effective, not to reduce fear but to increase his focus and stamina when he's in drive. This dog is very easy to inhibit, so his owner felt that his dog's subdued behaviors were an appropriate response to his confrontational approach to dog training. However, the dog really only learned to give up his drive and become submissively nervous, rather than learn what to *do* with his drive.

Therefore, when the dog rolls on his back, the handler should neutralize this reflex by running away and commanding the dog to jump up and make contact.

The running will relax his nerve; as he gets the urge to roll over, the handler, the object of the dog's maneuvering, is long gone. What we're doing here once again is converting nervous drive into clear or calm drive. If the dog wants to focus on the handler, he will only get to do it by being pure in his drive activity, running after and plugging into the handler. Immediately after making contact, the dog is rewarded with food.

From the emotional standpoint, going up to the handler's level is the opposite from being prostrate on the ground, so the dog is learning to occupy the opposite polarity in the group mind than he normally seeks to be in.

When the dog can stay focused on the food and remain resilient to a shock, he can be shocked for this nervous display of submission, and the shock will actually convert the nervousness into being poised for a drive behavior. After the dog becomes calm about staying, be sure the shock is then followed by the pure drive activity of chasing the handler.

In this way the dog can start to choose drive over nervousness. He will work to avoid the shock by self-inhibiting his nervousness. Then he will learn that the calm position of lying down in a focused manner on the handler and the food ends up causing the fun and pure drive activity of chasing the handler, the highest rate of flow.

Also, the handler is disassociating himself from the nervousness—which he probably helped to create in the first place—and that will make life calmer for the dog.

THE OVERDOMINANT DOG

Finally we have the "dominant" type of dog or, more accurately, the dog who becomes unsure when made to change his mood. Since his response to resistance is straightforward, he is compelled to assert himself. He'll push back when he feels the left hand on his shoulder blade, and since he's stressed, he most likely won't show any interest in the food. His "sense of self" is totally jamming all the pleasure circuits, so any type of ingestion other than a snap at your hand or the lead isn't possible. He will also probably bristle and growl.

This dog is very much misunderstood. Since he's active and direct by nature he's run into a lot of emotional dead ends in his dealings with people, and so he interprets all change as bad, relative to humans. He attributes a negative change to the person who entered his critical area, who, by doing so, asked the dog to create a new social order. From the dog's viewpoint this person, be it family member or stranger, is acting provocatively toward him! But what is this dog's true nature? Most likely he is extremely social in some positive group setting, and this is the pure core we want to develop. In fact, most owners see their pet as a kind of Jekyll and Hyde character because of this seeming paradox.

Profound hunger is definitely advisable in the early stages of training. When the dog is hungry enough he will go down smoothly. Improving the contact training is important because the resistance between the dog and the handler is the central issue in this dog's temperament. We want to relax the dog about the status issue (from the dog's point of view, this is a disconnectedness issue) and have him learn that flexibility to change is an opportunity for high drive flow.

Then I try to address the problem more directly, because sooner or later we will have to work the dog without food. But first he must learn suppleness to the touch, just as if he were a puppy. Then, when it's time to train without food, I will put my left foot on the lead while I hold on to it with my right hand. I will exert an uncomfortable degree of pressure on the lead by stepping down on it with my foot, but slowly enough so that I don't provoke him, and from here I will patiently play a waiting game. As long as the dog doesn't overload or panic I slowly increase the pressure downward on his neck.

A big mistake is to position your head close to this kind of dog. That will intensify his problem and increase his need to resist (as with any dog, but particularly in this case, it may very well get your face bit).

As I notice the dog start to tire or think about lying down to get more comfortable, I start to talk sweetly to him. (Up until this point we haven't commanded anything, but have made subtle suggestions that the dog might like to consider *Down* by once in a while tapping the floor beneath his snout.) This generally weakens resistance, and now I amplify the softening sensation by starting to scratch his topline and his ribs, suggesting that a good tummy tickle is a distinct possibility. With this kind of temperament you want him to sense that by lying down he becomes the focus or center of the group and that his station and potential for flow have improved. We aren't trying to make ourselves dominant—that would only reinforce his unsureness and reconfirm his negative assessment of humans who make him change his mood. We want instead for him to learn that becoming subordinate (from our human point of view) leads to his highest experience of flow.

This gives the dog a good reason to switch polarities, and when he lies down I rub his belly and give him a really soothing experience. It's OK for this dog to roll over because he's getting the experience of flow that I'm eager for him to have and I want to energize him in this moment so that his topline is positively affected. His back is absorbing positive contact with the ground through the prey circuit, and he's associating the handler with such a positive drive flow; so we're doing a lot to teach the dog that down is a harmonic pathway. If his topline becomes supple and absorptive, each repetition will see him go down faster and with less resistance.

It's vital to realize with such dogs that the problem is not that they're dominant but that they're brittle, yet at the same time they have a strong sense of themselves. They don't adapt well and usually like to avoid new things if they don't think they can get to the high level of experience their sense of self requires. Because they're brittle and change slowly due to a strong sense of place, they appear to be tough dogs, which leads to their being misinterpreted. Consequently, in training they are pushed too fast and too hard. Since they have a strong sense of their place they inevitably *have* to learn to push back.

I take care not to raise my voice or assert myself in any way. I'm just going to be around to be a positive variable when the dog decides to lie down by my nonconfrontational influence. I keep my style neutral until he drops, and then I pay homage to him.

After his belly rub, I'll jump up and get him to chase me. Usually, after the dog has decided to follow and plug into you, his drive to eat even if he's not hungry will start to increase. Employ food as soon as possible to reinforce his growing flexibility. As his resistance starts to melt, you will notice more joy and pure drive activity in his manner of contacting with you. The dog will start to enjoy the work.

We can spend a lot of time in contacting with the "dominant" dog so that the flow into the handler becomes a harmonic pathway. Remember that when the dog is on a harmonic pathway he is easy to shock, which is the final device needed to teach the dog to drop very quickly as we did in the *Training the Dog to Down* chapter.

Dropping quickly is particularly important with the dominant/ sharp dog because he will tend to be defensively aggressive to outsiders. This is because he is in conflict over a change of moods and becomes flooded with social resistance. A growl intermixed with his barking is indicative of this condition. When the handler can drop such a dog quickly, he removes the dog from a state of conflict. This will set up the possibility to form a new group according to the harmonic guidelines. When a dog drops smoothly, then the element of danger has been reduced from wildlike proportions to the domestic.

As you progress with these three different temperament types, whenever you do something too new or give the dog too big of a problem to solve, you will see the initial form of resistance come back to the surface. Don't be disheartened; such a regression means you've accessed the earliest negative lessons on the learning computer. Instead of seeing it as a setback, recognize it as an opportunity to help the dog solve the original problem in a new way. If you're unprepared and the dog is successful via his traditional nervousness this is indeed a setback to the training program.

It's in the nature of problem solving that you have to put the dog back into the moment of conflict and then provide an alternative way out than the one he originally learned. A lot of people try to avoid the problem and so it grows deeper in the dog's character. The right way is to back up the dog slowly and help him learn a new strategy wherever he has problems.

When you make a mistake with these temperament types, it's equivalent to making a lot of mistakes with the others. When you do some good it's equivalent to only doing a little good, so you will have to accept a slow rate of progress.

It's also more difficult for the dog to learn because the new behavior you are creating has to compete with an old behavior that has a priority in his memory bank. This is why it's so critical to raise puppies without negative training; that original programming is very hard to displace.

28

Training the Down/Stay

STANDARD

THE DOG WILL LIE DOWN on command from his handler out of the heeling position. He will stay in that place, without nervousness, and will maintain a clear focus on his handler no matter what else may be going on. Furthermore, when his handler goes out of sight, he will patiently wait and focus on the place where he last saw his handler.

CONCEPT

As with sit/stay, the dog has the same three basic problems to solve: duration, distance, and distractions. And, as before, the dog will learn that the group mood is the key to his success.

Another vital point the dog is learning with this exercise is to listen to his handler at a distance, with the lead playing absolutely no role in the handler's control over the dog.

When the dog learns to lie down he's learning to give up his drive to his handler, and he's low or poised in drive after that point. A dog can't go from low to high drive under these conditions in a snap. He has to go through gears; slowly, over several moments, his drive will build up again. Perhaps the dog sees another dog at a distance, or hears or smells something intriguing in some bushes. The handler will have ample time to see the dog start to get back into drive, and he can use the *Stay* or *Down* command to reinforce the desired mood of low and poised drive. Since the dog is mostly in that mood and only a few moments into the higher drive state, he can easily learn to give up that little drive energy to his handler and over the distance involved.

TRAINING PROGRAM DURATION

This phase won't take many sessions because such a strong foundation was laid in the sit/stay training. What we need to do, however, is to build up the dog's patience level to at least thirty minutes. While dogs don't have a concept of time, their bodies do have a rhythm that's cyclical, making them appear to be time-sensitive. A dog has to learn to resist urges to urinate, or bodily discomfort, and to repress frustration instead of getting up. Note that his tolerance to these urges are raised by the flow of drive.

If the dog is dropping without any hesitation on a *Down* command, he can be built up to *Stay* for a half hour in three or four sessions.

Show the dog a piece of food and command *Down*. Wait for at least a minute, then give the dog the food. Since he's on the ground he can clean up the area around his forepaws, but don't allow him to do any exploring for more distant morsels. On the third time, rather than giving the dog the food, command *Heel*, then make contact, and end the session by throwing a ball. Repeat this exercise, patiently stretching out the time you make the dog wait.

The down/stay exercise isn't hard work for a dog because it doesn't involve rapid mood changes, and the session can easily last a half hour.

DISTANCE

The first training step is to review what the dog learned in the sit/stay exercise; *Stay* means the handler comes right back. However, in the down/stay we will use much greater distances and eventually the handler will go out of sight.

First, we get the dog high in drive in his group mood by heeling. When you're out in a clear area increase your speed to a controlled run. Abruptly stop, commanding *Down* at the same time. As the dog hits the ground, have your left hand extended into a *Stay* command toward the dog's eyes and say *Stay* in a firm but reassuring tone. This tells the dog that this position is the right choice for safety and that you are still near.

Keep your hand extended and walk around your dog at a three-foot distance. The circular pattern instinctively suggests to the dog your imminent return.

As you return to the heel position, bend over and lightly press down on the dog's shoulder blades, massaging in a neutralizing fashion. Unlike the sit/stay exercise, down/stay when attracted to the handler at first is a very tentative emotional balance, so be more subdued in your praise so as to not excite the dog. Repeat the *Stay* command if necessary.

When I circle the dog I always go in the same direction, counterclockwise, in order to be consistent, and with the dog at the center of my orbit. This makes him the focus of the group; therefore, he is not in conflict as the group seems at first to be moving away from him.

After the first orbit, give the dog a piece of food. Later, try to go around the dog several times, slowly working up to distances of ten to fifteen yards.

As you walk around the dog pulse your hand signal in a cadence consistent with your gait, maintain eye contact, and calmly say *Stay* periodically. These signals reinforce the dog's assurance that he's in the center of the group.

You will find that your dog has a certain limit where he becomes anxious or excited about how far away you are. Pay close attention to this breaking point, and make it your training objective to slowly push the breaking point out farther and farther. If the dog doesn't do well near his limit, be very patient and spend the time necessary to build up his self-confidence.

In this beginning phase we don't want the dog to get up because then we are allowing nervousness into the formula. Many people don't see the dog's nervousness; they go beyond the dog's limit and end up doing too much correcting. The dog learns that *Stay* involves his avoidance instinct, and he learns to be in conflict about being with the group and his chances for success. All of these factors will compel him to break the down/stay when pressure gets too high later in a moment of conflict.

When you have a dog that's very fidgety about staying put in one place, try to raise the dog's nervous threshold by drive flow training instead of through corrections. The more secure the dog is in being with his handler, the more calmly he will later react to being shocked for acting in a nervous way.

A common mistake is to give the dog verbal praise for maintaining the stay while the handler is at a distance. This may be logical as the dog is behaving nicely, so why not tell him so? But the praise only energizes the dog, and instead of helping him to remain calm, it puts him into conflict about staying and being apart from his group, and therefore is counterproductive. In his eyes, he's no longer at the center and he grows nervous.

The movement of the handler along a circular orbit *is the praise*. It's a positive arousal of the dog's group instinct that implies the return of his handler. Once the dog has learned that the orbit precedes the return of the handler, we can actually run along this orbit to raise his group instinct higher and therefore give the dog more and more praise for remaining calm and holding the down/stay.

For example, if I'm going to go out farther than before, I will jog and break into a run when the dog shows some concern at the increased distance. This is a very powerful reward, as you will discover.

At some point when the dog shows patience to your return we need the dog to break so that we can increase his resolve to wait. He has to learn from direct experience that nervousness is not successful.

Go out to your dog's distance threshold and bend over to tie your shoe. When the dog gets up, calmly walk up to him and gently *praise* him.

Then, break into a fast heeling pattern, stop abruptly, make a shock with the lead, and command *Down*. This sequence of events is much more effective than correcting him for getting up, as the problem isn't that he got up, but that his attraction to his handler wasn't pure enough. At any rate, this is the first step before we deal directly with breaking the down/stay. In a later training session, should the dog break the down/stay, immediately command *Down* and walk or run directly at the dog, depending on how sensitive he is. When you get to him, give him several strong jerks and repeat the *Down* command and then the *Stay* as you walk around him, this time in a tight orbit.

Should the dog lie down as you're advancing, immediately reward the dog with a *Stay* command and resume your orbit at that particular threshold point where he decided to lie down again.

Another training moment is when the handler returns to the heel position after being away for a long time, or after going a long distance away; you must be very sensitive as to how you reenter the dog's critical distance.

As I return I always take care to complete the pattern of the circle by going behind the dog and coming up beside his head, well within his peripheral vision. Don't return by walking directly at the dog. That will overload a pack instinct.

As I get close, I'll give him a glimpse of a treat, extend my hand into his field of vision with the *Stay* signal, then lightly edge the rest of my body up alongside the dog. I'll use the *Stay* command in a tone ranging from hard—if I see the dog is getting stimulated—to firm but reassuring, if I see the dog is a little unsure.

Ideally, we don't want to see the dog make any bodily reaction to our return. The optimal response is a calm, expectant look. The dog should be poised for action yet clear about staying put.

I don't praise the dog when I return; I simply become still for a good five or ten seconds and then reward the dog's calmness either by contacting or heeling away, the food to follow shortly.

Save all your desire to praise the dog for performing well in his training for exactly this moment and then pour your heart out to your dog as you heel him out of the down/stay.

With this sequence of events, heeling begins to represent the fulfillment of all the group energy stored up in the down/stay exercise. Heeling becomes a powerful stimulant and inducement in itself and strengthens the dog's pure focus on his master.

Since heeling means high drive flow in the group instinct, we can start to think of the down/stay exercise as analagous to putting a trickle charge on a battery. By making the dog stay down for a prolonged period we are "charging" up the dog's attraction to his handler. This has a strong therapeutic effect for dogs that have developed a lot of resistance to their owners.

DISTRACTIONS

Any change in the dog's perception of what's going on is a distraction, so start with a change of your body height. Working within the dog's distance threshold, bend down to one knee while projecting your left hand toward the dog and commanding *Stay* in a firm tone. Get up and walk around the dog along the orbital path and repeat. After several times you can return to the heel position, and praise the dog with a heeling session. Heeling is the best way to praise the dog; it's a very focused expression of drive in the group mood. We were using a group instinct a moment earlier, when we bent down, so we don't want the dog to blur the distinction between the control and the praise.

Repeat this training with family members. Stand next to your dog, who is lying down, and have someone else walk around, talk prettily to your dog, then bend down to adjust his shoelace or find a four-leaf clover. As the dog gets calm with these distractions the handler can start to move around the dog and use the verbal command *Stay* to neutralize what the distracting person is doing.

Next, the best way to really harden the down/stay exercise is to use the ball.

Out of heeling, drop the dog into a *Down* and command *Stay* as you produce a tennis ball and give it a little wiggle. Step out briskly into your circling pattern. Periodically wiggle it and repeat the *Stay* command. When the dog looks calm bounce the ball every so often and again repeat the *Stay* command. Return to the heel position, pause, command *Hup*, then *Heel*, and then, after a short distance, OK, and throw the ball.

As the dog starts to form an overall mood impression linking these events—the return of the handler, the channeling of drive into the handler, the opportunity to make prey—I go to a final step.

After circling and returning to the dog I'll roll the ball ten feet in front of the dog, command *Hup*, then after the dog makes contact I release him to get his ball. You can build on this exercise in a limitless array of variations: slam the ball off the wall of a building and, as it rolls by the dog in a down/stay, command *Hup*, and release, for instance.

At some point use a second helper with a playful dog as we did with the sit/stay. However, omit the pulling on the lead aspect with a second handler as it isn't necessary when a dog is in a down mode.

GOING OUT OF SIGHT

As a dog is a group animal, when you go out of sight his drive will be aroused to a very high level. To train the dog to deal with this situation calmly, he has to learn that even when you're out of sight, *you're still nearby.*

A good place to start this training is in a big field with tall trees and clumps of bushes so that you can momentarily go out of sight and quickly reappear in sync with the orbiting pattern that the dog was grooved into when he last saw you.

Out of a fast heel, down the dog, command *Stay*, and start to orbit him, making the circle very big. As you approach a tree that's between you and your dog, command *Stay* and pick up your pace to stimulate the dog's group instinct before slipping from sight. As you emerge from the other side of the tree, command *Stay* and continue along the orbit.

If the dog seems calm, at the next tree pause for a few seconds behind the tree, then emerge, going even faster, repeating the *Stay* command. Then slow to a walk along the original trajectory, as if nothing had happened. Repeat the same routine with other trees along your path. Return to the heel position and heel the dog with a lot of praise.

If there's a large clump of bushes or a small building, eventually that can be used as a screen as well. The dog is learning, here, that the handler leaving his sight is a heightening of his group instinct, which is an even stronger indication that your return is imminent.

On another day and preferably in a different field, drop the dog into a down/stay and step out into another orbit. End up fifty feet away from the dog, downwind, and stand still a half step before a tree. Wait there without paying attention to the dog or displaying any body language that suggests you're about to duck behind that tree. As soon as the dog looks away (you may have to do this work in an area with some distractions if the dog stays focused on you), duck behind the shelter of the tree.

Peer around the other side so that you can see the dog's head, tail, or at least the lead. We need to see how the dog is feeling. (One can even build a blind with a peephole for this exercise.) You will notice that since he didn't see you step behind the tree, he feels you have vanished. It doesn't occur to him that you're behind the tree, because of your neutral and relaxed body language when he last saw you and because dogs can't analyze data logically, only through drive flow.

Read your dog very carefully and *before* he breaks, step back into view and repeat the *Stay* command. Continue the orbit as before.

Do this training as often as you must so that the dog becomes very calm when he can't see you. This behavior gets very hardened when the dog learns that even when he can't see you, you must be nearby if he feels attracted to you and remains focused on his group instinct.

The next phase is to train the dog that when he loses his

focus on his group instinct—he's nervous or sees an interesting distraction—and breaks the down/stay, you can rematerialize out of thin air.

For this training I like to use a building with two corner windows so I can see the dog out in the field on a down/stay without him seeing me. We must be aware of which way the wind is blowing so that the dog can't smell us. As always, I start with heeling and drop the dog into a down/stay. I walk straight away from the dog alongside the building. As I go beyond the corner of the building away from the dog, I start to arch back so that the corner I've passed starts to block the dog's view of where I'm going, yet he can't see that I'm about to change direction to sneak back around the building. From the dog's perspective, I'm still walking straight away.

As soon as the dog can't see what I'm up to, I turn back and run around the other side of the building, slowly easing up to the windows to view the dog. If there aren't any windows to take advantage of, you can still peer from the building's corner; the dog won't have the faintest idea you're that near.

Be prepared to wait for thirty minutes or for whatever duration you want to train your dog.

It's possible that your dog won't budge even after a long time. In that case, I have a ball and lob it over the building so that it lands about fifty feet away from the dog. As soon as he gets up, I charge back into view and command *Down* in a strong voice. When the dog drops I orbit around him a few times, saying *Stay* as I head to the distant corner, from which I disappear again as I did in the first place. Once I'm out of sight I double back to the windows.

This time I'll throw the ball, and right after it lands, I'll step back into view and command in a firm but softer tone, *Stay*. Conclude the exercise with heeling, contacting, and a good ball throw.

The dog is now learning through contrast. Breaking the down/stay by being in conflict over a moving ball doesn't end up yielding drive flow. A moment's calmness produces my return and, ultimately, high drive flow.

When the dog is really good at this exercise, go to new places (always with the dog on a long lead) and arrange for someone to meet you there with another dog for distraction purposes. Build up your dog's tolerance so that another dog can come up and sniff him, but he will still maintain the stay reflex. However, never train your dog to remain down and passive if a strange dog acts in a threatening way. For distractions, use dogs that exude sociability as opposed to social tension.

As the dog grows very confident about this learning (which, to repeat, is: 1) when you're away and he's in a group mood, in his mind you're still nearby, and 2) when he's in a nervous mood you can rematerialize instantly and enforce the *Down* command, and the dog remains calm)—you have an amazing training tool. You can go out of sight to *praise your dog*.

I used this technique to give a woman control over her pit bull, who had badly injured another dog who started a fight with it. This pit bull was bred from southern fighting stock, so its prey instinct was pronounced.

I secured an aggressive dog to a post and made the pit bull drop and lie near it, but out of range of its lunging attempts to bite the pit bull.

The woman ran out of sight so as to train her dog that the group instinct outweighs the dog's prey instinct even toward strange dogs that are provocative. In this case it was necessary, as the dog had severely mauled another dog. The reward for this self-restraint was for the dog to hear its name and come past the belligerent dog to its master. Needless to say, the foundation work that leads up to this step must be perfect.

If you have a dog that's giving you a problem with the down/ stay, ninety-nine times out of a hundred there is an unresolved conflict over either the down or the heeling training, so review that work right away.

However, you may run into a chronic problem with a "creepy-crawler." Ultimately, this problem runs back to the dog's need to show submission or dominance to either a dominating or a permissive owner. All the corrections the dog gets actually reinforce his nervousness, so he's hard to train to have a calm focus with a group instinct. Social resistance is distorting his learning.

With dogs of this kind that chain of nervousness won't be broken until we get to this point of the down/stay exercise.

Basically what you have to do is give the "creepy-crawler" enough rope to hang himself with. The dog has to learn that getting up isn't an acceptable cost of "doing business as usual."

What I do is leave such a dog in a down/stay and go out of sight a short distance away. Usually I use my office and look around the other side through a window, leaving the door open. I can see the dog, but he can't see me.

When the dog gets up I don't come out right away. I let him get twenty feet or so into smelling the grass and meandering to a bush to mark. Then I go very calmly, without saying anything, to the spot where he was left on the down/stay. It's important not to make any notice of the dog no matter what he does, even if he lies down again. I pick up the lead and I administer twenty feet worth of shocks without saying anything until the dog is back in the down/stay at the original spot.

Then I calmly command *Stay*, and I go back out of sight and wait for the dog to get up again.

In a short time, *if the shocks are severe enough*, the dog will start to be calm.

Now I want to train the dog right away that calmness produces my return. I step back into view as soon as the dog looks clearly focused and is not in any conflict. I walk back into view, orbit, and return to the dog, and then heel, contact, and ball play.

PRACTICAL APPLICATIONS

Down/stay is a very important exercise because through it, we can tune the dog's temperament to exactly the right frequency in which we need him to operate. The dog can be taught to ignore squirrels, joggers, or strange dogs and yet still be highly aroused and enthusiastic in his group mood.

With the techniques we've discussed in this chapter, the dog is actually absorbing energy from the environment around him, even from all the normal distractions, and storing it up for later group drive expressions. This means that his attraction to his owner is clear and unencumbered with resistance. That's the emotional balance we need so that our dog learns how to *control himself*. A well-trained dog is easy to live with; he doesn't need to be constantly repressed, only fine-tuned.

The other beneficial effect of a long down/stay exercise is the phenomenon of raising the dog's nervous thresholds. The dog can grow with this training to be more resistant to stress and less destabilized by inappropriate stimulations.

This exercise gives the handler ample opportunity to read his dog's mind, because dogs don't just get up from a calm down/stay and take off. As a distraction or a situation starts to summon up a dog's drive, he has to go through some gears first. This preparation to get up will range from pricking ears toward the horizon, crawling, pouting, whining, or simply avoiding looking at the handler. By paying close attention to his dog, the handler can read his dog's mind and condition the way his dog feels instead of reacting to what his dog does. As I've indicated before, this is the most effective way to train.

Also in this exercise, we are showing the dog for the first time that his handler can control him by making him stay down at a distance, without a lead in hand, using only voice commands. This is the halfway point to training the dog to drop into a down at a distance when he is high in drive.

29

Down/Stay with Recall

STANDARD

THE DOG IS LYING DOWN, calmly focused on his handler, who is facing him fifty feet away. On command *Scruffy, here!!* the dog runs quickly and directly to his handler and sits in front of him.

CONCEPT

This exercise is only part of what the dog needs to know relative to coming when called, since he's already focused on his handler when he hears his name, as opposed to chasing something in the opposite direction. It is, however, developing and strengthening the reflex to respond with high drive when he's distracted and commanded to come to his owner. Our specific intention in this exercise is to teach the dog what to do after the handler commands *Down* when he is indeed chasing something. This, then, is the halfway point to that final objective in our training program: coming when called off lead.

The recall from the down/stay gives us an opportunity to assess how our dog is doing and from there predict how he would do in a natural context. For example, the dog may come slowly to the handler, and this indicates that there's still a lot of resistance between them, and much improvement is needed before the dog will be reliable. Or, a dog may come very fast but then start to veer off the straight line that leads directly to his handler. Another variation of this theme is when the dog comes directly toward the handler, but then runs past him, preferring to make contact by coming up from behind. These two behaviors indicate that the dog, while attracted toward his handler, will opt for a more powerful stimulation if it's available and when he feels a little more free.

Finally, when the dog comes to the handler, it's important that he sit close and in front so that the dog feels fully focused on his handler and committed to sustaining the contact.

FROM THE DOG'S VIEWPOINT

The central problem for the dog to solve in this exercise is to be able to switch from the calm, down/stay mood, to an explosive charge toward his handler. This transition can be very difficult for many dogs because the compulsion of being made to lie down may neutralize some of their drive attraction to their handlers. They may be reluctant to get up when called, or they walk or trot slowly to their handlers once they do get up, because they've had a history of attributing resistance to humans. If the dog has difficulty making the transition when he's low in drive and looking at the handler, he will have much more difficulty when he's high in drive and headed away from his handler. This exercise is the perfect place to address the issue of transition from low to high drive focus on the handler.

PHASE ONE: THE HAIRTRIGGER

Engage the dog in some brisk contacting and heeling. When the dog is fired up and strongly motivated, drop him into the down position. As soon as he hits the ground, extend your left hand toward him in the *Stay* signal and gather your body into a poised position, as if you're about to run away. Keep the lead in the right hand. The dog should be highly attracted to the handler at this point and just on the verge of breaking the *Stay* command.

Don't worry about enforcing the *Stay* command; instead, concentrate on reading the dog, and when his drive is at its peak but before he breaks, call him by name and run away, engaging him in contacting when he catches up to you.

Should you misread the dog and cause him to get up prematurely before the command to come, call him anyway and run away as above.

After the dog's drive is strongly channeled it's easy to backtrack and shock the dog for anticipating the command. Nevertheless, it's better to read the dog properly and not create the problem in the first place.

If you have a friend or relative as a helper, a motivational technique can be used to really build up the dog's drive. Put the dog on a long lead attached to the dead ring of the dog's flat or choke collar. After the dog is in a down/stay, give the lead to your assistant or double handler, who is standing at six o'clock behind the dog as you orbit him.

The handler comes into the twelve-o'clock position and gathers himself into the poised position, about five feet away. Slowly, the helper gathers the lead up snug without the dog noticing. When the dog looks ready, the handler calls him. The dog springs up, but is restrained from making contact by the long lead, held tightly by the double handler. The handler moves from side to side, encouraging and enticing his dog with praise and with the ball. Then the handler runs away, being sure to keep the dog focused on himself. When the handler gets fifty feet away, he turns and faces the dog. Wait for one moment, then command the dog again: *Scruffy, come here!!* At this point the double handler releases the dog; the dog runs to the handler and makes contact, and the ball is thrown.

The frustration of being restrained while his handler runs away will greatly intensify the dog's attraction to his name, so another exercise can be to have a friend play with a ball or another dog near your dog, who is in the down/stay position. As the dog starts to get more and more attracted to this distraction, make a fast orbit of your dog, get into the poised position at twelve o'clock a short distance away, and call your dog.

PHASE TWO: REINFORCING THE STAY

After several sessions of three or four repetitions, the dog's drive should be sufficiently channeled so that he is starting to become very calm about exploding from the down position toward the handler. Now the stay portion of the exercise can be reemphasized.

In these more advanced sessions the lead can be dropped and the handler can orbit the dog one or two times. Then, as he nears the twelve o'clock position in front of the dog, about ten feet away, the handler extends his left hand and issues the *Stay* command simultaneously, slowing down and gathering himself into the poised position. He makes the dog wait a few moments, and then commands: *Scruffy, come here! Yaahoooo!* The handler runs away, engages the dog in contacting, then throws a ball to conclude the session. In subsequent sessions the distance between the dog and the handler can be made gradually longer and longer.

Finally, when the dog is in a down/stay, orbit the dog at about a distance of ten feet and at the twelve-o'clock position show the dog the poised position. Then stand straight up and face the dog. Wait several moments, then call the dog, running away as soon as the dog breaks from the down/stay position. Engage the dog in contacting and throw the ball.

When the dog is calm about this lesson, orbit him in a fifty-foot circle. Instead of the poised position at twelve o'clock, show the dog the ball and command *Stay*. Facing the dog, cup the ball in your two hands at your middle so he can't see it but senses that it's there, wait for several moments, and then command, *Scruffy, come here!* Have the dog come in and make contact with you and then throw the ball. Should the dog not have much ball drive, use food and tease him to the breaking point while you're exaggerating the poised position.

PHASE THREE: MAKING THE VERBAL COMMAND MORE IMPORTANT THAN THE BODY LANGUAGE

Up until this point the dog's drive has been mobilized by the attractive body language of the handler and by his prey attraction toward the ball. We've contrived events so that the dog's name has been the final releaser that allowed the dog to take action, but the primary stimulus that has attracted the dog's drive remains these overt, instinctive reinforcers. Now we want to tone down these instinctive energies so that the verbal commands begin to stand out in the dog's experience. If one isn't precise in this regard, the dog will never be trained to respond to voice alone. This is important because when a dog is chasing something, the only stimulation of his handler he can notice is one he must hear.

Drop the dog into a down as before and begin to orbit him. After several orbits, approach the twelve-o'clock position, repeat the *Stay* command, and get into the poised position. Make a few false starts to load the dog, but each time repeat the *Stay* command, with a heightened emphasis on the hand signal. If the dog gets up, quickly grab the lead and shock the dog back into the down position. As the dog grows calm about remaining in the stay position, bounce the ball a few times and repeat the *Stay* command as necessary. The dog may be a little confused—he's getting a lot of instinctive releasers for drive—and one verbal signal to stay.

Orbit the dog again, returning to twelve o'clock facing the dog about ten feet away in a fully upright position. If the dog is high in drive, call him and engage him in contacting when he comes to you. Then the ball can be thrown to end the session.

If when you called the dog's drive was low and he got up slowly, the next time when you come back to the twelve-o'clock position and face the dog, flex your knees, suggesting the poised position, then call the dog. Slowly ease up on the degree of body language you use to attract the dog so that the verbal command becomes the primary inducement that both raises and releases the dog's drive.

PHASE FOUR: TRAINING THE DOG THAT DIRECTNESS WORKS; INDIRECTNESS IS UNSUCCESSFUL

As we increase the distance the dog has to cover to get to his handler, many dogs will start to veer off the straight, direct line to the handler or run past the handler and then make contact from behind.

This problem can be easily corrected. As soon as the dog starts to deviate one inch off the straight line, or as soon as he goes past and avoids the handler one millimeter, the handler instantly commands *Down!!!* and charges the dog.

As soon as the dog drops, the handler stops his advance and orbits his dog at that threshold. Make the dog lie down for several minutes as you slowly orbit him, then slide back into the heel position and release the dog into a contacting session.

Gradually start to stretch out the distances again in the recall and keep a mental note of the point at which the dog starts to have trouble. Do a little motivational work at short distances and then go a little past the problem threshold, using the hairtrigger approach to get the dog over that hump. In the next chapter the runaway will be used as a motivational method with this kind of a problem dog.

PHASE FIVE: SITTING IN FRONT

The dog has already learned that sit is a replacement activity for contacting, so we can use the food or the ball to break the dog's drive to make direct physical contact with the handler as the dog is running in after having been commanded to come.

With the dog in a down/stay, go to a distance of about ten feet and wiggle the ball or food to entice the dog toward it. Then cup the food in your middle, out of his sight, wait for several moments, then call the dog.

When the dog gets about five feet away, show him the food or the ball and command *Sit*. When the dog sits, command *Hup* and engage the dog in contacting. Then command *Sit* again and throw the ball behind you so that the dog doesn't get in the habit of backing away from you in anticipation of the ball throw. The contacting reflex will also serve to keep the dog glued close to the handler when he's sitting. As the dog grows calm about this lesson, increase the distance and phase out the contacting command, throwing the ball right after the dog sits close.

When the dog is fully channeled, command *Sit* without showing him the ball as he closes. The last step in this phase is to shock the dog if he makes contact without sitting automatically.

PHASE SIX: DISTRACTIONS

Have a friend hold a dog as a distraction about twenty feet off the straight line between the dog and you as you call him from the down/stay position. Should the dog break away from the straight line to the handler, he is made to down, commanded to stay, orbited closely, and then called over a short distance.

30

Training for the Down at a Distance

STANDARD

THE DOG, WHILE CHASING something at full speed, will instantly drop into a down on command, ending up facing his handler, calmly waiting for a new command.

CONCEPT

This exercise is training the dog to give up his drive to his handler when he has committed his drive to a prey instinct outside the group's focus. Up until this point we have trained the dog to lie down out of the heel position on our left side, or when the dog is away from but still focused on his handler. Now we're going to train the dog to instantly drop into a down no matter where he is relative to the handler and no matter how highly committed he is to a hunting instinct. This training is the halfway point to training the dog to come when called.

The most vital key in this work is that the dog shows drive to make contact with his handler after he's been dropped. When the drive flows back into the handler, the dog *doesn't know how he was made to lie down*. That makes the transition to off lead very easy; the dog never learns how he was controlled.

FROM THE DOG'S VIEWPOINT

When a dog hunts he gets fully absorbed in his prey instinct to the exclusion of all distracting stimuli. Were he to take note of nonessential factors, the prey would have a better chance of getting away. The only time it pays to be sensitive to other group members is when he needs them to kill a large prey animal, or when he is not so engaged and the body language of his fellows telegraphs that they are closing in on prey themselves.

Using the dog's innate sensitivity to the group mind through his prey instinct, we can train the dog that by switching rapidly from a hunting instinct to the group mood he will come to experience his highest drive flow. The dog learns that his master both causes and heightens the hunt, so from the dog's point of view he is controlling the environment by learning to control himself. Because he's controlling the environment by dropping down, he'll do it quickly, and he'll eventually come to interpret the handler's command as a natural part of his drive's rhythm.

Remember, hunting is the drive to make contact with any stimulus (even other people or dogs) outside the intimate pack. It doesn't necessarily have to directly involve an obvious prey animal.

The First Phase

If the dog's drive to the ball is high enough, we will proceed with the steps as described below in this section. If your dog has low interest in a ball but is playful with other dogs, you may go ahead to the second phase in this chapter.

Starting here with the ball is ideal because it's a prey that's in the possession of the handler, as opposed to one that's naturally occurring. (A dog looks like prey at a distance to some dogs, a new social order that holds the potential for a hunt to others.)

Hold your dog by the lead on the dead ring of the collar and tease him with the ball. Roll it ahead along the ground while you restrain him by the collar. Encourage the dog to try to pull ahead to get to the ball. Then release him to pounce on the ball.

Do this several times, and on the third time, touch his shoulders and help him to lie down. Next, release him to get his ball. In the next training session repeat the sequence but on the third time, don't touch his shoulders, release your hold and immediately command *Down*, shocking him if necessary. Wait for the dog to grow calm, then release the dog with an OK signal and let him play and carry the ball around.

Switching gears from the prey instinct, before the prey is captured, to a group instinct is a hard transition for dogs, so it's important in the first session to do it on a tight lead where the dog still feels connected to his handler and the dog's drive is highest.

As the dog grows clear on this phase, play out the lead as he's pulling to get the ball you've rolled ahead. Let him pull out farther and farther before releasing the lead, which allows the dog to chase and grab the ball.

The next time, let the dog pull twenty feet out, and boom out the *Down* command.

After the *Down*, come up to the dog, and when he's calm command *Hup* so that he must make contact with you before he will be released to get his ball.

The next step is not to hold the dog at all, but to throw the ball for the dog. When the dog is ten feet away command *Down* and make a jerk on the lead if necessary. Wait a moment for the dog to grow calm in each control setting before commanding *Hup* and releasing him to get his ball.

In two or three sessions you should be able to let the dog get twenty feet away on a loose lead, drop him cleanly into the down position, pause, then make contact and release him to get his ball. Do four or five motivational chases for every control episode so the dog doesn't lose his love of the chase or start anticipating the *Down* command. If your dog is sensitive, you may have to have two or three sessions without any control episodes for every session where the dog is dropped into the down position.

The Second Phase

In this phase we're going to use another dog that your dog is friendly with. Using a dog for a distraction involves a complex web of social feelings in one's own dog. Also, another dog represents a social order to which your dog would like to gain access. The owner is not in possession of the "preyful aspect" of this new social order (the other dog is), so it's hard for the dog to see that the owner is vital to his immediate success.

In using other dogs we'll be teaching our dog that the handler is indeed in charge of all new potential social orders and therefore, he's the key to the dog's hunting instinct.

We start by dropping the dog close to us when he's highly distracted by another dog, as we did with the ball. As he gets excited by this dog, and before he's dropped, hold him by a tight lead and praise him. Then we'll start to increase the distance we'll let the dog get toward the distraction before he's given the *Down* command.

All of this training is done on the long lead, although by this point you should be able to let the lead drag loosely along the ground and just keep hold of the lead in case you have to shock the dog.

The dog you use as a distraction should be very playful with your dog. If none is available, another family member can serve as the distraction.

Let the two dogs, both on leads, begin to sniff and then start to play hard. (You don't have to make your spouse or other family member get down and sniff; she or he only has to run around and tease the dog.) When the two dogs are fully engaged, have your helper pick up the distracting dog's lead and run away from you and your dog. Tell your dog OK and run along, encouraging him to keep up with them, then the entire entourage reassembles to resume the play session.

Each time you allow your dog to break away, let him run farther and farther ahead of you.

The next time, as your helper runs away let your dog get five feet into pursuit and command *Down* in a strong voice. Be prepared to shock if necessary. As soon as the dog drops, command *Stay* in a reassuring, firm voice and orbit the dog. Return to the heel position, command *Hup*, then release your dog to catch up with his buddy after he makes contact with you.

The next several times allow your dog to keep up with the rolling frolic, and on the control episode command *Down*. If the dog doesn't respond, make a shock.

Most dogs will drop on the mere voice command, but if yours doesn't, don't give him the chance on your next control episode. The next time *first make the shock*, then the command. The dog has to learn that you have valuable information and by being responsive to your voice and then by making contact with his handler, his drive always gets to its target. He has to stay in the old group mind in order to link up with this new social order.

Keep a mental note of what your dog is likely to do each successive time based on what he did the last time. If you are always reacting to the dog, giving him chances and then responding, you are only going to train him that the lead is the means of your control, and it will be very difficult to wean him off it.

The next step is to train the dog to down while he's in the middle of playing with the other dog. Wade into the fray and grab your dog by the flat collar to break his concentration in a positive way. Praise him to arouse his group instinct toward you and then release the dog and command *Down*. Wait for a few moments, have him make contact with you, and then encourage the dog to resume playing. The best way to get your dog fully released is for you to go ahead and try to be the first to engage the distraction dog in play yourself.

The next step is to drop the dog from a short distance away while he's playing, then come close, contact with the handler, and then release the dog to continue his play.

Continue the training to the point where your dog is playing hard with his doggy pal at a great distance and in mid pounce he will drop instantly on the command *Down*.

After a few sessions it should be quite clear to you how your dog is going to respond, and if he is very calm about this exercise, it's time to take him off the fifty-foot lead and repeat the entire sequence.

Since the dog hasn't been seeing you making the shocks on the lead it's not really a big step for him to make. However, we have to remember that there's a sensation of drag on his neck from the long lead, and the dog has to learn that this feeling isn't an important variable. That's why it's very important that the dog doesn't lose his drive to the distraction by dropping him too often. If his drive to the other dog or family member remains high, your training program will be 100 percent relevant to naturally occurring situations when the dog is away from you and free of any restraint. You won't have to wonder what your dog will do. Keep your dog's drive high by spreading this training out over several weeks.

In conjunction with this training, you can take your dog out into parks, parking lots, and other places with natural distractions, again always trailing his long lead. Let him get several steps into a chase, make the shock, and command *Down*. When the dog is reviewing something familiar, but in a new environment, always repeat the first lesson because it's new from the dog's perspective. Of course, out in public we can't allow the dog to fulfill his drive and make contact with whatever he was chasing, so be sure to displace his drive into ball or stick chasing if possible, and certainly food or contacting otherwise.

If the dog has little ball drive, take heart: The chance to follow you around the park still constitutes a hunt, and to that extent the dog's drive is being channeled into the group mood. This theme will be more fully developed in the chapter Coming When Called.

When a dog chases something and he's made to lie down, that

instinct, usually prey, didn't come to a fulfillment and will start to lose its value. The dog won't become frustrated unless he was improperly trained to down. Instead, he will start to channel his drive back into his handler, because drive has to go somewhere. Furthermore, we're allowing the dog to learn that channeling his drive back into his handler allows the hunt to continue, albeit in a different direction.

Because the potential for a dog to be hurt is so high when he's out in public, the shock must be made before the command *Down* is given. The dog needs to learn that leaving his handler's sphere and zooming off into a new hunting mood is a dangerous action. The shock is the danger, one he has been amply prepared to deal with, and we don't want to avoid giving the dog the opportunity to learn this lesson in a controlled situation. The *Down* command then stimulates the reflex to make contact with the handler, which erases any negative overtones.

When a dog is doing very well on these outings I usually carry along a shorter ten- or fifteen-foot lead that I'll switch over to. As I shorten my lead I lower the amount of drive I'll allow the dog to get into, especially when I take the lead off completely.

It's vital to remember with dogs that have developed a problem about being off lead that these dogs have to learn calmness about being free of a lead. If they've been in this situation before, they've inevitably been put into conflict about their group and hunting moods.

With these dogs, I usually emphasize that the lead is coming off with a loud click of the snap. The instant I see any nervousness, which can even come in the form of play solicitation, I make the dog lie down. Then we walk along, and if he shows a determination to be in front of me more than a few feet or to "tune" me out, he must lie down again. If the *Down* command weakens, the long lead comes back on. The dog learns that calmness provides his free opportunity to hunt with his handler; nervousness is not successful. Since it took the dog a while to learn that nervousness was his ticket to have fun, we have to go just as slowly for him to learn the opposite.

But, in all candor, such residual problems mean we have to go back and review the fundamentals. When a dog is clear about what *Down* means, his owner has been transformed into a master.

Also, when a dog is very nervous about being off lead, its helpful to run with the dog around a park or his yard with a sense of urgency, so that his nervousness is neutralized by such drive activity. Don't meander; demonstrate through your body language that you're up to something important.

Sometimes when you drop a sensitive dog he will lose his drive and act very subdued. In that case I let him remain down for a long enough period so his drive can regenerate. Sensitive dogs are very easy to inhibit, but they're hard to motivate. To successfully train such a dog, one must spend more time on the motivational end to raise the dog's drive. The higher a dog's drive, the easier it is to train him.

31

Coming When Called

STANDARD

THE DOG, WHILE IN HOT PURSUIT of something, will instantly stop his chase, turn around, and come all the way in to his handler when his name is called. He will stay in close contact with his handler until released with an OK signal.

Otherwise, as the handler walks along, whether it be in a wide-open or a congested area, the dog will range freely around the handler, investigating and exploring things of interest to him. The dog will stay as close to the handler as the situation warrants. However, under no circumstances will the dog leave the handler.

CONCEPT

This section of the book represents the most essential exercise in our training program. Generally speaking, the dog is learning that by being attentive to his handler he gets the opportunity to investigate the glories of the outdoors and the chance for simple prey making. The handler will take the time to reinforce this by throwing a stick or a ball and giving the dog a good workout when the dog is properly focused.

In a philosophical sense, we can say that the hunting and the social instincts come into harmony through this training. The dog can be a dog and have doggy fun and still be part of the group that revolves around the handler. This balance of instincts parallels the one condition in nature where the wolf in the wild can be said to be "free."

On a more specific level, the dog is going to learn how to channel his drive from a prey instinct—for example, chasing a squirrel—to a group instinct, the drive to make contact with his owner. This requires significant mental gymnastics.

When a dog is moving he is hunting; millions of years of evolution are compelling him to find something to chase and then to follow the chase to its conclusion. *In nature, there is no instinct to break off a chase in deference to another being.* That is, unless the prey decides not to run. An alpha wolf would never call an inferior off from a chase; he would always join in. Therefore, nature hasn't equipped a dog with any mental faculty or physical reflex with which he can break off a chase and return to his owner. There's nothing inherent in a dog's nature that we can appeal to. As dog owners, we have to artificially create and then strengthen this desired behavior through our training regime.

One of the misconceptions that contributes to the high delinquency rate in training dogs to come when called is that people think a dog's intelligence and sociable nature comes into play in this type of training. Nothing could be further from the truth. Because the point of being social is to hunt, and because canine intelligence is concerned solely with figuring out how to make prey, the dog will use every reserve of social drive and canine intelligence to figure out how to avoid a repressive owner rather than how to listen to him. Therefore, training the dog to come when called is strictly an issue of channeling the drive from the hunting mood to the group mood.

In this section we're going to break down the complexities of training a dog to come when called into its simple components, and then train the dog to be proficient one step at a time. Half of the training program is designed to motivate the dog, and the other half is designed to control him using the obedience skills he has mastered so far in our program. In this bifold approach, as the dog learns that his hunting instincts only come to a successful conclusion through making and sustaining a degree of contact with his handler, *the dog will work to control himself!*

I recommend doing the motivational portion of the program from day one of training, and you will find a slower-paced version of it recommended in the puppy section as well. The motivational material is positioned this far along in the text mainly for organizational clarity.

Also, once the dog has mastered coming when called, he can be trained to the boundaries of his yard.

FROM THE DOG'S VIEWPOINT

The important thing to realize in training the dog to come when called is that from the dog's point of view, it involves two distinctly different problems. The first problem is to give up an exciting chase.

When a dog is running away he is in a hunting mood, and his drive is flowing toward a prey stimulus. Since there's no instinct to return to the group until the chase is abandoned or the prey is caught, anything that happens during the chase will serve to heighten the dog's commitment to catch what he's after. For example, when the dog hears his name and senses his owner approaching, this will increase his drive to continue as he feels the group is joining him in the chase. Also, he will be stimulated to go even faster when he senses the approach of his group, so that he gets to the prey first. And if the dog is really deep into the chase, he may be so focused on his quarry that he can't hear his name in the first place.

The second problem is to return to the owner. The dog's drive has to be redirected from a prey instinct to a group instinct.

Even if the dog should hear his name, he still has these problems of being high in drive, in conflict about what mood to be in (whether to continue to chase or to return), and, finally, making contact with someone who's acting confrontational and demanding (hence unattractive, especially compared with a juicy rabbit).

When these issues are lumped together—stop chasing and return to the handler—the dog has a problem that's impossible for him to solve. As we've discussed in the puppy developmental section, confrontation, while appealing to our human, logical nature and seemingly effective in the early going, is actually only confusing the dog.

I'm reminded of a dog I was trying to train when I was younger, using traditional dominance techniques. The dog was excellent on lead, but when he got a certain distance away from his handler he'd take off. Nothing worked, but as I discussed the problem with the owner, she mentioned that the dog never took off when she was horseback riding; as a matter of fact, he came whenever he was called. Remarkably, as it then occurred to her, he even came to his name when he saw deer, which he regularly chased at other times.

That dog reversed all my ideas about dog training because I realized that a dog could only be reliable about coming when called when his prey instincts were brought into harmony with his need to be connected; in other words, a group mood. Because the woman on horseback could move rapidly, the dog could be high in drive on a nasal adventure and still be *with his owner*. When the dog's instincts were so harmonically balanced the owner could assert her control over the dog, and the dog learned that he could only become complete (high drive flow) by being with his owner. She found that rarely did she even need to command the dog, which is why the whole process had escaped her attention.

Now that we see the problem from the dog's point of view, this is what the dog needs to learn. These lessons are really just extensions of what the dog has learned so far.

1) To plug into his owner when he's high in drive. Many dogs are inhibited about this because their pack instincts are overly emphasized.

2) By making contact with his handler the dog will get to make prey (chase a ball); this allows the dog to become calm and learn that he did the right thing.

3) The dog will be trained to be attentive to his owner's command even if he gets deep into a chase.

4) In outings into the real world and off lead, the dog learns to orbit his handler. The hunting instincts are to revolve around the handler just as a bird dog orbits the bird hunter.

BUILDING THE GROUP INSTINCT

The first step is to test the dog's group instinct and see how much drive it can handle. Anything short of an optimal response will be due to social resistance that has accumulated over the dog's life. Out in the real world, such resistance will cause the dog to disobey the command to come when called. Even if the test shows that the resistance is slight, the force of evolution on the natural flow of the dog's drive will cause the resistance to develop over time into disobedient behavior. By testing the dog, we can find where we have to focus our training effort long before the dog ever learns to be disobedient. Later, as the dog gains in his proficiency, we'll put him into conflict in controlled settings so that the desire to break away from the group can be shocked. More important than the shock will be its conversion to a stimulation that will heighten and strengthen the group mood. This lesson will be highly specific, positive, and of lasting and practical value.

This test has nothing to do with the degree of affection the dog has for the owner. It simply tells us how much drive the dog can channel into his group instinct, and how much resistance there is between the handler and the dog over the dog's drive. Of course, as we clear up this issue, the bond between dog and owner grows stronger and calmer.

The test will categorize dogs into either low-, medium-, or high-drive types. After the dog is identified, specific techniques will be recommended to develop the dog to the optimal level.

The first step is to get the dog excited to run after and make contact with his handler, and this is best done with a helper. If a helper isn't available, refer to the puppy section on channeling hunting instincts into the group mood for some alternative suggestions.

The dog is placed on a fifty-foot lead and held by the helper. The helper's role is to be as neutral as a post, and to simply release the dog when the handler calls him. After the testing process, when we move into actual training, we'll give the helper a more active role.

As the helper holds the dog, the handler arouses him to play for a moment, and then abruptly runs away, teasing the dog as he goes. As the handler is running away, note the dog's reaction. Is the dog disinterested, or watching but standing calmly, or is he excited with much barking and/or straining on the lead? These possibilities show us how much drive the dog can express in his group instinct; naturally, the more, the better.

The handler runs about fifty feet, turns around, faces the dog in an upright posture, standing motionless, and commands the dog, *Scruffy, come here*, in a loud, demanding tone.

Don't use casual language such as, "OK, Scruffy, come on buddy." That isn't the way you're going to call your dog in the real world in a crisis. The language used in training must be very precise so the dog associates all of his drive with that command.

As soon as the handler commands the dog, the helper lets the dog run to him but holds on to the lead for safety purposes. Once released, it's important that the dog doesn't feel any tension on the lead so that this variable will be very easy to phase out when we go to off-lead work.

If the dog is sensitive and inhibited by the helper, the helper might have to run alongside the dog to get him to run ahead.

Repeat the test three times to get a true reading. If the dog shows weak drive, does it build with subsequent exercises? If the dog displays strong drive, does it weaken as you go along?

Another aspect to the test is how the dog responds in different places. Dogs who are confident enough to hunt for themselves will be the most distracted in new places and will test better on familiar ground. Dogs who are more unsure will display a stronger attraction to the owner when they're in foreign territory and are less attracted when they're in their own yard. Do the test in a familiar and then an unfamiliar setting to get an overall picture.

How the dog runs from the helper to the handler and then makes contact will complete our evaluation.

LOW-DRIVE DOGS

If one's dog shows little interest in chasing the handler, the first order of business is to build up the dog's drive. One way to motivate the dog is to fast him, then tease him with food as the handler runs away. Or, if the dog is enthusiastic about the ball, use that to heighten his enthusiasm. I would like to reemphasize that fasting a dog can do wonders in producing high drive, no matter what his inclination may be.

When the dog is released by the helper the handler should go only a short distance on the next repetition and should also kneel down. The smaller and more submissive you make yourself (this emphasizes your "preyful aspect"), the more attractive you become to the dog's drive. Praise the dog lavishly simply for looking at you, and as the dog starts to come closer, encourage him to make physical contact with you to get to his prize. But don't force yourself on the dog by leaning forward or by trying to snag him. If the dog is looking at the handler, especially if he's moving toward the handler, the dog is attracted; it's just that he can't see an opportunity to plug in should he keep his distance. If the handler instead of the dog closes the gap, we're only reinforcing the dog's avoidance instinct. Lean away from the dog as you praise him so that he is taking the initiative by coming closer to you.

Over time, as the dog's drive starts to flow at a higher and higher level and the dog is making contact readily, start to stand more and more erect, using less praise as an inducement to get the dog to close the gap.

Eventually, we want the dog to make contact with the handler who is perfectly still and upright. But even as the dog is learning to take the initiative, remember always to praise and reward immediately after the dog shows that drive, not just when he gets to you.

MEDIUM-DRIVE DOGS

The medium-drive dog will be attentive to the handler running away but won't start after him at full speed. He gets into high gear only after he gets rolling. He's having trouble overcoming the initial resistance he feels about being in the group mood and becoming high in drive. This dog needs to be encouraged in the same way as the low-drive dog so that he doesn't have any hesitation to the handler's command to make contact. He will respond more quickly to the inducements, and as his full drive emerges the opportunity to shock the dog for being distracted will come faster as well.

Another medium-drive possibility is the dog that starts to trot toward the handler but never gets committed to the group instinct and veers off the straight line before closing the gap. Such a dog looks for a bush to urinate on, or tries to avoid his predicament by smelling the ground.

This kind of dog has learned a lot of resistance to his handler either by having the opportunity to hunt on his own or through disciplinary training. He's trying to avoid discomfort as well as look for some natural stimuli that can satisfy his hunting mood. His drive has been aroused by the handler's running away, but it's trapped because he perceives his handler via a pack instinct. With this dog we have to proceed on two pathways. As with the low-drive dog, he needs to learn that high drive in his group instinct is successful. Spend a lot of time using food and the ball in the early phases. If this effort is successful, we can proceed to the channeling when in conflict phase, farther on in this chapter.

However, if after this phase the dog doesn't show much improvement, we have to shock him for his avoidance behavior. The following technique can be used once the dog is trained to heel, sit, down, and stay.

In a training session the handler runs away and calls the dog. As soon as the dog deviates from the straight line that leads to the handler, the handler commands *Down* and charges him to the point where the dog lies down. Then, we proceed with a down/stay exercise that the dog has already learned in obedience training. The dog can remain in a down/stay as the handler orbits the dog, returns to a twelve-o'clock position several feet in front of him, and calls the dog and rewards with food or a ball. The longer the dog has to wait, the more drive will be available.

In future motivational exercises, only run a short distance from the dog; you know the problem exists and the shorter distances will give the dog quicker success. As the dog grows more clear about the exercise, start to increase the distance the dog has to cover to make contact both in the runaway and after the down/stay.

Be very patient in the developmental work because the dog didn't cause his problem; he learned the behavior from the environment.

However, for all the patience shown in the developmental phase, one must not have any patience with the avoidance behavior. Although the dog didn't cause himself to learn avoidance, only *he* can unlearn it.

HIGH-DRIVE DOGS

In the case of the high-drive dog there are several possibilities we can expect when the dog is released. The optimal response is an all-out flat run toward the handler and then an uninhibited drive to jump up and make contact. If that's the case, our work is to simply channel this enthusiasm into a controlled manner of making contact. A ball or food can be used to shape the dog's manner of making contact from jumping to calm sitting.

A very likely possibility that presents a problem with high-drive dogs is that the dog runs right at the handler at top speed, but then runs right past him, headed for the next county.

A less severe version of this problem is the dog that runs past the handler and then approaches him from the rear.

The mildest form of this problem, particularly with young dogs that haven't gained their hunting self-confidence yet, is a shiver of submissiveness or playfulness as they close in and have to give up their "critical distance" (about one yard) before the actual moment of contacting. This happens very quickly, so pay special attention as to how your dog closes the final gap should he come directly at you. Even though the result may seem near perfect, the germ of a problem may be showing itself.

These variations of high-drive dogs are in various stages of learning in which they can't be high in drive and also be with their handler. They still have a lot of drive in their group instinct given their outgoing temperaments, so they remain very easy to train.

The best way to motivate this dog when you see these kinds of behaviors is to run right past *him*, back toward your helper, as the dog closes to within one yard. Run as if you really want to get away. Then let him catch up, lower your height, praise, and reward.

Do two or three of these sessions to motivate the dog and to neutralize in this positive way the avoidance instinct.

CHANNELING WHEN IN CONFLICT

Finally, when the low-, medium-, and high-drive dogs are built up so that they're high in drive and calm about making contact with the handler, it's time to train the dog.

The dog will be put into conflict between coming to his handler or running toward another dog that has been set up as a distraction. If the dog chooses to run to the other dog, he will be shocked by the helper holding the long lead.

Depending on the sensitivity level of the dog, have him on either the pinch or the choke collar (the pinch collar is recommended for most dogs). Go with your helper to a busy area, or tie another dog up a hundred feet away. Run away from the helper, directly at the distracting dog or some other commotion, ending up about fifty feet away from your dog and at least fifty feet away from the distraction.

Command, *Scruffy, come here!!!* Stand upright and motionless, without offering the dog any inducement. The dog is likely to run right past the handler; at that instant, the helper makes a shock on the long lead with a strong snaplike force that halts all forward motion. At the same time, the handler runs away in a straight line back toward the helper. The dog will be turned around; there he'll behold his handler running away in an attractive manner, so he'll quickly run to catch up. When he gets there, he can be rewarded with contacting and a ball throw.

The essential thing here is not to say anything when the dog gets shocked. The command was given at the onset of the exercise, and that's sufficient. We want the dog to attribute the shock to the other dog that was 100 percent occupying his mind when he blew by his handler. Don't hold back on the shock. We need the shock to serve as a durable insulator between the dog and the distraction when he's under command. A severe shock is the only way to neutralize the emotional value of the distraction so that the dog in the future can easily put it out of his mind. Giving the dog a small shock is not doing him any favor; it will only serve to correct his spirit and inhibit his character by keeping him in a constant state of conflict. The dog must experience the maximum shock effect that's prudent in order to learn the most positive of lessons.

After the dog experiences the shock, he turns around; there he sees his handler running away. This is a powerful attraction to his drive. Since the handler is 100 percent positive, the dog's drive will be magnetically drawn back into his group mood; all his drive energy, previously targeted toward the other dog, has to go somewhere because nature abhors a vacuum. Furthermore, because no negative influences are present, there isn't any way for the dog to internalize the drive into stress. No one is bellowing at him or standing still glowering at him for being a bad dog. The handler is being totally positive as he's running away, and the other dog remains a positive variable in the environment: He didn't cause the shock either.

All the drive the dog felt for the distracting dog was cleanly channeled back into the handler. *The shock has been converted into a stimulus to be with the handler!*

The hunting instinct the dog selected in his own mind (instead of the group instinct to make contact with his handler) to get to the distracting dog is where he finally attributes the negative in this learning process. This makes the final effect of the lesson incredibly specific. The dog learns that high drive is good, that avoidance or hunting when under command is unsuccessful, and that plugging into his handler under command is successful.

The only negative aftereffect of the lesson is a split second of pain that quickly goes away as the dog immerses himself in the drive activity of chasing and making joyous contact with his handler. The dog is left feeling high in spirit, learning a lesson of lasting value.

Repeat the lesson several times over several days, varying the position of the distracting dog around the field. Drive flow is very sensitive to spatial dynamics, and while the dog is learning not to run by the handler, for the moment it's only in that one direction. The stronger the dog's hunting drive, the more this rule is true.

This sequence of events has to be repeated in a variety of situations and directions in order for the general lesson of *always* inhibiting a conflicting hunting instinct to permanently sink in.

The main thing to be careful of is keeping your dog high in drive and happily making contact with the handler. End the lesson after five minutes or whenever the dog's drive starts to subside.

ORBITING THE HANDLER

Now that the dog has learned that committing his drive 100 percent to a hunting instinct outside the group's focus is not successful, the dog can learn to orbit the handler.

In this phase the dog learns that he can run around his handler, smelling and investigating, if he stays 50 percent in a hunting instinct and 50 percent in his group instinct. The dog gets to do doggy things as he moves about as long as he doesn't commit to leaving this "orbit" around his handler.

We can test that the dog is in the proper emotional balance by making slight attractions to the dog's group instinct as we move around: by making a low whistle or simply by changing direction. It's a mistake to command the dog if it's not really necessary because the command must arouse 100 percent of the dog's drive in this early learning stage. As the dog grows calm about how he is to orbit his handler, he can learn a middle way about these outings, as he did with his leash training.

The handler has to be able to recognize when the dog is committed to a hunting instinct. Getting high in drive is a telltale indicator, especially with problem dogs. The dog could be smelling something a little too intensively even though he's close and not moving away. Or he could be air scenting with his nose high into the wind and starting to grow excited. Or he could be just trotting away in a straight line in a little too determined a manner. All of these high-drive behaviors mean the dog will grow nervous about being in a fifty-fifty group mood ratio, and that nervousness is what has to be inhibited before it expresses itself into running after something. So even though a stimulus to chase something may not yet be in sight, the dog is getting loaded to run. Five minutes later you may encounter another dog or a squirrel, and by then nervousness has its releaser. If the dog seems to be growing distracted, make him lie down and stay, then orbit him and call him, and then move out rapidly in a new direction.

The next training exercise is a simple variation of the one before. Ideally, we would like to use a helper who will hold another dog on a short lead and another helper to work the long lead.

After these first sessions don't do any training for several days. Then take the dog to a new place or try using a new dog as a distraction. In this session we're going to give the dog the contrasting lesson to select the group instinct before he breaks out after a distraction.

Have your helper hold your dog and run toward the distraction as before. The helper releases the dog as you turn around and stand still, but this time you don't make any command. As the dog closes in, run at an angle past your dog and then give the command, *Scruffy, come here*. Reward the dog as he makes contact.

In this sequence the dog is helped to choose the group instinct over the hunting instinct, which brings about high drive and success.

Repeat the exercise. Then start to walk around the field with the helper acting totally neutral but in position to shock the dog should it start out for the distracting dog.

Every so often, start to run away from the distraction; each time the dog mirrors your movement, kneel down and praise him. If the dog fails to see your motion, the helper should shock him; the handler can then give the command and run away.

The final step in this phase is to wait patiently for your dog to become emotionally immersed in the distraction and then command, *Scruffy, come here,* and run away. When the dog makes contact, praise and end the training session with a good ball-throwing session. Use several balls so that the dog has a chance to relax and you don't have to harp on his name. Nevertheless, the dog isn't allowed to reinvestigate the distraction should he lose interest in the ball. If his drive tires to the ball, conclude the session.

An important training point here is to not rush the dog. Let him naturally work himself up in high drive toward the distraction so that the session has a natural tone to it instead of a contrived atmosphere. This is especially important with dogs that have been made overly sensitive by previous training or handling and for those dogs that are low in drive.

To complete the dog's training, all one has to do is take the dog to a busy park, let him drag his long lead, and go for a walk. Since the dog already knows how to down at a distance, whenever he starts to show undue interest in something on the horizon of his visual field, drop him into a down. Make him stay and orbit him. Return to twelve o'clock, pause, and then call him.

After the dog makes contact start to cruise through the area at a very brisk pace to show the dog that the group mood brings about a lot of investigatory pleasure. Then go slowly and watch your dog carefully.

The dog will quickly learn that keeping 51 percent of his mind in the group instinct is very successful, while 51 percent of drive flow in the hunting instinct brings on the *Down* command. A simple way to test this emotional balance, as I mentioned, is to reverse your direction or make a little whistle as you're walking along. If the dog notices, dog and handler are both on the right track. No matter how well your dog is doing, always review the motivational portion of this training, since our final product is the reversal of millions of years of evolution and genetic propensity.

32

Retraining the Problem Dog, and Boundary Training

IF YOU OWN A problem dog, I suggest you be sure to read the puppy developmental section carefully for a better understanding of how he came to learn to run away and to appreciate what developmental exercises the dog missed out on while he was young. This way the owner can better understand the nature of the problem and how to go about solving it.

One way dogs with strong spirit are made problematic is if they're trained to come when called by being put on a long lead, commanded, and then reeled in like a fish. When you make eye contact with the dog, give him a jerk on the lead and then make him come to you. In the first instance the dog is only learning that the lead is an agent of repression and that to be attracted to the owner means to feel submissive, since he's being made to change moods. When the dog finds himself in high drive and attracted in a prey instinct, he can't possibly come when he's called; not only was he not trained to, he was trained to do quite the opposite.

Many people feel their dog needs to run and blow off steam. That does seem to have a calming effect. The dog goes out for a jaunt of several hours through the neighborhood and comes home contented and infinitely easier to live with. But the therapeutic effect is illusory and far outweighed by the way in which the dog's drive is being channeled away from his owner and how nervous the dog is destined to be when his owner makes a demand on him.

It's widely written that a dog can be trained to come to his name strictly by using positive reinforcements such as food or a ball. Once again, this is a serious error. The dog can't be conditioned to respond to his name out of context with the way the need to hunt makes him perceive and feel. A dog is always attracted to the number one variable in his environment, but it's relative to the mood he's in. If a dog is attracted to a cat with his prey instinct and his owner is offering him a piece of cheese as a counterbalance, there's no way the dog can come to the owner. The dog will go after what the number one variable is in his perceptive field, which will be the cat and which will be consistent with all the cheese training the owner has done. When the dog was in a group or pack mood, the cheese would have been the number one variable. He never trained his dog what the purpose of the group was.

The group purpose is best demonstrated through a prey item, but with a problem dog the training inducements such as this have absolutely no attraction for him and so we have to take drastic measures. The first step is to deprive the dog of all drive activity until our artificial prey inducements start to take on a high-drive value. Then get a group of people together and with the dog tied to a tree on a five-foot chain lead, tease him with the toy and throw it to another person. Roll it past him just out of reach so that it's a game of monkey in the middle. As you see his interest mount, roll a ball through his area so that he can snag it. Immediately the group should start a round of applause so that the dog gets all pumped up about his treasure. The toy could be tied to a light string, and when the dog loses interest you can sneak up and steal it to resume the game again. If you're alone, you can bounce a tennis ball off a fence or a building to generate the same kind of intense frustration.

Meanwhile, as you're trying to develop pure expressions of drive, acclimate him to the long lead. He should drag it around at all times, outside on the full fifty-footer and then indoors with a fifteen- to twenty-foot version. Eventually, he will become as oblivious to its presence as a football player is to his helmet. Note that on football teams, all drills are conducted with helmets on even when pads aren't worn. This way the helmet feels like part of the body and won't be an irritant or distraction when the player has to execute a difficult move. After a while, the player forgets he's wearing it.

Sooner or later a dog who won't respond to his name is going to be killed or badly injured on a roadway, so we're justified in using any kind of training aid. In many instances I recommend the use of an electric collar as the final step, but it's a subject that requires more discussion than we have time for here. Briefly, I use it as a tool with which to build the dog's attraction to his handler rather than as a more draconian means of punishment.

One way to arouse the dog's drive to be with his handler is to take the dog for a car ride to a strange open area where there aren't any distractions. Enlist the aid of a helper who can hold the dog on a fifty-foot lead. The helper holds the dog as the handler goes back to the car and teases him either with a toy or food, or with praise, whatever gets the dog the most excited. Then hop in and drive away several hundred yards, get out, and call the dog. If the dog is straining on the lead, the helper can release the dog to chase after you. Open the car door and let the dog hop in. Repeat several times and then continue this over several months.

Finally, have the helper hold the dog while you run away. If the dog's drive is high in this less dramatic exercise, you have made a strong degree of improvement. Now you can build on this attraction by running away, hiding, and then letting the dog be released to work to find you, always, of course, on a long lead. As his persistence and enthusiasm for this work improves, start working him in his own yard. The next step would be to have the helper hold the dog while the handler runs into the house and the dog is released to go indoors to find his owner. Play heartily with the dog and then take him outdoors right away so he's not confined after responding positively to his name.

Another problem area is desensitizing the dog to certain flight releasers such as open doors or gates. Prearrange for the door to be left open with the dog on his long lead. If you can arrange for a distraction to be beyond the open threshold, that would be the most ideal of circumstances. The dog is let into the hallway or simply allowed to wander there on his own in the most natural of fashions. The dog must be on a pinch collar, and as he blasts through the door he is to receive as hard a jolt as is possible. No command is given. You should be around a corner out of sight in case the dog comes to find you after the shock. Play with him, take him back to the open door, and make him lie down. Shut and then open the door several times while commanding *Stay*. Then command the dog to make contact with you and let him run out the door. Go outside and play with him or let him make contact with the distraction and then make him lie down again. Command *Stay*, go indoors, and then call him. Play with him when he makes contact with you and then let him break away and head for the door. When he gets to the threshold command *Down*, and when the dog is on the ground, command *Stay;* make him wait for a few moments, and then call him. After you make contact release him with an OK signal and allow him to go out the door.

It will probably take several months of this kind of work and exposure to a wide variety of distractions before the dog can be considered reliable. In the meantime he is to be considered in training, so he must always be wearing his long lead. If your household is very active and doors and gates are always left open, the dog needs to have a kennel within which he is to be kept until he's trained. Remember, the dog's response to his name is a matter of life and death.

Take the problem dog for lots of walks on his long lead, allowing him to orbit you as conditions allow. As soon as he gives you any indication that he's about to embark on a hunting foray, command him to *Down*. He must stay for a minute or two until you call him to you; then release him with the OK signal. A problem dog can't be allowed to get too deep into a natural hunting mood so he can only learn that flow occurs by orbiting you at your pace. As the training tools start to elicit pure drive, the connection and the bond will be made between dog and owner. The dog at this point is trained.

Be mindful of this dog in new situations, since the first lessons ever learned have priority in the computer. Whenever you take the problem dog to a new area, drop him into a down/stay to emphasize that his handler is the number one variable in the new environment.

BOUNDARY TRAINING

Unless your yard is fenced, I don't recommend leaving the dog outdoors alone when the owner is not at home even if he's well trained to his boundaries. However, as long as the owner is home, either indoors or out in the yard, it's reasonable to expect a trained dog to stay near the house no matter how temptingly a distraction may beckon to him from the street traffic or some nearby woods.

The first step is to identify for the dog what the boundaries are. I prefer to take mason's twine made from cotton so that over a period of time it will rot away and the dog will have that duration to generalize the lesson to the area so defined. The dog is only going to be allowed a zone around the house of about a hundred to two hundred feet. Just because you may own a beautiful stretch of woods behind the house, the dog can't be given this as part of his domain;

his distance from the house will be too great a burden on the training process. Lay the twine out around the house at nose height, about six inches off the ground.

The most important training principle is that we don't want the dog to associate his handler with the shock he's going to receive when he violates the boundary. Also, we are only going to shock the dog when he is high in drive toward a powerful distraction, either a dog going by or a jogger or cars if he's a car chaser. The biggest mistake people make is to emphasize their role in the dog's learning process by commanding *No* and letting the dog see how he's being corrected. Additionally, the dog is corrected for violating the boundary when there's no distraction, which just fills him up with resistance and, if he's of strong enough temperament, is actually training him to need to flee from his yard.

The first step in training is to take the dog out on a short lead and walk him around the boundaries. Let him go up to the line and smell it, even smear parts of it with bacon grease to attract his attention to it if necessary. When he investigates, get close to him and praise and touch him so that he gets excited, and then run with him toward the house. Once there, give him a food reward or a ball throw, depending on what turns him on the most. Repeat this in a number of places around the entire perimeter so the dog is cognizant of the boundary and his association of the boundary with his owner is a pleasurable one. There are absolutely no shocks to be made in this phase.

Next, put the dog on a long lead and pinch collar and prearrange for a helper to hold a sociable dog on the outer side of the boundary. Let your dog go full bore to make contact; right before he gets to the white string, give the dog a strong jolt. Then run away, and when your dog catches up give him a robust play session. Meanwhile, your helper has run up to you with the distracting dog. Now within the boundary, the dog gets to make contact and play with this dog. On following days repeat this exercise at other points around the boundary so that the dog generalizes the lesson to the overall perimeter.

In the next phase several weeks later, let the dog outdoors while you stay indoors, watching vigilantly. Once again your helper jogs by, preferably with another dog if possible, and if your dog commits to leaving, storm outside and command *Down*. However, if the dog demonstrates restraint, step outside, praise him, and then have the helper come into the boundary so the dogs can play. As they're playing, pick up your dog's long lead and have the helper start to lead his dog back outside the boundary. If your dog bumps into or goes over the string, shock him and run back toward the house as before. Again praise and let him play with his buddy and repeat the exercise until the dog shows restraint on his own initiative.

The final phase is simply to watch the dog like a hawk when a jogger or a neighborhood dog goes by when your dog is outside on his long lead. If he starts to show a commitment to chasing the distraction, step outside and yell *Down*. On the other hand, it's hoped that by now the dog will display a calm focus without any drive activity, in which case, step outside and play with him. Then when the dog is outside, and eventually when he's progressed to being off lead, step out and play with him every five minutes. Gradually lengthen this to ten minutes, twenty minutes, and so on to expand the dog's threshold. Every couple of months it would be prudent to review the first phases conducted on the long lead.

33

Special Training

THERE ARE TWO AREAS that merit special attention: training a dog not to jump on people and training a dog how to behave when company visits.

The two areas are closely related, but we'll start with the more basic issue of jumping. The objective here is to train the dog to make contact calmly. It should be noted that if this issue isn't confronted when the dog is young, and if his drive is deflected into sitting for food, then he never really needs to learn not to jump. He simply grows up and loses his yen for inappropriate contact as a natural outgrowth of his maturity. However, where a dog's nervousness about how to make contact is the source of the problem, remedial measures need to be taken.

The basic premise is this: We're going to give the dog a clear focus for his drive, a ball or a piece of food, while simultaneously allowing the dog to learn that nervousness causes him discomfort. With dog and stranger sharing the same focus (food or ball), the dog can readily learn that sitting patiently is his avenue for success. The negative element in the situation has been reduced from making contact when hyper-charged, to gaining access through something positive. Locked on to the target in this way, how and where the stranger positions the reward activates the proper reflexes within the dog's temperament. The harmonic instincts then surface to command the dog how to behave and, finally, we associate our verbal commands with these reflexes.

With the dog on the lead, have a helper show the dog that he is holding a piece of food. The handler's role in this training sequence is to be as neutral as possible in his handling so that the dog learns to behave calmly, independent of the handler's presence. Ideally, only the helper will talk to the dog or physically praise him. The handler can, however, touch the dog's rump and pull up on the lead to guide him into a sit. Should the dog be sensitive to the presence of the handler, then the handler should indeed praise him extensively so that he shows himself attuned to the dog's needs, which makes for a strong impression of the moment on the dog. An indication that the dog is learning properly is if he stays constantly focused on the helper and the food. That is, by far, the most important component of the exercise.

The helper draws the food up to his chest with the hand slightly open to expose the food, and with his free hand he pats his chest, thereby baiting the dog into jumping. The handler immediately chokes up on the lead so that the dog never succeeds in making contact. The dog experiences a moment of discomfort.

After the dog registers a degree of discomfort, help him into sitting. However, no command is to be given; The dog should sit on his own. Quickly reward him with food and then bring the food back up to chest height, clasping his hand tightly around it to demonstrate that he has complete control over the food. When the dog displays a look of calm focus, immediately reward him with a morsel. Repeat this exercise, eventually getting to the point where you can coo at the dog and bend over and touch him without the dog breaking his sit position. However, should the dog start to look shaky, immediately reinforce his focus with a tidbit, thereby promoting calmness. When the dog is strongly focused, use more and more energy to bait him so that he can be made uncomfortable, as before, when he gets nervous and jumps up. Deciding when to reward with food and when to inhibit with the tight lead is a fine balance that needs to be adjusted for each dog's temperament.

When the dog is performing well in close, it's time for him to learn not to jump on someone, even after running toward them in an excited state. The helper moves a distance away, which should raise the dog's drive, and the dog is released on a long lead to run to him. As the dog closes in, the helper shows him the food, inducing him to brake his speed. The lead must be loose.

At the moment the dog reaches the helper, the handler should be prepared to shock him if necessary. The helper should hold the food a little above the dog's head to prompt him to sit. Tightening the lead at this point will encourage sitting as well.

When the dog sits, relax the tension on the lead. As the dog progresses, slowly wean him away from the prompters. Eventually, put the food in a pocket, out of the dog's sight.

As the helper periodically feeds the dog, he can give the dog lots of physical praise so that the making of contact becomes that much stronger.

In the case of a stranger coming to the door, all of the dog's training can be put into practical effect. When he knocks or rings a doorbell, it is a moment of disorder, and most dogs become highly energized. Excited barking is a natural and appropriate reflex.

The handler arrives and praises the dog so that both dog and handler are on the same wavelength, the first step to encouraging the dog to being attentive to his handler.

Before the guest is admitted, the dog is sent to his place. Training the dog to go to his place must be done as an exercise apart from any interaction with a stranger. Once completed, the unfamiliar visitor may be added. The dog's place should be clearly defined either by a raised landing or a mat or rug of some sort. Train the dog to go to his place by using food. The quickest way is to feed the dog daily at its place, and you will find your dog beating you into position in no time. At this point you can start commanding the dog to go to his place and then reward him with a biscuit. As the dog learns that by leaving you he ultimately gets to his food, so can he learn that by leaving the visitors he is actually getting closer to making contact with them.

When the dog arrives at his place, he is commanded to lie down and stay. Then the handler opens the door.

Greeting the guest is the most critical moment for the dog. He is still charged up, and the previous social order is being disrupted by the exchange of emotional energy between the two people. Therefore it is best to use a family member in the beginning and repeat the exercise over a and over so that the dog is learning when not hypercharged over a real visitor. The biggest handling error is to fail to notice a dog's mounting nervousness, which results in his breaking the down/stay. It is more important to pay attention to the dog in order to build a strong foundation in his training than it is to be a good host or hostess.

After a few moments, the dog is called by his handler. How the dog reacts at this point allows the handler to monitor what is on her dog's mind. Does he come quickly and directly, or is he in conflict? By making the dog come straight to her, the handler is ensuring that a calm social mood pervades her dog's temperament.

The handler heels her dog around the helper as an intermediary step to making actual contact. This is especially important with aggressive dogs.

The dog is positioned to make contact with the stranger by sitting. Since the dog has closed the gap between himself and the stranger, as opposed to the stranger breaching the dog's critical distance, aggression or nervousness hasn't been aroused, making calm contact more likely.

After making contact, the dog is sent back to his place. This reinforces the handler's control and the dog's calm disposition.

The dog should be conditioned to allow guests to have their own place by leaving them alone. This is especially therapeutic for nervous or sharp dogs. After lying down for five or ten minutes, the dog can socialize with the group if the owner desires. If he is a problem dog, he should first be called to the handler. If he's calm, then he can be released from his place by a simple OK signal.

Conclusion:

Born Wild, Train to Be Free

"I DON'T WANT TO KILL my dog," the man said. He was near tears. He stood in my office telling me that this should be the happiest time in his life. His newborn son had just come home from the hospital, but his dog was aggressive toward strangers and, even worse, with children, and now he was torn between his love for the dog and his deep concern for his child's well-being. His son was the main concern but, nevertheless, the man couldn't bear to have his pet destroyed.

To his credit he accepted the fact that he had made every mistake in the book with his dog. But what had he done that was so different from the way most dog owners respond to dog problems? He thought that love meant hugs and kisses and that discipline meant a whack every now and again. He approached training by thinking that getting his dog to sit and lie down was all that had to be done. His dog was treated as most pets are, except that his dog, a pit bull cross, would tend to learn aggression, given these common handling errors.

As I studied the dog for a few minutes, the overwhelming message coming from the animal was one of fear. I moved my hand above his topline and his hair stood on end instantly, rippling along the spine in anticipation of my touch. It is commonplace to call such a dog a "fear biter," for he is indeed afraid, but such a term misses the truth that lies beneath this dog's potentially explosive reactions. When a dog lashes out, for one brief instant he feels free of his fear. While he may be compelled by stress to bite, he is motivated by freedom.

Biting, as well as the countless other behavioral problems which send ten million dogs to their doom each year, is completely avoid-

322 / Conclusion: Born Wild, Train to Be Free

able. No matter what the temperament of the dog may be, genetics doesn't mean that a behavior is predetermined. All dogs can adapt to any environment if their wildness is acknowledged, appreciated, and then channeled into expressions of freedom that are appropriate. Such adaptability, broadened and deepened through domestication, forms what I call the dog's "harmonic quotient."

The pit bull owner in my office was deeply perplexed. Where had he gone wrong? Had he been too tough on his dog, or not tough enough? While there are a lot of handling errors to focus on, there is one simple answer to this dog's problem that is also the common denominator in any other breakdown in the dog/owner relation. The owner had fallen into the usual trap; he had formed a pack with his dog. His mind-set had been to tame his dog so that he would be lovable. Since this approach ignored the prey instinct, the dog's cooperative spirit was undeveloped and their homelife revolved around the tension of a pack rather than the harmony of a group.

This man was not aware that a dog is biologically and emotionally designed to absorb and store stress, and that this occurs whenever the prey instinct isn't fulfilled. In the wild, this behavioral mechanism ensures survival, which is why social tension is typical of pack life. In the absence of any prey, pack members have no target on which to vent their aggression. Thus inhibited, the stress level builds to a high pitch, finding its ultimate release when another individual acts out of place, causing a shift in the pack order. In this moment, all of the imprisoned passion in the pack is released toward the hapless pack member. Of course, the social tension of the pack may also find a release in an attack on a vulnerable prey animal.

As I moved my hand toward the dog all the confusion he had experienced in his life with regard to his prey instinct surfaced merely by the extension of my hand. The possibility of a stranger's touch made this dog go beyond his breaking point—were I to have gone further, I might have provoked an attack.

Interestingly enough, this dog's stress level was directly proportional to the strength of his attraction to me. The more attraction a dog has, the more aggressive he'll be if the harmonic pathways are blocked. Nothing in nature can occur in a vacuum—a dog's behavior always has its reasons, but it can't be predicated on a negative motivation, such as being afraid. A dog can't dislike, he can only like, he can only be attracted. Therefore the pit bull's fear of me isn't a motivation to bite me. The germ of his mood was one of longing, an uninhibited urge to be with me, its purity long since scarred by incorrect handling. This is why it is incorrect to say that, genetically speaking, pit bulls are problem dogs. Pit bulls that experience flow along a harmonic pathway are wildly *social* toward strangers.

Wildness is an innocent, unabashed attraction to that which is positive in nature. In young pups this innocence is reflected in their every impulse, which is why they are so outgoing. But of course, such an undiscriminating attitude is not a successful survival trait in the forest, and so it is that wolves must live in packs and with stress. It is necessary that each member be made extremely nervous so that he won't ever forget an unpleasant experience. With a tautly strung nervous system, he's less likely to be surprised by a predator or be insensitive to any power shifts within the pack. Additionally, he will be highly charged to chase and to bite a large prey animal.

Because life in the wild is so oppressive, we must recognize that there is really no such thing as real freedom in nature. Canine survival is intimately connected to all other forms of life, and it is as a result of this interdependence that life and death always hang in the balance. However, the incredible beauty of the prey instinct is revealed with the realization that *freedom* and *harmony* are synonymous. When the group is coordinated by the master prey instinct, that is the sensation of freedom. That is unity. That is life.

In the wild, freedom is short-lived, for as soon as a kill is made, the group becomes a pack once again. Nevertheless, that fleeting spark of harmony is what bonds each member to the group.

Our task as dog owners is to capture that transient surge of freedom and expand on it until it occupies our dog's entire range of reference. This is not hard to do, but it seldom happens because we're constantly seeking to tame our dogs while under the misconception that their wildness is a destructive force. Although we don't want our domesticated dogs to be wildlike, this natural wildness is not the problem. The problem is how to get a dog to open up and to be receptive to calming influences. Calming the dog through the prey instinct is how you gain access to his most innocent and vulnerable essence, arousing his spirit in such a way as to be channeled away from a survival instinct and onto a harmonic pathway. The purpose of a pack, however, is to make each individual nervous in order to catalyze the survival instincts. This brings me back to the central theme of this book. I wish to guide the dog owner in how *not* to be part of this instinctive plan.

We do not want to duplicate life in a pack. The stability of a pack is destined to falter, since balances are constantly shifting over even the smallest daily occurrence. One pack member might stumble onto an object that another one treasures; an adolescent might naively press against a bitch in estrus; a nursing puppy might nip his mother's nipple too hard. These innocent actions are out of order in a pack and unleash the pack's warehouse of stress. In the wild, this is appropriate. Each individual must become a prisoner to the survival instinct in order for the species to endure. However, in man's world, such stressed or overly charged reactions to change spell disaster. Dogs, unlike wolves, need to learn to adapt more fluidly if they're to live peacefully with modern man.

While stress is inevitable, it can also be an ally, because the ultimate function of stress is to implement the harmonic plan. Stress brings focus and intensity to behavior, and by using it carefully and creatively we can tune our dogs to our domestic specifications. But first our dog must have a clear mind. By being with his owner, at some point the dog will get to experience prey making. In other words, prey making and being in harmony with his group need to be defined as one and the same.

It is rare to find a good rapport between dog and human. Often I reach out to touch an excited dog, and he flinches as if I'm about to swat him. Or I see a dog whose face is so sensitized by repeated whacks, or hypercharged by inadequate socialization, that whenever he's around strange dogs his muzzle bristles. Finally, the saddest situation is when a child approaches a strange dog, or even a family dog, and the years of pent-up stress are unloaded on this innocent youngster. Such an incident is not evidence of an unpredictable or a mean dog; unknowingly, the child tripped a wire that had originally been set by an owner locked in a struggle with his pet. The child is merely the final domino in a chaotic chain reaction. The owner topples the first one with a confrontation, or blow, and the child ends up being the victim.

Dogs are not trying to test us, to dominate us, or to put one over on us, and handling a dog is not a matter of just getting tough. That's an old-fashioned attitude toward discipline. All the social angst in a wolf pack is not evidence of a leader struggling to the top in order to bring peace and balance to the pack. What is actually going on is the transferrence of stress from one individual to the next in line. It is the timeless rule of instinct, the relentless reign of stress imposing order on its subjects.

While there must be order and balance in a dog's life, we must recognize that it is through harmony that they are achieved. Without the flow of emotion released through hunting, these qualities by themselves serve no purpose and are merely suffocating. The reason wolves need to be in balance within the pack *is to remain connected to the group*. Only through hunting as a group can there be freedom.

Owning and training a dog affords us the chance to make contact with our dog's wildness so that he can live free in our lives. The experience can only help us to be more human, more deeply connected to nature. To refrain from hitting a dog is not, in itself, enough. His prey instinct must also be actively developed, for it controls a valve within him that, once opened, makes him innocent and amenable to any group purpose. It isn't how much love you try to give your dog, it's how much of your love your dog is *open* to receive. A master's role is to expand on that brief snippet of freedom that nature affords in life until it becomes fixed as a character trait.

A dog is born wild, he learns stress, he must be trained to be free.

INDEX

about-turns, 229–231
affection:
  appropriate forms of, 91
  social resistance and, 293
  unstructured, 83
aggressiveness:
  conflict training and, 217–218
  defusion of, 91–93
  drive recovery and, 213
  female hormones for reduction of, 19
  as stress release, 321–323
alpha wolf, 71, 84, 290
American Kennel Club, 185, 186–187
animal shelters, 18, 188
arm, gripping of, 199–200
association, learning by, 73–74
  see also disassociation
attention span, puppy development and,
  127–128
attraction, 44–46, 54–55, 59, 322–323
attribution process, 108–111, 116, 184
automatic sit, 215–217, 227–228

ball playing, 149–155
  with children, 176–177
  connectedness and, 149
  in contacting training, 196–197
  in down/stay training, 268, 270
  for fast down training, 254–255
  fighting instinct and, 152, 153
  in heeling training, 211, 212, 220
  lesson plans for, 150, 151–155
  prey instinct exercised in, 76, 119, 149,
    150–152, 155, 158, 254–255, 282–283
  puppy development and, 150–153
  as pure drive behavior, 149, 150, 152
  release command taught in, 153–154
  return skills developed in, 150, 154–155
  standard of performance for, 151

  tennis balls for, 119, 149
  as useful distraction, 147–148
barking, 68–69, 182
beagles, 48
Behan, Agi, 41
Behan, Cara, 37
Behan, Sonora, 109
behavior:
  as emotional response, 20–21
  theories of, 80–85, 118
bird dogs, 77, 152, 157–158, 186, 292
biting:
  attraction as root of, 44, 54–55, 59,
    322–323
  breeding practices and, 186
  children's play behavior and, 142, 172–174
  confrontational reactions to, 170
  curiosity exhibited in, 42
  emotional energy released by, 43, 44–45
  feeding habits and, 177
  group connection and, 45
  ingestive reflexes and, 44, 54
  of lead, 194
  pleasure principle and, 51, 52, 53
  puppy development and, 44, 52, 56, 128,
    130, 132, 169–170
  sensory information from, 40
  sexuality vs., 55–56, 59
  social behavior and, 43, 44–45, 51, 59, 62,
    170
  training techniques for, 169–170
bleached character, 85, 86
body language:
  of authority figure, 62, 63
  of canine self-confidence, 132
  drive stimulated through, 97, 120
  verbal commands vs., 72, 236–237,
    278–279
body-mind connection, 47, 48

contacting, 195–203
attention held by, 196
at chest level, 196
collective purpose reinforced through, 202–208
desire cultivated for, 119–120
disengagement process and, 198, 215–217, 227
at ground level, 166–167, 196–197, 198
in heeling, 210
Hup command for, 196, 197, 205, 206
judicious use of, 202
with nervous dogs, 199, 200
with overdominant dogs, 260, 261
with sensitive dogs, 198–199
sit in, 202, 217, 280
strong hunting drive and, 199–201
sustained focus developed in, 213–214
cooperation:
for group order, 53–54, 57
harmonic pathways and, 14, 57, 63
in wolf pack, 24–25
correction:
as focus shift vs. prohibition, 106–108, 112, 129
handler disassociated from, 108–112, 201, 203–204
in housetraining, 136, 184
as shock, 112–114
coyotes, 26
crate training, 18, 180–183, 184
Crisler, Lois, 44
curiosity, 42

dachshunds, 31
danger, down response to, 246, 255, 262
defensive behavior:
breeding practices and, 186
discipline linked to, 135–138
in feeding habits, 177–178
friendliness as, 34, 43, 44, 59, 257
from survival instinct, 13, 44
den instinct, 180, 181
desire to please, 76–77
disassociation:
mechanism of, 108–112
praise used for, 201
from shocks, 154, 201, 203–204, 307
discipline:
defensive behavior linked to, 135–138
defined, 115–116
dominant/submissive model for, 324
Down command vs., 245
improper, 321
see also correction
distractions:
channeling vs., 100
collective purpose vs., 203
to coming when called, 297–298
in conflict training, 217–219, 231–232

in down training, 283–286
sit/stay and, 233, 240–243
dog pounds, 18, 188
domestication, 23, 29–32
adaptability deepened by, 322
prey instinct amplified by, 55, 56
of puppies, 167–169
dominance:
down training and, 259–262
judicious use of, 116
in learning process, 70–71
from survival instinct, 13, 44
tension manifested in, 57–59
as training technique, 84, 291
dominant-submissive social structure, harmonic pathways vs., 163–164, 171–172, 324
doors, open, 305–306
down, 245–255
as automatic reflex, 14
basic concepts of, 245–246, 281
calmness induced by, 245, 250–251, 255, 272
as danger response, 246, 255, 262
from distance, 281–287
distractions overcome with, 283–286
from dog's viewpoint, 246, 281–282
food and, 247–249, 250, 257–258, 264
from heeling, 247, 249, 252–254
incentives used for, 247–251
interruption exercise for, 251–252
mood change necessitated by, 246, 262
off lead, 285, 286–287
performance standards for, 245, 281
for problem temperaments, 257–262, 271–272
six-step training program for, 246–255
Down command:
barking and, 182
introduction of, 248, 249
Lie down vs., 245–246
other incentives supplanted by, 251, 255
timing of, 248, 282, 283, 284, 285
vocal inflection used for, 246, 248, 253
down/stay, 263–265
basic aspects of, 263–264
distractions and, 263, 267–268, 280
from dog's viewpoint, 276
duration of, 263, 264
handler's location in, 264–267, 268–272
performance standards for, 263, 275
practical applications for, 272–273
premature breaking of, 266, 269–272
problem behaviors and, 271–272
with recall, 275–280
reinforcement exercise for, 277–278
sit/stay training vs., 243, 263, 264, 265, 268
drive:
attention span and, 128